SCIENCE/TECHNOLOGY EDUCATION IN CHURCH-RELATED COLLEGES AND UNIVERSITIES

Proceedings of a Workshop co-sponsored by

The Institute For Theological Encounter with Science and Technology (ITEST)

and

Saint Louis University

October 27-29, 1989

Robert A. Brungs, S. J., Editor

Published by ITEST Faith/Science Press, 1990

Published by:
ITEST Faith/Science Press
3601 Lindell Blvd.
St. Louis, MO 63108

ISBN 0-9625431-0-1

Printed in the United States
of America Versa Press

Table of Contents

FOREWORD

Robert A. Brungs, S.J.
Director: ITEST

Thanks to the administration of Saint Louis University, especially the President, Father Lawrence Biondi, S.J., ITEST has been able to sponsor this very important Workshop. I also thank the essayists and the participants who shared their experience and wisdom with us. Although many of the comments during the discussions involved local or national situations, I feel confident that the underlying themes are important for Christians worldwide as we all cope in varying degrees to help the church in a technological (and increasing secular) cultural age.

The papers and discussions are a mixture of the local and international, the theoretical and practical. It would take far too much space here to try to summarize the Workshop. But as I was editing the discussion material, I noticed that, despite the seeming lack of focus, there was a deep-running coherence to the meeting. There are interrelationships between the purpose and goals of science/technology education in church-related schools and such seemingly mundane issues as curriculum and the role and importance of undergraduate research, between professional competence and service, between the pursuit of science and our belief in our Creator and Redeemer.

Drs. Gerard Magill and Charles Ford of Saint Louis University have captured the more profound issues involved in the meeting. This volume begins with their essay, Imaginative Learning in Theology, Science and Technology. That excellent theoretical summary stands on its own and needs no comment from me. I will comment on the more practical issues of the Workshop.

Dr. Charles Ford of New York furnished us with the data base needed to begin our conversation. Note that I have designated "Ford of New York." This meeting furnished both the moderator, Dr. Robert Bertram, and myself with the challenge continually to distinguish between the Drs. Charles E. Fords, one from New York and one from St. Louis, one an educationist turned Dean and the other a mathematician deeply immersed in the faith/science encounter in the Soviet Union. Dr. Ford (NY) devised an instrument designed to give us a view of the state of science/technology in church-related colleges and universities. With that data, and our own local experiences, we were able to consider issues as they actually exist.

Father J. A. Panuska, S. J. accomplished what all good keynote speakers are expected to do, namely, discussing the issues at hand in a way that encourages the exchange of ideas. There is no doubt that he accomplished this task exceptionally well. His talk effectively combined the ideas of the essayists and his own reflections in a manner to provoke further discussion.

Dr. Chase of Wheaton College eloquently described the excellent faith/science connection in one college. That essay complemented Dr. Ford's evaluation of the more general situation, showing what can be done by the students, faculty and administration working together in an atmosphere of cooperation, dedication and trust. Comments throughout the meeting confirmed the existence of such qualities in other schools.

The other essays ranged over questions (and answers) about church-related schools' involvement in science/technology education. Conventional wisdom (usually more conventional than wise) separates science from religion. In the assumptions (and in some cases, the conclusions) of all the essays there is a recognition that Christianity must remain incarnate in the world if it is to be faithful to its incarnate Lord. That <u>demands</u> an intimate involvement in the scientific search for understanding. From this assumption, the essays and discussions ranged from models of knowing to the need for more scientific publication, from the nature and content of the core curriculum to the need for undergraduate research. Equally wide ranging were discussions of the vow of chastity taken by religious to the clear indications that the Christian laity will be carrying more of the burden (and joy) of Christian higher education.

Discussions on the "uniqueness" or "special characteristics" of church-related colleges and universities revealed some of the riches of our educational legacy and the challenges we have and will have in the foreseeable future. One of the manifestations of this "special character" of church-related institutions was seen in the freedom to discuss seriously the interaction between faith and science. As I listened to the tapes and then edited the discussions I noted a strong sentiment (perhaps stronger among the scientists than the theologians) for a serious <u>faithful</u> search for meaning.

Underlying the entire weekend was the question of the advisability and the need for some future meeting on this whole question. I think there is a clear consensus (approaching unanimity) that there should be such a meeting or meetings. Beyond that the consensus fades when it comes to the practical questions of who should be included or what the topic or theme should be. A multitude of possibilities was offered; unfortunately they are sometimes contradictory. Some suggested a general meeting for all science educators in church-related schools, K through graduate. That, however, I would classify as definitely a minority position. More support surfaced for inclusion of high school teachers. That too, in my opinion, represents a minority (though larger) opinion. The more commonly held view would include only higher education personnel, preferably with a strong representation from the liberal arts faculties.

As editor, I made an initial attempt to edit the discussions strictly along the lines of themes and topics, skipping from one session to another in the pursuit of logical connections. After doing this for two or three themes, I concluded that I was seriously disturbing the rhythm and the flavor that were so important in the discussions. Consequently, I fell back on the alternative of a "real-time" edit, following the sequence of the interventions as they in fact occurred. This is not, I admit, satisfying in a logical sense. As Dr. Bertram noted out at one point, many of the provocative statements were not pursued. This can be frustrating to a reader. Nonetheless, I decided to offer the sequence of interventions as they occurred in order better to represent the actual development of the Workshop. Like so many things in life, the Workshop was not an exercise in consecutive logic. To portray it as such is a fatal distortion. These Proceedings then represent a "judgment call" on my part for which I do not apologize.

ITEST is determined to continue to pursue efforts in this area. The Board of Directors, once they have had the opportunity to refresh their memories by reading these Proceedings, will develop a strategy thought to be consonant with the opinions expressed by the attendees at this Workshop. All of you will be informed of the plans that will be developed. This topic is so vast and so crucial that ITEST will have to reach out for help in pursuing it. Should any of you who are reading this book have any suggestions to make or any help to offer, we would be grateful to hear from you.

My own opinion, developed from almost twenty-five years of work in the faith/science apostolate is that this is the most critical issue in church-related education. It subsumes, in one way or another, all the issues that arise in other frameworks. I am not, of course, proposing that science/technology education dominate church-related education. I am proposing that it must be strengthened across the board and at all levels of church-related educational effort. Our students need it; our society and nation needs it; our world needs it; our church needs it. I've worked myself up here to the point where I'm almost ready to shout with Pope Urban II, when he called for the Crusades, "God wills it!"

KEYNOTE ADDRESS

SCIENCE/TECHNOLOGY EDUCATION IN CHURCH-RELATED COLLEGES AND UNIVERSITIES

Rev. J. A. Panuska, S. J.
President, The University of Scranton

Father J.A. Panuska, S.J., currently President of the University of Scranton, is former Provincial of the Maryland Province of the Society of Jesus. Father Panuska has a PhD in Biology from Saint Louis University. His scientific specialty is cryobiology.

INTRODUCTION

I am honored and delighted to be able to address you as keynote speaker of this workshop which will consider science/technology education in church-related colleges and universities. Myers Briggs profiles me as an "extrovert," so it is wonderful to be able to give a keynote to a distinguished group like yourselves. I would hate to miss a chance like this. As an "intuitive," I will enjoy the speculations involved in this workshop, the conflict of theories, and the various approaches to our topic. Even though a "T," or a "thinker," in this context I will have great difficulty in overcoming my feelings about the subject which are very strong due to my lengthy background in science and my almost equally lengthy background in educational leadership, not a term most faculty use to describe administration.

Also, as a "T," wondering seriously if I was the logical person to give this keynote, I resisted the invitation and challenged Bob Brungs to demonstrate that I was suitable. Having once been Bob's so-called Superior in religious life, and knowing how stubborn he can be, I knew that would be a losing battle. At any rate, I tried. You will experience the result.

As a "J," or someone in the Myers Briggs "judgmental" category, I have a passion for planning things well ahead of time. For the sake of the workshop, this means that we do have a keynote address tonight. It also means that I have prepared my comments before reading all of your papers. Had I seen them early enough, I would have insisted that one of you give this talk. I have now read all which were sent to me and I realize that there will be some overlaps in presentations. At any rate, that would have been unavoidable. I hope that this evening will reinforce your own thinking and possibly challenge both your thinking and mine. Your papers challenged me.

CONGRATULATIONS AND THANKS

On this twenty-first anniversary of the Institute for Theological Encounter with Science and Technology (ITEST), I believe that we owe much gratitude to Father Brungs for founding and maintaining ITEST. I know that this struggle has not been easy. Surely, there was always that sticky question of a black bottom line. I know how hard it is for ventures like this to succeed over the long term. But Bob persisted through the years. I congratulate and thank Bob, and I thank Saint Louis University for co-sponsoring this workshop.

TWO ASPECTS

My paper will be divided into two sections. In the first part I will reflect on our topic in a more or less philosophical manner and in the second part I will present a series of observations, which may not appear particularly connected at the moment, but in the course of this workshop I suspect that relationships will develop.

TWO FORMS OF THE SAME REALITY

Just about everything I have to say in this first section can be summed up in one clause from the Constitutions of the Society of Jesus with which at least a few of you are familiar. This is a clause for which I have great respect, so much so that I had it engraved on a heroic statue of St. Ignatius which was dedicated at the University of Scranton as a "second cornerstone" monument during our centennial year: In Omnibus Quaerant Deum -- "In all things let them seek God." In my view, God is blended with the world in a way which, while not pantheistic, is indeed intimate. It is no surprise, therefore, that the relationships between theology (and religion) and science are many. And the relationships between science, technology and education in a church-related institution are many.

This conference will reveal many interrelationships, as can be anticipated from the various perspectives identified in the title of the papers: an administrative perspective, ideals and limitations, why church-related institutions should be involved in science, the feasibility of developing adequate science programs, our present situation, ways in which science/technology education can enrich the more general liberal arts emphasis, the ideal venue for teaching the relationship of science/technology society in human values, the importance of research and publication.

At least there should be no conflict between two things which are, after all, only two forms of the same reality although using quite different models for understanding: the direct (theology) and the indirect (science) revelation of God. And further, there should be no conflict between science and the liberal arts tradition. They too are ultimately about the same reality.

When Father Paul McNally, S.J., was director of the Astronomical Observatory at Georgetown, he often presented a popular lecture in which he spoke about finding God in the stars and in the atom. It was an apologia of sorts, but it was more. It was a proclamation of the potential of the human intellect.

Father Matthew Ricci, S.J., has always been honored for bringing Christianity to China by means of science. What is too often forgotten is that Father Ricci had done great things for the Chinese before he spoke to them one word about religion.

Let me give you another instance. The Jesuits are thought to have brought new musical forms to Paraguay (we claim many things -- in our humility). On the wall of the old Fordham University Community Refectory there was a colorful painting of Jesuits floating easily down a river, keeping their balance on a raft with apparently no effort (naturally!), intent on their music and their instruments, while the Indians rushed out of the jungle seeking the charming sounds. You will note that sometimes bishops react to Jesuits this way! Much was done for the natives before a relationship to God ever arose. Ricci gave knowledge which should have been a part of the Chinese culture; he shared with the Chinese some of the store of divine knowledge just as the Paraguayans received an insight into that beauty which is one manifestation of the divine.

In a similar context, the New England Province for years sent outstanding teachers to Baghdad where they could teach, expand the minds of students, but could not speak of theology. Relationships, however, developed. Other groups have done this in many parts of the world.

In other words, relationships develop from the simple communication of knowledge. There is a natural compatibility, a unity. There is bound to be, after all, it seems to me, an exploration into God. It is good that we have left behind us that vision of a great confrontation between the worlds of science and religion. That collision disrupted thought and paralyzed minds in 19th century England when Darwin stunned believers and destroyed religious peace.

The human mind was born to know and its restlessness for knowledge is akin to Augustine's awareness that our hearts "can never rest until they rest in Him."

MORE DIRECTLY TO THE QUESTION

Now let me speak a little more directly about the role of science in a church-related university.

One could have a whole conference on the nature of a university or, to be more complicated, a church-related university. I'm not going to talk about either one in terms of definition, but I would like to say that, in my opinion, any Church relationship should be, and in most cases is, more behavioral than juridical. Of course, behavioral and juridical relationships are not mutually exclusive. Recently within the Catholic tradition, there has been considerable discussion about juridical relationships. I do not consider this unimportant, but I believe that it is very far from the heart of the matter. In such considerations, shared purpose and purposeful behavior are far more effective than unwelcome and unenforceable juridical ties, but a juridical tie naturally can influence behavior.

GOOD FOR SCIENCE

Science within the Church-related educational context is good for the progress of science itself. I do not mean to suggest that pure science can be accomplished better in a church-related environment, but I believe that this environment could lead scientists to investigate questions which have great human value and which might possibly be overlooked in another type of environment. I believe that a church environment can have an integrating effect, or a broadening effect, on the scientist. This is something that is hard to measure since it is based on a subjective judgment, but I think that it is real. There is something psychologically stimulating that comes from a diversified environment.

In a church-related environment, the scientist may be less likely to have a perspective of the world that is overly dominated by scientific methodologies. The door is open to other approaches to reality. Life is less likely to be exclusive. Intense concentration on any research, whether it be in science or the arts can be narrowing. Broader visions and challenging experiences tend, in my experience, to encourage imaginative thinking, something which can only enhance the productivity of the scientific effort. Sciences should have an integrated view of the world, especially those sciences which touch the human person.

The cohesion of science and church-related universities should be mutually nourishing, both because of the science/church relationship and because the institution is a university.

GOOD FOR CHURCH

What are the advantages for the church-related aspect of this question? There is the advantage of the continuity of a tradition. From the very beginning of education in church-related schools there was scientific education. And just as the church-related environment assists scientists to an integrated view of the world, so the presence of science helps the Church maintain an integrated view of the world. Churches do not deal simply with things of pure spirit, but of spirit acting through flesh and blood, with psychological, sociological and economic human relationships. Being "other worldly" is incomplete, just as being simply "worldly" is incomplete.

A complete university setting provides the Church with a special opportunity to influence students and professors in both scientific and theological disciplines. The more complete and honest the relationship, the stronger that influence will be. If there are to be any apparent conflicts in the human mind between religion and science, it is far better that those conflicts appear in an environment where there can be a healing, where there is time and intelligence for integration.

For these and other reasons, some of which I am sure will emerge in the course of our workshop, the presence of science and technology appears to me to be very important within the church-related aspect of our question. Indeed, I believe that science is necessary for the full development of the church.

AN EDUCATIONAL NECESSITY

Now to the easy part. For me it is inconceivable to think of a university, especially one dealing with undergraduates, which does not have strong scientific programs as a part of its basic environment for learning. All of our school catalogues claim in one way or another that we strive to produce well-balanced persons, persons with an integration of knowledge, professionally competent -- ready for graduate schools or professional schools, ready for life. In my mind this means there should be a strong liberal arts base so that the view of the world is broadened and the past respected. Sensitivity to all of the elements of the present should result in future steps to be taken in the context of history, present knowledge, and a long-range vision. I do not believe that in the world today, any more than in the world of the middle ages, one can have this balanced view, this integration of knowledge which leads to a fuller life and the capacity for fuller service, without science.

I believe that there should be serious science taught even in general programs, not merely soft introductions which could be obtained equally well from popular reading. Science is too important a part of our world to be given light treatment. As educators we have an obligation to see that this integration is accomplished.

I think that in order to achieve a balance even for the general student, it is important to have strong science departments, departments which are not only knowledgeable and can provide a solid major, but also are involved in scientific research. And, of course, there must be an integration and a balance within the university itself.

To repeat what is probably an already clear opinion of mine: there is no complete university without science. Therefore, there is no complete Catholic university without science. Without science it is impossible to be in adequate contact with the world.

Universities have a responsibility to perpetuate scientific knowledge and add creatively to it. Religiously-related universities can add a perspective which broadens vision. Their scientific activities not only give them credibility, which is very important, but also help them to achieve their purpose both as a university and as a religiously-related university.

ADDITIONS

Let me add a few other practical comments and then draw this keynote to a close.

Although there have been cutbacks in federal support for science in recent years, external funding for scientific works through research grants and development of facilities is greater than for the humanities. Despite my affection for science, I believe that this is unfortunate, but nevertheless it is true. The presence of science in our schools opens the door to research opportunities and has the capacity to set a tone which can have a very positive effect on the creative aspects of university life in other areas.

When I first came to the University of Scranton one of my primary goals was to intensify the spirit of scholarly inquiry. I thought that this was healthy for the faculty themselves and certainly for the entire university, reaching both the graduate and undergraduate levels. The movement of one portion of the faculty in this direction is truly a stimulus to the entire faculty. I must admit that such a movement applies pressure on the administration to provide the necessary course loads, equipment, and other means to support this. It is not inexpensive, but I believe that it is both healthy and essential.

Another thing that I would mention is that at least for a number of universities, including church-related schools like the University of Scranton, excellence in science and technology can assist our outreach to the community at large in a practical way, which is truly helpful to our neighbors and also increases the appreciation of our communities for the value of having a vital university in their midst. This can often be helpful. At my university we have been intensifying this relationship dramatically over the past few years and I expect that movement to continue.

AND FINALLY

Let me conclude by once again thanking Father Brungs and St. Louis University for co-sponsoring this conference. Congratulations to ITEST on its 21st year. Thanks to all of you for participating in this workshop.

God gave us a world full of wonders, beautifully integrated, remarkably balanced, but ever changing and sometimes confusing. In order to understand God and to become a gift ourselves we must move forward in our own lives and in our schools as best we can with that integration of knowledge that leads to imaginative discovery. Such an integration in our church-related schools, such a remaking of ourselves and the keeping of our churches on course is not possible without the presence of science as a significant part of our educational systems.

I hope that this keynote will help to open doors to our discussions this weekend. I look forward to our sharing of ideas.

IMAGINATIVE LEARNING IN THEOLOGY, SCIENCE AND TECHNOLOGY

Dr. John Cross
Dr. Charles E. Ford
Fr. Gerard Magill

Dr. John Cross is Professor of Psychology at Saint Louis University. He is a member of the Saint Louis University Internal Review Board and a member of the ITEST Board of Directors.

Dr. Charles E. Ford is Professor of Mathematics at Saint Louis University. He is a member of the ITEST Board of Directors and is deeply involved in researching the faith/science interaction in the Soviet Union.

Gerard Magill completed his doctoral degree in 1986 at Edinburgh University, Scotland, having previously completed his Bachelor degree in Philosophy and Licentiate in Theology at the Gregorian University, Rome. In 1988 he joined the faculty at Saint Louis University as assistant professor of Theological Studies. His specialty area is foundational questions of Moral Theology, and, in addition, he has recently developed a new course in Business Ethics for the School of Business and Administration.

We reach the high ground of wisdom, especially in matters of the academy, all too often with hindsight. After struggling with a morass of data we find ourselves hesitatingly promoting an argument, hitherto unnoticed. A review paper on conference presentations and discussions provides the security of such a vantage point. Despite the attractiveness of such an approach, this paper attempts a more precarious route.

In light of the dynamic interaction during this ITEST conference, it seems more suitable to preface the published papers with an interdisciplinary reflection on the selected topic, Science/Technology Education in Church-Related Colleges and Universities. A systematic examination of some key issues in the papers and dialogue can be a helpful lens to focus the plurality of opinions that characterizes a successful, scholarly meeting. These initial remarks attempt to capture and examine the central concern of the participants about modes of learning in Theology, Science, and Technology. Here, the introduction of Theology reflects the widespread interest in a faith community as characteristic of a Church-Related College. In each of these disciplines two fundamental questions arise: how do we interpret data as a learning process, and what significance do the similarities of interpretation have for a liberal arts education? Underlying both questions is the complex relation between Nature and Grace, and so, with this we begin our reflection.

NATURE AND GRACE

Science and Technology seek to investigate and harness the complex reality of nature. The ensuing dilemmas of when to control nature by rational dominion and when to celebrate it by supporting its fragility and enhancing its environmental evolution inevitably introduces the scientist into the realm of ethics. Theology seeks to understand and explain the mystery of God relating to human nature as creator and redeemer whose grace transforms our human potential for spiritual flourishing. This includes the ethical dimension of responsible action within the empirical possibilities for developing nature. Therefore, the scientist and theologian alike must address the reality of nature from an empirical and ethical perspective. Yet the borderline between the material and spiritual world is not so clearly delineated in a technological age that faces the urgent distinction between what can be done and what should be done.

In the Christian tradition there is no single understanding of how God's grace relates to nature. In particular, the explanation of the Fall, Original Sin, and God's Salvific Grace has significantly divided the Roman Catholic and Reform traditions. Without entering the complexity of these debates, some common ground in theological anthropology (the meaning of the divinity-humanity relation) cautions the theologian against naive interpretations of nature. God cannot be easily perceived in nature. For example, even the most benign explanation of the optimistic Catholic view that nature was not basically disturbed by the Fall bids us beware. Such a view explains that nature and Grace are harmoniously related in a way that enables God to transform nature without changing it, akin to the proverbial cognac lacing the gâteau. Even here, the glory and majesty of God cannot be directly discerned. If, for example, we claim that in the beauty of molecular structure we recognize the face of God, what sort of God is portrayed in the AIDS virus? Even in the finest natural beauty, the mysterious presence of God appears only vaguely, confusedly, and at most, analogously. All the more does humanity's holiness arise only through God's forgiving mercy.

The process of secularization has emancipated reason from any religious connection. This triumph of reason has generated a sort of control over nature that appears as the hallmark of modern technical science without any religious connection whatsoever. In such a context, the domination of nature by emancipated reason can become an end in itself.

Yet, God's supernatural grace urges us, through the flourishing of nature and humanity, to participate in the divine creative purposes. To do this, Theology investigates and explains the religious significance of scientific progress, especially in the ethical dimension of the proper use of nature (e. g., the impact of industry on the environment), and in resisting the propensity for depersonalization by technological development (e. g., causing financial havoc for society through computer controlled investment planning). Not every scientific advance is humanly liberating. The inevitable trade-offs between costs and benefits must be resolved within an ethical perspective that relates nature to God's supernatural purposes. In a religious context, the pursuit of science is the means to both human and divine purposes. There are two crucial aspects in this theological process of interpreting empirical reality; first, the relation between salvation and stewardship, second, the relation between faith and reason.

Salvation and Stewardship

To seek God in all things entails our stewardship of creation. If Salvation has opened the possibility of yearning for God by enabling nature to flourish, we stand responsible before God; the greater our scientific technology, the more demanding our responsibility. This encourages us to reverse the secularizing tendencies in society today by identifying our religious belief as both legitimate and meaningful for scientific and technological growth. The integration of the truths of Revelation and Religious Tradition with the truths of Science and Technology is the demanding contemporary task of Theology.

As religious thought seriously engages new scientific insights, scientists may also engage the human and religious realities in the context of responding to the divine call. The call of Christ encompasses not only personal relationships but, also the relationship between scholar and science. The total nature of this call demands unqualified response of the whole self to the entire domain of reality, religious and scientific. And, as science and religion are destined to blindness without such a response to the divine calling, so too will human freedom flourish in the quest to recover the original relation with God.

Faith And Reason

How we discern the balance between dominion and acquiescence, between active control and passive acceptance of the manifold opportunities in nature, will remain the function of reason in the context of faith. The insights of Teilhard de Chardin center upon this integration of Religion and Science as the one act of knowledge. While we approach these as separate specialties we ought not lose sight of their underlying cohesion. Speaking of God is strewn with the difficulties of mystery. But less so with Science, and in particular with its ethical dilemmas; we hope that the unknown is within our rational grasp, though this may be a false hope as we stand before the transcendent mystery of God.

When faith and reason are united there can rise a harmony of meaning that yields the capability for mutual enlightenment and for enriching the autonomy of each. This interpretation is possible because Theology and Science advance their learning in remarkably similar ways. At least at the foundational level, both seek truth not so much by proof but by persuasive argument. This occurs not so much by the classical scientific paradigm of deductive reasoning but by the more inductive interpreting of the available data and tentative suggesting of hypotheses to understand what we see, and thereby to reach forward to new knowledge, predicting and testing as we progress. If this is an acceptable comparison, the interpretation of data can be the linchpin in relating Theology, Science, and Technology in Church related colleges.

THE INTERPRETATION OF DATA

Christian Religion cannot be reduced to hand-down phenomena that is exhaustively tied to the Revelation of Scripture and the authority of past Tradition. Rather, the dynamic development of Religion requires Theology to reflect upon the past, in the present, by anticipating the future. Simply, this is a task of interpretation that employs sound reasoning within the context of faith. This interpretative function also appears to characterize empirical research in Science, although the significance of a faith horizon requires careful explanation. To undertake such an interpretation, which includes an examination of historical experience in Theology and of empirical reality in Science, raises the important question of different methods and models of knowledge.

Method And Models

Language influences our understanding of reality, whether spiritual or natural, and manifests an inseparability of the knowing subject and object known. When we interpret data there is always a personal dimension to our knowledge that reflects our education and culture and thus influences our perception. This personal element of knowledge is less noticeable in the deductive method of reasoning, yet it is required for the selection of discursive premises and the determining the direction of deduction. Yet, the more obvious advance of knowledge does not occur in this abstract fashion because reality cannot be reduced to a set of postulates. Rather, most research progress occurs by accumulating and interpreting data by a method of reasoning that transcends the systematic limitations of deduction and includes a distinctly personal element in perception. There is in deduction a similar openendedness (Gödel's incompleteness argument) to that in induction (Popper's falsification argument).

This personal method of reasoning is most apparent in the adoption of schemata or models by Science and Technology. Models help explain the insights that arise from experimentally verified data, by carefully organizing all the details and coherently formulating their meaning. Though these models bear a distinctly subjective element they are indispensable for advancing our learning. No aspect of education or scholarship is neutral in the sense of being without personal influence. Models, each implying some subjective view, enable us to retrieve and develop past knowledge in light of new data, and thereby anticipate the future by predicting results and seeking ever-new discoveries. The success of a given model lies in its capability of tentatively explaining and predicting the complex reality of natural phenomena.

Theology also adopts this evolving process of discovery in its development of religious doctrine. In this sense scientific empiricism and religious doctrine are remarkably similar. As Science uses models to give meaning to the accumulation of empirical data, Theology uses models to understand our ever changing historical experience as a window onto the divine, thereby enabling us to further explain the mysterious reality of divine-human interaction. Theology retrieves the doctrines of the past to invigorate and develop them in light of reality today in order to reach into the future by anticipating what we can be and do ethically and morally. The historical and transcendental features of contemporary theology focus on these issues where truth and value embrace the whole range of human development. Discovery and development lure us forward in both Theology and Science as the unfolding of the creative and salvific acts of God allowing nature to flourish. This occurs in our labors in which we create things and values in accord with the divine mandates that are manifest in God's action in creation. And these labors bring both the glorification and service of God. It is the fulfillment of these divine purposes that enables us to participate in these creative acts as we seek to regain a lost union.

Certainly, Theology and Science deal with different object-materials because they are divergent specialties and therefore use some very different models. But they both adopt a remarkably similar learning procedure: they select methods of reasoning that employ models to explain and predict the complexity of reality. And in this process the question of interpretation (hermeneutics) is central to these disciplines.

Interpretation And Imagination

The interpretation of data is possible only within a larger horizon. Even the selection of specific models reflects this broader vision. A holistic perspective promotes our understanding of the relevant data in every academic field. Central to this synthetic overview, whether as the foundational context for all knowledge, or as a particular horizon for understanding specific data, is the assimilation of past truths and future possibilities with present reality and insight. For example, when we decide to marry our future spouse, the discernment, or insight, arises only by integrating our past experiences with hopes for what lies ahead in relation to present reality; and the married couple enter into God's creative and salvific process, thereby giving glory and service to God. Both Science and Theology employ hypotheses to understand reality and also participate in the creative and salvific purposes of God. From the accumulation of relevant data we construct hypotheses, and the process of verification entails finding data that fits these hypotheses to advance knowledge step by step. The recognition of truth occurs when we perceive the data fitting together, converging upon a conclusion which may take a long time to discursively unpack by logical discourse alone. This procedure of interpretation requires an appeal to the imagination.

The imagination has three features in this process of interpretation. First, it enables us to synthetically grasp the data at hand. Second, it recognizes when the data converges upon a conclusion even though it remains logically short of it (as hypothesis). Third, it gives meaning to the conclusion in relation to the interpretative horizon of objective data and subjective understanding, and thereby avoids the danger of randomness or whim; and subsequent verification of the conclusion requires an ongoing quest for data to fit the hypothesis. This applies as much in Theology as it does in Science and suggests a horizon of mutual interaction that will advance our understanding of nature within a religious context and thereby develop our awareness of the mysterious presence of God. How these insights are formulated by language in scientific principles or religious doctrines is a complex matter. Suffice it to say for the present comparison of method and interpretation that both are open to subsequent insights and the development of doctrinal and scientific formulations.

Imaginative learning in Theology, Science and Technology is the corollary of the interpretative similarities in these subjects. If this is so then an appeal to the imagination becomes a central function of education, especially in church-related schools and therefore should be a characteristic feature of Liberal Arts education.

LIBERAL ARTS EDUCATION.

This emphasis upon imagination is important because church-related schools explicitly acknowledge a religious context for their academic commitment. On the one hand, this religious context provides an interpretative horizon for Science and Technology in faith communities. On the other hand, imagination enables Science and Technology to explain reality in more historically relevant models and thereby both reinforce and challenge religious and scientific doctrine and belief. This imaginative interaction not only highlights the independence and integration of the disciplines, but also in Liberal Arts education sharply focuses the important distinction between the possible and the ethical.

Independence and Integration.

Certainly Science and Theology must retain their independence because each has specifically different object-materials and resources to study. As Science advances our understanding of nature by investigating empirical reality in relation to the inherited insights of past research, Theology examines experience in relation to the communal wisdom of past tradition of understanding God's action in history in order to develop our explanation of the relation between divinity and humanity. The autonomy of each specialty warrants its own rules and restraints, and ought not to be burdened by restrictions that may be legitimate within other specialties. However, I have also suggested that their underlying methods, models, and interpretations can be remarkably similar. Therefore, the legitimate integration of these disciplines can be coherently proposed, especially by appeal to the imagination. This integration resists confrontation between the disciplines and can be described both from the perspective of Theology and that of Science.

First, from the perspective of science, the faith community of a church-related school legitimizes Theology as an interpretative horizon for Science and Technology. If the verification of hypotheses in scientific research receives meaning from the model adopted, an interpretative process is needed both in the selection of the model and in the perception of the hypothesis from converging data. In this process the horizon of religious belief has an influence, not in determining the outcome of the hypothesis and data, but in discerning the broader significance of each scientific insight. Not only does belief give impetus and stimulus to further research in fulfilling God's creative and redemptive purposes, but much more importantly, it enhances the sense of ultimacy and mystery of the transcendent God in every scientific discovery. The meaning of technological advance varies according to the horizon of interpretation. A faith environment not only brings a religious motivation but broadens the meaning of scientific results. To glimpse, albeit dimly, God's presence through the flourishing of human nature is no small human accomplishment, even though, as mentioned earlier, caution must constrain overly optimistic claims for perceiving transcendent mystery.

Second, from the theological perspective, the integration of these disciplines in the Liberal Arts education of church related schools enables Science and Technology to challenge religious belief and doctrine. If imaginative interpretation legitimizes giving a religious significance to a scientific discovery, in turn it also warrants the contribution of scientific discovery to the development of religious belief and doctrine. To maintain a reciprocity between the analogical narratives of language about God and ongoing human flourishing, theology must integrate the ever-changing portraits of nature depicted by scientific research. The holistic character of this creative interchange will ensure that Science will maintain a harmony between its broad view of nature and its many research specializations that progress demands. For the imagination not only provides models of interpretation within the specific specializations of each discipline but also enables each to reach above its detailed research with a panoramic view of its materials and discoveries. At this generic level we require a cultivation of the imagination to facilitate the integration of Science and Technology with Theology in reciprocal influence, yet with each retaining autonomy.

Within such an integrative framework between technological literacy and religious commitment, Liberal Arts education will not only continually evolve its curriculum by encouraging creative teaching and innovative research, but will also reach out to its local community. This integration enables students to appreciate the factors at work in today's complex world. If specialist training is fundamental for clear thinking, interdisciplinary study is as important for imaginative thinking, not just between academic specialties but also within the community, between different levels of education, and different segments of society, to provide a full panoply of imaginative learning experiences within cultural diversity. To maintain a balanced curriculum in a world where scientific sophistication and religious education compete for diversity and autonomy, requires a sensitivity to the difference between what is possible and what is ethical. This paper suggests that developing the distinction between what is scientifically feasible, what seems socially deirable, and what is religiously justifiable is most possible when there's a dynamic integration of Theology, Science and Technology.

The Possible and the Ethical.

The question of moral imperatives is foundational to the imaginative balance between scholarly diversity and personal integrity in a Liberal Arts education. If the dynamism of education demands we be attentive, intelligent, reasonable, and responsible, it is the imagination enabling us to reach a deeper self-awareness that imbues empirical knowledge with ethical considerations. The synthetic and creative functions of the imagination enable us to obtain a holistic view of self and transcend the present reality to what is possible. In a society faced with scientific and technological dilemmas (gene control, brain surgery, etc.), a church-related school can relate the empirical and ethical within the interpretative horizon of religious ultimacy. The vision of a faith community that takes scientific study seriously can provide a celebration of the divine and human where their intermingling cultivates an awareness of transcendent mystery as significant for ethical deliberation. The need for the formation of Christians to sensitize the scientific community, which remains predominantly pre-Christian, becomes more urgent every year.

Theology contributes to the critique of Science and Technology by discerning the borderline between what science can do and what ethics permits. The coherence between these disciplines will become more complex as progress leads society onward, and the temptation to allow each to go its separate way will increase. Without a Liberal Arts education Science and Technology are impoverished by the lack of the interpretative horizon of at least Philosopy and more ideally Theology. Thus, a central function of Liberal Arts education will be to maintain dialogue between Theology and Science and to avoid a dichotomy arising between orthodoxy and orthopraxis. Church-related schools' mission statements will contribute substantially to this collegial undertaking of developing critically informed moral judgments and ensuring that Science and Technology remain alert to ethical considerations. These statements can't diminish the primary responsibility of each discipline to continue collaborative research in their comparative methodologies, and to promote the reciprocal integration of each discipline's insights in teaching, research and publications. This paper suggests that Liberal Arts education in church-related schools has a dynamic future in developing an imaginative interaction between Theology, Science, Philosophy and Technology. The following papers and discussions provide suggestions for implementing the appeal for the collaborative integration of Science and Technology Education in Church-Related Colleges and Universities.

A PILOT STUDY OF THE PRESENT CONDITION OF UNDERGRADUATE SCIENCE AND TECHNOLOGY EDUCATION IN CHURCH-RELATED COLLEGES AS PERCEIVED BY DEPARTMENT CHAIRPERSONS

Dr. Charles E. Ford

Charles E. Ford, Ed.D., Dean of the Graduate School of Health Sciences, New York Medical College, Valhalla, New York, lives in Bridgeport, Connecticut. He earned an Ed. M. in Higher Education and History from Saint Louis University in 1956 and an Ed.D, from Washington University in 1962. At Sacred Heart University in Bridgeport, he served as Academic Vice President and Dean from 1972-76 and as Provost from 1976-1980. During his tenure at Saint Louis University Dr. Ford was Associate Professor and Director of Center for Higher Education.

METHODOLOGY

1215 Chairmen of Biology, Chemistry, Physics and Natural Science departments of 794 church-related colleges were asked to complete and return a thirty seven item opinion questionnaire; designed to assist ITEST efforts to determine the current and projected status of science and technology education on the undergraduate level in church-related colleges. This study is intended to be exploratory i.e. a pilot. Respondents were asked to select one of five levels of agreement - disagreement or no opinion. Information was requested on the number of baccalaureate degrees awarded in 1988. Four statements designed to elucidate respondents opinions on science and technology education within their college or university were included. 301 responses (24.7%) were received: from chairs of Biology (94), Chemistry (96), Physics (74), and Natural Science (35). (Nineteen responses were received too late for inclusion in tabulations).

190 respondents volunteered the names of 28 denominations and 127 did not specify their college or university denomination. Geographical distribution was national.

Responses to 37 questions were scanned and converted into a continuum scale based on 5 as the highest value of agreement with each statement: (5) strongly agree; (4) agree; (3) no opinion; (2) disagree; (1) strongly disagree. The five levels of responses were also combined into agree, disagree and no-opinion and are reported as percent distribution. Results are contained in Appendix #1. Of the four opinion statements provided for respondents comments, 274 were returned. Of these, 68 diverse and provocative statements were selected and are reported in Appendix 2. Chairpersons also sent twelve mission statements and seven offered additional opinion statements.

RECOMMENDATIONS

Following is an abstract of the survey based on review of responses to the 37 statements in tandem with the essay or opinions offered by the respective chairs. The investigation suggests that church-related colleges' faculty and administrators should upgrade their denomination's and the public's perception of the unique mission of church-related colleges' role in the education of generalists' and professionals' ability to integrate and act on scientific and theological knowledge and insight.

1. ITEST should conduct a follow-up study focused on

the educational philosophy of church-related colleges; the desirability of integrated course(s) that address:

(1) ethics of sci/tech per se (2) sci/tech based issues on social justice and ethical matters concerning man, earth, environment, space); (3) comparative methodologies of science, technology, religion and social sciences.

2. Plan a 1990 conference organized to develop curricular materials designed to assist church-related colleges faculty to interrelate theological and science and technology instructional goals and objectives through courses, seminars and lecture series.

3. Encourage the formation of denominational and college consortia focused on science and technology, theology and public policy. Note this should be pursued in conjunction with the executives of church-related higher education groups, council of independent colleges and the various denominational college and university organizations.

4. Participate in initiation and support of legislation designed to support education of scientist and technologists with special focus on facilities, training and scholarships, including recruitment of minority faculty and students.

ABSTRACT

1.1 - 1.5

Church-related Colleges are committed to preparation of Baccalaureate level graduates for advanced studies in the sciences and technology. Respondents consider science as essential to the Liberal Arts and science degree programs offered by their respective institutions. However science and technology instruction as a component of religious education or within their colleges denominational tradition is minimized.

The concept of methodological comparability between science and religion is apparently denied, which suggest that instruction in theological methodology is missing thus diminishing the basis of conversation amongst and between scientists and theologians. (The investigator assumes that scientific methodology i.e., beyond technical competence is paramount in undergraduate science instruction regardless of the role of the department, i.e., pre-professional, devoted to liberal education, per se and/or to the religious and philosophical rationale of the respondents college).

A more positive attitude is expressed when the inquiry is focused on ethical aspects of religious practice.

1.6 - 1.8

The "priority" of sci/tech as measured by recruitment, support of students, and curricular status viewed more positively by biologists with natural scientists the least, with, however, a low margin of difference among the four disciplines. (Do church-related colleges with limited resources imperil professional, liberative and integrative goals by reliance on a multi- -science department's limited faculty and curricula, in spite of the conviction that instruction is adequate for admission to Graduate School)?

2.1 - 2.5

Contrary to prior investigations (Oberlin, NSF), proposed Federal college facilities legislation, institutional advancement agenda and philanthropic strategies, respondents believed that the overall church-related colleges' science infrastructure is adequate.

3.0 - 3.4

Church-related colleges' faculty are well qualified and committed; compensation is adequate; church-related colleges' sci/tech departments might be enhanced with additional members. Note the increasing number of projections of faculty and replacement into the next century.

4.1 - None too complimentary.

Respondents assessment of pre-college (secondary school) preparation is provided for comparison:

CHAIR	BIOL	CH	PH	NS	AV
PRE-COL					
4.1 Math	2.46	2.50	2.37	2.31	2.41
4.2 Bio	3.34	3.88	3.45	3.40	3.51
4.3 Ch	2.85	2.98	3.20	2.68	2.92
4.4 Ph	2.67	2.39	2.64	2.22	2.48
4.5 Other Sci	2.86	2.94	3.01	2.71	2.88
Average	2.84	2.94	2.93	2.66	2.84

5.1 - 5.10

Church-related colleges were founded to manifest an impressive range of values from intellectual, education of clergy and laity, evangelical and salvational. And, as scientific and technological advances have cascaded through our culture and institutions, increased sensitivity to the fragility of the earth and people has followed. That entering students score lowest on global issues and relatively higher on life style choices suggest that definition of church-related college's mission to its students lives and to global issues is more critical now than in less informed times:

6.1 - 6.6

Polarization characterizes section 6. Church-related colleges' chairs are clearly dedicated to the function of scientific and technological literacy and competence within faith-based liberal arts and pre-professional Baccalaureate degree programs. Items 6.1 - 6.4 suggest a strong commitment to the CRC mission. Item 6.5 dispels assumptions that there is a unified or organic approach to the pedagogic integration of disparate intellectual systems. As to Item 6.6, ITEST'S mission is one of encounter i.e., to come upon face to face. This survey suggests that ITEST is uniquely qualified to pursue the dynamics of encounter in that precious environment, the church-related college. Over 300 CRC/CP's are amenable to a dialogue and in need of support.

CHAIR

ISSUE	BIOL	CH	PH	NS	T
5.1 Med. Waste	1.87	2.56	2.58	2.42	2.35
5.2 Deforestation	2.05	2.62	2.63	2.54	2.46
5.3 Global Warming	1.89	2.75	2.66	2.62	2.48
5.4 Green house	1.92	2.86	2.72	2.65	2.53
5.5 Acid rain	2.09	2.92	2.81	2.48	2.57
5.6 Toxic waste	2.25	2.73	2.79	2.88	2.66
5.7 Nuclear waste	2.21	2.89	2.85	2.88	2.70
5.8 Food supply	2.27	2.82	2.78	2.94	2.70
5.9 AIDS	3.63	3.77	3.74	3.77	3.72
5.10 Drug abuse	3.74	3.96	3.77	3.88	3.83
AVERAGE	2.39	2.99	2.93	2.91	2.80

SUMMARY

1. CRC'S are committed to preparation of scientists and technologists.

2. CRC'S are committed to teaching science and technology within the framework of liberal education.

3. CRC respondents are not convinced that science and technology instruction is a component of religious and liberal education.

4. Science and technology programs and courses generate a mixed response in rating of their priority within the CRC'S liberal arts and science degree programs.

5. A medium response on the issue of the commitment of resources to the recruitment of superior high school graduates to enter 5 tech undergraduate degree programs.

6. Disagreement with the notion that science and technology instruction and religion courses are interrelated, that is, that the methodology and content are viewed as a whole with the goal of teaching the undergraduates that both are exploratory scientific evidence-based disciplines.

7. Total concurrence in the idea that the ethical aspects of their respective religious persuasion includes knowledge of the science and technological basis of public issues.

8. It is essential that CRC'S maintain a strong presence in science and technology education within American higher education.

9. Respondents are convinced that church-related colleges can compete with public and non-sectarian institutions in recruitment and training of undergraduates to enter or prepare for graduate study in science and technology.

10. Public concern for ethical issues cannot be maintained by the community at large, the legislative, or judicial process.

11. An informed public will not suffice for well-trained, church-related, college graduates competent in the basics of science and technology in pursuit of ethical norms in issues facing American and worldwide society.

12. In keeping with prior comments on the inter-relatedness of science and religion information and methodology, respondents also indicate students are not made aware of the relationship between scientific discovery as it relates to understanding of the respective faith traditions. That such a relationship should occur was not contained within the survey and should be discussed by ITEST participants.

13. Almost total conviction that instruction is adequate in terms of admissions to graduates of church-related colleges to graduate programs in the sciences and technology.

14. through 22. All highs on the positive scale in terms of the quality of the faculty, the commitment of the faculty, 99.1, are adequate.

16. Disagree that faculty are adequately compensated for their efforts or that church-related colleges compete effectively with industry for qualified committed scientists, technologists who could be lured into collegiate teaching professions.

17. Medium agreement on the number of full and part-time faculty available for science instruction.

18. As with Oberland and other studies, middle of the road response to the adequacy of buildings and classrooms, total space available, number and quality of laboratories, support by provision of supplies, and number and quality of books and journals available in respective college libraries relevant to science technology instruction.

23. through 27. Basically low end of the scale and significant disagreement with the notion that students are adequately prepared to enter courses in mathematics, the biological sciences, chemistry and physics, or are adequately prepared for courses in other areas of the sciences. We would note that the lowest level on this scale is in mathematics and the highest level of preparation is in the biological sciences, with chemistry and physics holding the middle ground.

28. through 36. Attempt to assess student awareness of various science and technology issues yields two observations Students are minimally aware of the impact of global warning, acid rain, the greenhouse effect, tropical deforestration, toxic waste disposal, and nuclear waste storage and medical waste disposal. They score very high in the respondents sense of the students awareness of drug issues, i.e., typical undergraduate most aware of what effects them directly, less informed on national and global environmental issues.

In response to the topic questions treated in some of the pre-papers we have the following points to make from the survey:

Is science technology education on the part of church-related Colleges really feasible, with subsets on the issue of finance as applied to the application of human and physical resources?

While the responses indicate a high level of commitment of the faculty, which in my judgment reflects commitment within the framework of the institutional mission, to support science instruction, the level of support is mixed in terms of buildings, laboratories, equipment, and supplies. It is at this point where one could return to a more reliable study of this subject with the Oberland Report of 1987 which analyzed 50 colleges and was highly effective in influencing current legislation for the support of undergraduate science education programs. Nonetheless, the church-related colleges, though not necessarily in the Oberland group, or institutions supported by other public or private sector groups, are heavily committed to maintenance of a role in science education.

However, in what way can science technologies education enrich the more general liberal arts emphasis of Church-related colleges and in what way can liberal arts enrich the science technology training are somewhat disturbing? It would appear that in science and technology as related to religion, both in content and methodology, there is little effort, perhaps little interest as well as opposition to attempting to relate scientific data and progress to impact on the fundamentals of theology and to impact on state practice, other than in the realm of ethics, as applied to primary environmental issues.

APPENDIX 1

ITEST QUESTIONNAIRE & RESPONSES

1.0 <u>Mission and status of science/technology programs at church related Colleges</u>

SECTION I

1.1 At your college, the role of science/technology departments and faculty is to teach science and technology in order to prepare the next generation of scientists and technologists.

	SCALE	AGREE %	N	DISAGREE
BIOL	4.35	94.0	2.0	4.0
CH	4.50	97.0	-	3.0
PH	4.31	94.0	-	6.0
NS	4.32	88.0	6.0	6.0
	4.37	93.0	2.0	5.0

1.2 At your college, the role of science/technology departments and faculty is to teach about science and technologies component of a liberal education.

	SCALE	AGREE %	N	DISAGREE
BIOL	4.41	95.0	2.0	3.0
CH	4.26	90.0	1.0	9.0
PH	4.20	92.0	0	8.0
NS	4.34	97.0	-	3.0
	4.30	93.5	1.5	5.7

1.3 At your college, the role of science/technology departments and faculty is to <u>teach about science and technology</u> as a component of religious and liberal education within your college's faith tradition.

	SCALE	AGREE %	N	DISAGREE
BIOL	2.68	37.0	10.0	53.0
CH	2.62	36.0	13.0	51.0
PH	2.45	29.0	8.0	63.0
NS	2.66	37.5	6.2	56.2
	2.60	35.0	9.2	55.7

1.4 Sci/Tech and religion are interrelated, i.e., students are taught that methods and content of sci/tech are relevant to religion as a field of study.

	SCALE	AGREE %	N	DISAGREE
BIOL	2.58	29.7	12.7	57.4
CH	2.37	17.7	22.9	58.3
PH	2.29	24.3	8.1	67.5
NS	2.57	31.4	5.7	62.8
	2.45	25.7	12.3	61.5

1.5 The ethical aspect of the practice of religion requires that members of your college's faith tradition understand the scientific and technological basis of public issues.

	SCALE	AGREE %	N	DISAGREE
BIOL	3.63	63.0	22.0	15.0
CH	3.33	61.0	12.0	27.0
PH	3.62	68.0	11.0	21.0
NS	3.51	63.0	11.0	26.0
	3.52	63.7	14.0	22.3

1.6 Sci/Tech is a high priority as measured by sci/tech requirements for non sci/tech students.

	SCALE	AGREE %	N	DISAGREE
BIOL	3.05	47.0	12.0	41.0
CH	2.38	24.0	10.0	66.0
PH	2.64	28.0	14.0	58.0
NS	2.47	30.0	-	70.0
	2.63	32.2	12.0	58.7

1.7 Sci/Tech is a high priority as measured by active recruitment of superior high school sci/tech graduates and provision of scholarships and related support for such students.

	SCALE	AGREE %	N	DISAGREE
BIOL	3.26	56.0	6.0	38.0
CH	2.90	40.0	16.0	44.0
PH	3.08	43.0	22.0	35.0
NS	2.85	44.0	6.0	50.0
	3.02	45.7	12.5	41.7

1.8 Our college provides instruction that is adequate (as measured by admission of our graduates into M.S. and Ph.D. programs in the sciences) to prepare students for careers as professionals in the sciences and technology.

	SCALE	AGREE %	N	DISAGREE
BIOL	4.70	99.0	--	1
CH	4.67	96.0	2.0	2.0
PH	4.51	97.0	0	3.0
NS	4.48	94.0	0	6.0
	4.59	96.5	0.5	3.0

2.0 Resources

2.1 The total space available on campus is adequate for students in our college who are preparing to enter the scientific and technological professions.

	SCALE	AGREE %	N	DISAGREE
BIOL	2.86	63.0	5.0	32.0
CH	3.96	82.0	6.0	12.0
PH	3.68	72.0	7.0	21.0
NS	3.45	72.0	--	28.0
	3.48	72.2	4.5	23.2

2.2 The buildings and classrooms (age and condition) in our college are adequate for students who are preparing to enter the scientific and technological professions.

	SCALE	AGREE %	N	DISAGREE
BIOL	3.72	75.0	2.0	23.0
CH	3.94	80.0	4.0	16.0
PH	3.72	73.0	7.0	20.0
NS	3.45	68.0	3.0	29.0
	3.70	74.0	4.0	22.0

2.3 The laboratories on campus are adequate for preparing students who wish to enter the scientific and technological professions.

	SCALE	AGREE %	N	DISAGREE
BIOL	3.51	63.0	4.0	33.0
CH	3.65	70.0	5.0	25.0
PH	3.37	62.0	6.0	32.0
NS	3.48	74.0	--	26.0
	3.50	67.2	3.7	29.0

2.4 The biological and chemical supplies available on campus are adequate for preparing students who wish to enter the scientific and technological professions.

	SCALE	AGREE %	N	DISAGREE
BIOL	3.82	51.0	5.0	44.0
CH	4.06	86.0	5.0	9.0
PH	3.75	67.0	24.0	9.0
NS	3.65	77.0	3.0	20.0
	3.82	70.2	9.2	20.5

2.5 The library books and journals available are adequate for students who wish to enter the scientific and technological professions.

	SCALE	AGREE %	N	DISAGREE
BIOL	3.16	24.0	9.0	67.0
CH	3.31	22.0	12.0	66.0
PH	3.63	23.0	11.0	66.0
NS	2.91	24.0	5.0	71.0
	3.25	23.2	9.2	67.5

3.0 Faculty

3.1 The quality of our faculty (as measured by their advanced degrees) is adequate to prepare students for careers as professionals in the sciences and technology.

	SCALE	AGREE %	N	DISAGREE
BIOL	4.69	98.0	--	2.0
CH	4.70	98.0	1.0	1.0
PH	4.63	99.0	--	1.0
NS	4.68	97.0	--	3.0
	4.67	98.0	--	2.0

3.2 The commitment of our faculty (as measured by the time and effort devoted to training students in class, laboratory, seminars, journal clubs, and independent research) is adequate to prepare students.

	SCALE	AGREE %	N	DISAGREE
BIOL	4.66	99.0	--	1.0
CH	4.73	98.0	1.0	1.0
PH	4.67	96.0	3.0	1.0
NS	4.51	94.0	--	6.0
	4.64	96.7	1.0	2.2

3.3 Number of our faculty both full-time and part-time is adequate to provide instruction in preparation for admission to graduate school.

	SCALE	AGREE %	N	DISAGREE
BIOL	3.80	75.0	5.0	20.0
CH	3.48	61.0	4.0	3.5
PH	3.64	72.0	3.0	25.0
NS	3.37	60.0	8.0	32.0
	3.57	67.0	5.0	28.0

3.4 The compensation of our faculty (as measured by the college administration's awareness of the need to compete with industry for qualified, committed teachers) is adequate to prepare students for careers as professionals in the sciences and technology.

	SCALE	AGREE %	N	DISAGREE
BIOL	3.80	75.0	5.0	20.0
CH	3.48	38.0	7.0	55.0
PH	3.64	49.0	9.0	42.0
NS	3.37	31.0	9.0	60.0
	3.57	48.2	7.5	44.2

4.0 Students: Preparation

4.1 Students entering your college from high school are adequately prepared for courses in mathematics.

	SCALE	AGREE %	N	DISAGREE
BIOL	2.46	24.0	9.0	67.0
CH	2.50	22.0	13.0	65.0
PH	2.37	23.0	11.0	66.0
NS	2.31	23.0	9.0	68.0
	2.41	23.0	10.5	66.5

4.2 Students entering your college from high school are adequately prepared for courses in biology.

	SCALE	AGREE %	N	DISAGREE
BIOL	3.34	63.0	3.0	34.0
CH	3.88	58.0	34.0	8.0
PH	3.45	45.0	50.0	5.0
NS	3.40	60.0	11.0	29.0
	3.51	56.5	24.5	19.0

4.3 Students entering your college from high school are adequately prepared for courses in chemistry.

	SCALE	AGREE %	N	DISAGREE
BIOL	2.85	39.0	11.0	50.0
CH	2.98	39.0	15.0	44.0
PH	3.20	42.0	36.0	22.0
NS	2.68	32.0	8.0	60.0
	2.92	38.0	17.5	44.0

4.4 Students entering your college from high school are adequately prepared for courses in physics.

	SCALE	AGREE %	N	DISAGREE
BIOL	2.67	31.0	16.0	53.0
CH	2.39	11.0	32.0	57.0
PH	2.64	32.0	16.0	52.0
NS	2.22	15.0	11.0	74.0
	2.48	22.3	18.7	59.0

4.5 Students entering your college from high school are adequately prepared for courses in the sciences, other than biology chemistry and physics.

	SCALE	AGREE %	N	DISAGREE
BIOL	2.86	26.0	37.0	37.0
CH	2.94	22.0	55.0	23.0
PH	3.01	26.0	49.0	25.0
NS	2.71	15.0	49.0	36.0
	2.88	22.7	47.5	30.3

5.0 Students: Awareness

5.1 Students entering your college are aware of and/or concerned about medical waste disposal.

	SCALE	AGREE %	N	DISAGREE
BIOL	1.87	26.0	19.0	55.0
CH	2.56	16.0	37.0	47.0
PH	2.58	13.0	39.0	48.0
NS	2.42	23.0	18.0	59.0
	2.35	19.5	28.2	52.2

5.2 Students entering your college are aware of and/or concerned about deforestation of tropical rain forests.

	SCALE	AGREE %	N	DISAGREE
BIOL	2.05	30.0	21.0	49.0
CH	2.62	21.0	30.0	49.0
PH	2.63	18.0	37.0	45.0
NS	2.54	17.0	23.0	60.0
	2.46	21.5	27.7	50.7

5.3 Students entering your college are aware of and/or concerned about global warming.

	SCALE	AGREE %	N	DISAGREE
BIOL	1.89	24.0	27.0	49.0
CH	2.75	21.0	38.0	41.0
PH	2.66	17.0	39.0	44.0
NS	2.62	26.0	17.0	57.0
	2.48	22.0	30.0	48.0

5.4 Students entering your college are aware of and/or concerned about the green house effect.

	SCALE	AGREE %	N	DISAGREE
BIOL	1.92	29.0	21.0	50.0
CH	2.86	26.0	35.0	39.0
PH	2.72	22.0	35.0	43.0
NS	2.65	26.0	20.0	54.0
	2.53	25.7	27.7	46.5

5.5 Students entering your college are aware of and/or concerned about <u>acid rain</u>.

	SCALE	AGREE %	N	DISAGREE
BIOL	2.09	35.0	20.0	45.0
CH	2.92	43.0	27.0	30.0
PH	2.81	26.0	35.0	39.0
NS	2.48	31.0	20.0	49.0
	2.57	33.7	25.5	40.7

5.6 Students entering your college are aware of and/or concerned about <u>toxic waste disposal</u>.

	SCALE	AGREE %	N	DISAGREE
BIOL	2.25	33.0	27.0	40.0
CH	2.73	33.0	18.0	49.0
PH	2.79	23.0	38.0	39.0
NS	2.88	37.0	17.0	46.0
	2.66	31.5	25.0	43.5

5.7 Students entering your college are aware of and/or concerned about <u>nuclear waste storage</u>.

	SCALE	AGREE %	N	DISAGREE
BIOL	2.21	35.0	24.0	41.0
CH	2.89	34.0	25.0	41.0
PH	2.85	26.0	38.0	36.0
NS	2.88	37.0	20.0	43.0
	2.70	33.0	26.7	40.2

5.8 Students entering your college are aware of and/or concerned about food supplies in developing countries.

	SCALE	AGREE %	N	DISAGREE
BIOL	2.27	37.0	22.0	41.0
CH	2.82	32.0	23.0	45.0
PH	2.78	26.0	35.0	39.0
NS	2.94	37.0	23.0	40.0
	2.70	33.0	25.7	41.3

5.9 Students entering your college are aware of and/or concerned about AIDS.

	SCALE	AGREE %	N	DISAGREE
BIOL	3.63	76.0	12.0	12.0
CH	3.77	77.0	15.0	8.0
PH	3.74	72.0	22.0	6.0
NS	3.77	77.0	11.0	12.0
	3.72	75.5	15.0	9.5

5.10 Students entering your college are aware of and/or concerned about drug abuse.

	SCALE	AGREE %	N	DISAGREE
BIOL	3.74	80.0	12.0	8.0
CH	3.96	84.0	11.0	5.0
PH	3.77	73.0	23.0	4.0
NS	3.88	80.0	14.0	6.0
	3.83	79.2	15.0	5.7

6.0 <u>CRC:</u> <u>Religion, Science and Technology</u>

6.1 With regard to church related colleges' role and status in American higher education, baccalaureate level training of future scientists/technologists <u>is</u> <u>essential</u>, given the importance of faith and ethics within the sci/tech profession.

	SCALE	AGREE %	N	DISAGREE
BIOL	4.30	86.0	8.0	6.0
CH	4.17	89.0	6.0	5.0
PH	4.22	80.0	15.0	5.0
NS	4.00	80.0	5.0	15.0
	4.17	83.7	8.5	7.7

6.2 With regard to church related colleges' role and status in American higher education, baccalaureate level training of future scientists/technologists,the church related college <u>cannot</u> <u>compete</u> with public and non sectarian institutions in recruitment and training of undergraduates to enter graduate study in science/ technology.

	SCALE	AGREE %	N	DISAGREE
BIOL	2.73	11.0	5.0	84.0
CH	1.46	3.0	3.0	94.0
PH	2.05	11.0	4.0	85.0
NS	2.09	20.0	4.0	76.0
	2.08	11.2	4.0	84.7

6.3 With regard to church related colleges' role and status in American higher education, baccalaureate level training of future scientists/technologists <u>is</u> <u>not</u> <u>essential;</u> churches, the sci/tech community, legislators, judicial process and an informed public will maintain ethical standards on sci/tech issues.

	SCALE	AGREE %	N	DISAGREE
BIOL	1.57	9.0	0	91.0
CH	1.55	4.0	5.0	91.0
PH	1.94	4.0	5.0	91.0
NS	1.64	9.0	3.0	88.0
	1.67	6.5	3.2	90.2

6.4 Church related colleges were founded to educate laity committed to a faith tradition by emphasis on Liberal Arts, Philosophy and Religious Studies. As such they should not prepare graduates for those professions (especially sci/tech) which require substantial resources and commitment.

	SCALE	AGREE %	N	DISAGREE
BIOL	1.37	6.0	0	94.0
CH	1.28	3.0	2.0	95.0
PH	1.31	0	3.0	97.0
NS	1.45	9.0	3.0	88.0
	1.35	4.5	2.0	93.5

6.5 Students are made aware of scientific discovery as it relates to the understanding of your faith tradition and/or to the further development of that faith tradition.

	SCALE	AGREE %	N	DISAGREE
BIOL	2.60	35.0	25.0	40.0
CH	2.71	25.0	30.0	45.0
PH	2.67	29.0	22.0	49.0
NS	2.88	41.0	15.0	44.0
	2.71	32.5	23.0	44.5

6.6 Within your colleges faith tradition knowledge of Sci/Tech and practice are regarded as:

	CRITICAL	ESSENTIAL	USEFUL	NOT ESSENTIAL	IRRELEVANT	
BIOL	12 %	30 %	41 %	13 %	4 %	100%
CH	3	23	51	16	7	100%
PH	2	26	44	18	10	100%
NS	11	23	49	14	3	100%
AV.	7%	25.5%	46.2%	15.2%	6.0%	

7.0 BACCALAUREATE DEGREES AWARDED BY DEPARTMENT, 1988

	0-5	6-10	11-15	16-20	20+	
BIOL	13	22	16	15	27	93
	13.9	23.6	17.2	16.1	29.0	
CH	43	33	9	3	7	95
	45.2	34.8	9.4	3	7.5	
PH	43	15	10	1	3	72
	59.7	20.8	13.8	1	4.1	
NS	11.4	40	20	8.5	20	
	4	14	7	3	7	35
	103	84	42	22	44	295

APPENDIX 2

8.0 SELECTED RESPONSES TO THE QUESTION:

In what ways might the liberal arts enrich sci/tech education, in either context -- education in science or about science?

8.1 Science without liberal arts is poor science. A study of liberal arts without recognition of the process of science and technology is no education at all. Current societal problems have direct science and technology components, but the direction of society and the allocation of resources are traditional liberal arts decisions. Even the choice of problems on which to work by an investigator is an ethical decision. Thus one must conclude that the only responsible education of a scientist is in a liberal arts college and that a liberal arts education must have a science/technology component.

8.2 a) Do their classical job. (Several of the classical subjects included under "liberal arts" are sciences.)

b) Require more courses in the sciences to receive the A.B. degree. (The present two semesters required here is ludicrous.)

c) Professors teaching courses in philosophy and theology might invite science professors to give guest lectures in their courses.

8.3 Pass.

8.4 Our general education requirements have just been revised to include a course in science/technology to be taken by all students in junior or senior year. This course will be developed within an historical context and will address concerns such as those mentioned in items #27-36.

8.5 We offer a one-semester "Science and Religion" course, co-taught by a physicist and a theologist. Our analysis are from "historical" survey to "contemporary" but usually includes both.

8.6 The liberal arts (true liberal arts, not just some vague humanities requirement) would enrich science education by showing the destructive assumptions inherent in scientific thinking. The liberal arts should teach critical thinking about such problematic scientific notions as progress, efficiency, and perfectibility.

8.7 Science without being set in a broader context is a perilous enterprise, as our history attests. Hopefully a liberal arts curriculum provides future scientists with the moral/value context they need to be contributors to society rather than dangers to it.

8.8 There are many ways in which the liberal arts could enrich sci/tech education. Philosophy courses could emphasize how the Greek way of thinking led to science, starting with the pre-Socratics. Students could also be made aware of the Anthropic Principle which emphasizes the narrow range of values which our physical constants must have to enable life to exist. Philosophy would also point out the different causes, material, formal, final, efficient, and how predictability of the behavior of material does not imply a comprehension of the essence of material. History courses could include the religious motivation of many scientists, such as Newton, Duhem, Pascal and Alexis Carrell. History courses could also include Thomas Kuhn's emphasis on the role of the paradigm in science and the difficulty of changing it. History could show that modern science derives from Greek philosophy combined with the experimentation carried out by Renaissance man. Technology existed in Egypt, China, etc., but did not develop into science.

9.0 SELECTED RESPONSES TO THE QUESTION:

If you believe church-related colleges should offer baccalaureate curricula designed to prepare graduates to seek advanced degrees in science or technology, indicate a rationale specific to the mission of church-related colleges that would justify investment in preparation of future scientists. (This may be a broad philosophical or theological statement, or a statement descriptive of the theological statement, or a statement descriptive of the role and status of science within your faith traditions.)

9.1 If the undergraduate curriculum does not demand more knowledge of the sciences, especially the biological sciences, it will not be too long before the churches will have no parishioners, for life (human) may vanish from this planet.

9.2 Clearly, there are life and death issues facing mankind and earth (along with all its inhabitants) that require a thorough knowledge of the scientific/technological aspects, e.g., global warming, acid rain, nuclear weapons and waste disposal etc. Preparing competent scientists to deal with these issues is an absolute necessity. Preparing scientists who, by their training, are also alert to the ethical dimensions of these issues at the same time appears to be one area where church-related colleges can play an important if not unique role. If church-related institutions abdicate their responsibility to educate both scientifically literate as well as ethically well-formed individuals, who can be expected to do it? It appears to me that church-related colleges are contributing to an ethical vacuum if they do not invest in sound scientific education as well as value education.

9.3 It seems to me that science is increasingly concerned with the role of values in research and policy decisions. Issues such as environmental problems, scientific fraud, genetic manipulation, etc. raise ethical questions that students must learn to confront. St. Anselm College, as a Catholic liberal arts institution, can provide an excellent scientific education with significant opportunities for undergraduate research, while also emphasizing the importance of human values in the application and pursuit of technical knowledge.

9.4 Most historically Black Colleges are church-related. They are the prime providers of education for black people. Statistics show that the majority of the successful black graduates of colleges are graduates of historically Black Colleges. With these facts, HBC's have a responsibility to train students in all professions, regardless of the religious ties.

9.5 Education in our faith tradition should be Catholic and freeing. All aspects of our human lives are affected by science and technology; hence these are an essential component of a liberal education.

9.6 There is no conflict between science and the Methodist tradition of our college. Protestant (mainstream) and its emphasis on hard work to achieve desirable ends fits comfortably with the demands of science education.

9.7 I certainly do believe that church-related colleges such as ours should offer science and technology training. We have been doing such for many years and are noted for our accomplishments in this area and have not seen it as incompatible. We believe that it is a mandate to understand as well as possible the components of the world as we now know it. Science at this college has always been one of the two strongest areas available. The church has supported this and is willing to consider seriously what we pronounce. We want our students to think critically, to discriminate values, and be competent in problem-solving all of which can be enhanced through the study of science. We also seek truth, and science is certainly one of the places to attempt that.

9.8 As a Catholic I have always felt uncomfortable in the discussions which attend questions of responsibility, ethical behavior, prudent development of science and technology. Catholic Universities have, historically, contributed proportionally less to the education of scientists than they have to medicine, law and engineering. This lack of involvement is out of keeping with pronouncements concerning ethical dilemmas in science, an enthusiasm which Catholic institutions have felt appropriate and obligatory. For my part, we are not sufficiently involved in the education of research scientists to glibly comment on the value of science and its societal effects.

9.9 Scientists are consistently working to find proximate causes of events. All events, in the context of s Supreme Being are manifestations of God's Divine Plan and man's intelligence is the gift from Him by which we can see order in the Universe. It is incumbent upon us to use those gifts to the extent that we can, and with the expectation that it can benefit humanity.

9.10 This has nothing to do with a faith tradition but rather with a liberal arts education. We feel those with a liberal arts education are better able to grasp the implications and ramifications of their chosen fields.

9.11 First, liberal arts colleges (church-related or not) are a major source of scientists which the nation very much needs in the coming decades. It would be irresponsible for such institutions to shift their duty by giving up their historical role in this area. Second, these schools can provide the supporting environment needed to bring more women and minorities into the sciences, thus serving society in two ways at once. Such institutions should also serve to produce scientists with needed ethical sensitivities. All of these are well within the tradition of the United Church of Christ.

9.12 The entire realm of animal rights and human rights is broad enough to rationalize a role for church-related schools. Issues in genetics, reproductive technologies, drug manufacturing, (i.e. orphan drugs), heroic efforts to sustain life, ethical use of resources and toxic waste management, to name a few, all require an ethical and philosophical base from which we need to begin, implement, and refine our laws and statutes.

9.13 Our college is not the place to be asking these questions -- our church connection is loose at best. Our students' religious preferences match the state's demographics and our science faculty of 11 has only one member of our parent church. Even so, there is a campus-wide concern for Christianity and ethics. We teach -- live, really -- that there is something besides science and even our most focused majors must be different from those who graduate from the big state science factories, where the student can get by by taking only a few courses in areas other than science.

9.14 a) I do believe.
b) Churches have an obligation and a vocation to be countercultural prophets.

9.15 The church has the potential of instilling a humaneness to future scientists. It can provide an ethical framework for decision making and action.

9.16 If religion is to pervade all of human life, how can we ignore one of humankind's greatest philosophies: Science?

9.17 The world needs scientists motivated to:
a) help solve some of the world's problems
b) help bring the gospel to non-Christians in science
c) be role-models of Christ-followers, disciples, among others, including our youth.
d) be tuned to a high ethic in all areas of being.

9.18 It is important that sci/tech students encounter educated believers, who are competent professionals in a technical field, and also have a sophisticated and nuanced understanding of faith and theology. Such people have a witness value even if they rarely or never address interface questions between religion and science.

9.19 Scientific empiricism is antithetical to doctrine. When inquiry leads to conclusions that contradict doctrine, one or the other is forced to give way. Church-related schools are more or less bound by doctrine, and thus are forced to reject empiricism, no matter how compelling the evidence. In short, a Catholic liberal arts college is an oxymoron. When science is useful, it is acceptable. When science is neutral, it is tolerable. When science contradicts doctrine, it is ignored, or treated as mere opinion (occasionally, as in "creationism", it is distorted). There is constant tension between science and doctrine, and I see no way around it.

9.20 The mission of a church-related college should obviously be to seek and approach the truth, as outdated as that might sound. Science is a window to truth as are other disciplines, and any institution on such a journey should incorporate science into its pursuit, but reject science's triumphalism.

9.21 Our world is increasingly science-oriented, and scientists rather than other leaders are increasingly respected. Church-related colleges should be training B.S. level scientists so that ultimately the traditional viewpoints of Christianity make up at least a part of the voice of the scientific community.

9.22 If the practitioners of science do not espouse a religion, the influence of positivism will increase due to the positive contributions of science. Religiously committed scientists are needed to serve as spokesmen for a theistic interpretation of the world. Modern science is confronted with many ethical decisions. These can only be reached from a philosophical or theological position involving values. Scientific thinking prescinds from such values. It is important for people with a religious belief to be trained as scientists so that they will be in a position to make meaningful contributions to the problems that confront us and that will be respected by scientists. The whole concept of pollution has an ethical dimension that can only be resolved in terms of value systems. Similarly, the very use of nature which involves the animal kingdom is predicated on the Old Testament interpretation that they are created for man.

10.0 SELECTED RESPONSES TO THE QUESTION:

Offer any other view point useful to the discussion of sci/tech education at church-related colleges.

10.1 As scientists, our main priority is to provide a first-rate education that will prepare our majors for graduate school and that will equip the non-science student to understand technical issues. The primary difference between St. Anselm and non-denominational institutions is the values-oriented environment in which we achieve these goals.

10.2 The development of critical thinking and problem analysis skills that is so essential for successful scientists is best accomplished in a setting of diverse fields of study. It would be a serious failing if the church-related liberal arts colleges were to abdicate their responsibility in this area.

10.3 Modern technology is presenting us with ethical problems and choices. The scientist in a church-related college is not a theologian, but depends on the theologian to offer some answers. It seems that theological training should keep a pace with technological information and advances. A tall order.

10.4 I believe science offers a humbling perspective in so far as it does not elevate man but allows theories and other work to be overturned as new information is forthcoming. Philosophy can build systems where the intellect can roam free of constraints, yet science places one in a situation of limited knowledge and the limits of experimental evidence. Religion also can be soft in its conception of reality and lead to a primitive mindset that is static and unfair to believers.

10.5 Ecological issues and the "new physics" are calling many to a new interest in the mystical and the religious. We seem to have come full circle!

10.6 Question #1.3 is one-sided. Of greater concern to us is how our Christian perspective can inform our understanding of science. Science describes and explains how things work. Our "religious" perspective provides insight relative to value, purpose, worth, origin of the natural world.

10.7 Extremist/fundamental colleges could very well be antithetical to open-mindedness necessary for the proper practice of science.

10.8 People are often polarized in their thinking. They feel either science is right or religion is. The barriers separating them should come done. Defense of "Turf" should be set aside and issues openly discussed in a rational manner.

10.9 We may be small, but we pack a "punch" that can be a stepping stone to a future individual who holds his own in not only science but also in communication and rational thought regarding issues in society.

10.10 Truth is instructive in any area and its knowledge is wisely governed when the holder has a moral/ethical perspective. A church-related college should balance the secular viewpoint required by science with a spiritual one, and be prepared to withhold a mis-application of science which is perceived to be contrary to God's intention.

10.11 Scientist have a splendid window on creation at its most beautiful and awe-inspiring levels. Through that window we catch glimpses of the glory, the majesty, the power, and the graciousness of God. To teach science is to bring others to that window (and also to remind them that despite all we see thereby, we don't see Jesus.) To see the grandeur and glory of God in history in its fullness we have to look to the cross. Hearing this from a scientist may (just may) reach someone not easily reached by others.) This work can happen at a church-related college.

10.12 If we become so heavenly minded as to be no earthly good then our religion isn't worth much. Jesus went about doing good and healing people. How can we be effective in bettering conditions if we are ignorant of scientific and technological issues?

10.13 It seems obvious that one cannot consider ones self educated in any sense of the word without some knowledge of science. If it then follows that the institution must hire scientists to teach the sciences, it is only a small step to offering majors. Many of these departments are small, understaffed and overworked and yet they are among the most productive in meeting the educational goal.

10.14 The relationship between science and church in college education MUST be one of mutual reinforcement. The church must recognize that sci/tech education IS THE PRIMARY MODE of preparation for economic survival in the world. Even the most visionary of church hierarchy must recognize that liberal arts alone will rarely support graduate and family. The job market is technological. The sci/tech educators must recognize that SCIENCE EDUCATION WITHOUT LIBERAL ARTS IS STERILE, ISOLATING, and OFTEN ARROGANT. It may lead to good, even great, personal income and position but it will not enable the graduate to appreciate or benefit from such attainment.

10.15 Our school views natural science as from God and also as a way in which God reveals Himself. We have every right to study it and ought to strive to be excellent in this attempt. Although this college is limited financially - the administration is attempting to increase the faculty and monies to better assist this division. The school is committed to a worthy program.

10.16 Science is not only a profession, it is a way of thinking and solving problems that every educated person should be familiar with. Ignorance in this area incapacitates one from making logical decisions in many areas of our daily life and in determining steps that should be taken by our government, as well as private industry.

11.0 SELECTED RESPONSES TO THE QUESTION:

Comment on the philosophy of education at your college as related to the sci/tech curriculum.

11.1 There is a deplorable lack of understanding on the part of the non-scientist faculty and administration concerning the necessity to increase the level of science knowledge of our graduates. The basic philosophy seems to be that science should be required only of the scientist and that the non-scientists can function in the world with essentially no science.

11.2 The centerpiece of the general curriculum at St. Anselm College is the Humanities Program, a two-year integrated course taken by all freshman and sophomores. The program explores the relationships between different fields of inquiry, such as philosophy, theology, history and science. In addition, all students are required to take two semesters of a laboratory science. Undergraduates thus receive training both in the methodology of science and in the human dimensions of science and technology.

11.3 There appear to be two perspectives, one a philosophical one and the other is practical reality. Philosophically, faculty recognize the importance of the sciences and the scientific method appeals to them. The practical reality of limiting the core hours for all students leads them to a compromising situation. Ultimately, it appears, the ability to verbalize a problem is more important than understanding the scientific basis of a problem. We commit all students here to the study of environmental science, yet the course is superficial by virtue of necessity. Perhaps the weakness of the faith mindset shows through. Science is perceived to be complex (as is religion) by the non-science faculty. Yet they see students and society as needing to take a stand and this taking of stands (right or wrong) becomes the critical thing in the end. If this is indeed true, I worry for society. Personally, I like to be skeptical of all things before and after I take a position, with constant reassessment being part of the process.

11.4 This institution (Jesuit) is quite unprepared to become significantly involved in science/technology education beyond the pre-health science level. It has excellent physical facilities for that level and a faculty which is better than one would expect, but it lacks administrative experience with science as a major component of society. There is a gulf between the scientific world as it acts internationally, and the experience and aspirations of those who make policy decisions. For this reason, it is very unlikely that significant change in the level of science education can (or possibly should) occur here.

11.5 This college has historically supported science and technology, to a lesser extent, well. In general, issues involving sci/tech are discussed in many different departments. Science and religion are largely regarded as independent here, although one can support the other in certain ways.

11.6 At present they are minimizing the importance of science for non-majors permitting only one lab course and one lecture science course which could be History and Philosophy of Science. They are looking for science courses on issues and not basics.

11.7 There is no consensus, there is also no demand for a consensus. There is no "Lutheran" position on issues in science and technology. I hope there never becomes one. [Time-conditioned statements on political issues are another matter]. Even here it's hard to find a way to condemn those who disagree by calling them "Un-Lutheran" or "Un-Christian."

11.8 There exists no conflict between the philosophy of Xavier University as it relates to the sci/tech curriculum. More than 55% of our students are pursuing degrees in the sci/tech disciplines. We feel a very definite need to produce individuals, rooted in our faith traditions, who will contribute to the forming of a more humane society, with these contributions being made in all possible areas of society.

11.9 a) Have a good masters program rather than a poor doctoral program.
b) Education in science is part of a liberal education.
c) Next January we shall have our Sixteenth Annual Physics Department Reflective Weekend.

11.10 Academic freedom and individual integrity of the teacher is highly prized and respected. I have taught at this institution for over thirty years. The institution has been associated with two different protestant religions and for a brief time, been independent. I have never been a member of the sponsoring church. I am reluctant to support most organized religions. Each seems to be a bit too self centered for my tastes. However, I think churches and religions have an important role to play in society and in science and science education. However, they must not inhibit science or critical thinking by closing areas of investigation as being forbidden because they are contrary to church policy. Such a move is fatal to both religion and science, in my opinion.

This has been my philosophy and experience throughout my professional teaching career. I think it is the correct one and has been, and is, the prevailing philosophy at my college. I have made this philosophy known to various administrations over the years and have never had the slightest suggestion that I change. One faculty member (in science) in the past, was counselled to keep his religion out of the classrooms and ". . . not confuse the commandments with the gas laws."

11.11 We have recently introduced a course entitled "The Impact of Technology on Women: Reproductive Technology". This course brings in experts from diverse areas including social work, anthropology, biology, religion, philosophy, psychology, art, literature and communications as well as a physician practicing the new assisted reproductive technology. (Partially funded by UCC). All students take one year of a laboratory based science.

11.12 We try to combine vigor with tolerance, but within a broad view of the nature of man and all his endeavors, which are seen to be affected by the fall.

11.13 I have a bleak picture of education in the future. Colleges that attempt to form the complete person, particularly in the context of biblical presuppositions, will have to compete for a decreasing number of students with publicly funded institutions with low tuition, splendid campuses, and headline football teams. In the space of a generation we can become a generation of specialists who have not the least notion of where we have come from or where we are going. I trust in God's providence that the outcome will be different, and that we who have labored to pass on the torch will be permitted to have a part in His solution.

11.14 I don't really see what this "philosophy" is as promulgated by administrators. Where the vision is to be just "church-related" and not Christ-centered, we are reduced to pushing the same secular standards as everyone else. What a sad, sad waste. If I asked you, "are you a Christian?" would you reply, "No, but I am church-related"?

11.15 Seventh-day Adventists place a heavy emphasis on healthful living. So of necessity our students need to have a good and solid exposure to science and technology subjects.

11.16 During my career I have taught at a large West Coast University, a very large state related University, a middle sized Catholic University, and at Stetson University which has a student population of 3000. There is no philosophical difference among these schools as far as teaching is concerned. We pride ourselves on the graduates in science who have gone on to many of the very best professional and graduate schools. The administration has remained out of the curriculum, and has increasingly supported the sciences with funds as available. There are no restrictions on recruitment of new faculty, and as a consequence we at present have no Baptists on the staff. I see no pending change in the future that might alter the present relationship.

11.17 The philosophy of education at our college, as related to the science/technology curriculum, suffers from the fact that the majority of our non-science faculty (who outnumber the science faculty) are either ignorant of the role of science and technology in a liberal arts education or are actually anti-science. Too many of them were educated during the past 20 years during which science and technology were portrayed as the source of much of the evil in the world.

11.18 The philosophy is under transition as the college re-examines its core requirements. Hopefully they will listen to the Math/Science Division and increase the sci/tech emphasis (it would be hard for the emphasis to get any smaller).

11.19 We have an administration that does not understand or appreciate the role of natural sciences in the curriculum of all liberally educated students. Hence we are woefully inadequate in terms of facilities and supplies and equipment.

11.20 The philosophy is great, the practice is poor with respect to the non-science/tech majors. The non-majors are very much shortchanged. There is no decent science requirement for them, and there is such a competition for students in the general education science courses that are required that no serious demands can be made on the students. The philosophy of education as applied to the majors is different. The majors get a fairly balanced education with a required liberal arts core of 39 out of 124 semester units in the liberal and fine arts.

11.21 At my institution the philosophy related to science is not on solid ground. We are in the midst of re-evaluating our goals statement, and relative to science our plan of action is not clear. The science faculty is divided as to the role research should play (undergraduate research), and what role publication should play in promotion consideration. In a Christian institution such as mine I feel that strong, if not total, emphasis should be on education for its own end.

11.22 The university recognizes the important role played by science and provides strong support for biology, chemistry, physics and psychology. It also recognizes the importance of a knowledge of science for all people and requires two (2) science courses of all students regardless of majors.

SELECTED REFERENCES:

National Institutes of Health: January 1989, "The Status of Biomedical Search Facilities: 1988"

National Science Foundation: "Scientific and Engineering Research Facilities at Universities and Colleges: 1988

Oberlin College, March 1987, "Maintaining America's Scientific Productivity, The Necessity of Liberal Arts Colleges"

American Association for the Advancement of Science, Projects 2061 "Science for All Americans Summary", March 1989

Communicator, Council of Graduate School, Data Sources, OTA Report finds education of scientists and engineers a diverse process, outlines Federal policy options to strengthen system. Peter D. Syzerson.

The Government-University-Industry Research Roundtable: "Nurturing Science and Engineering Talents", a discussion paper, July 1987.

National Science Foundation Program Flyer: "Ethics and Values Studies in Science, Technology and Society" (RST).

American Council On Education: "Higher Education and National Affairs," 9/11/89 Facts in Brief -- High school Graduates enrolled in more math and science courses.

The New York Times Magazine, January 22, 1989, "Higher Education, The Real Crises", Michael I. Sovern.

The New York Times, "The End of Forever, How Can the Environment Be Rescued?", Anthony Lewis, October 12, 1989.

The New York Times, May 21, 1989, by Adam Clymer, "Poles Show Contrast In How Public and E.P.A. View Environment".

The New York Times, May 9, 1989, "Colleges, Glad For Research Gifts, Are Asking More For Mortar"

Chronicle for Higher Education, "Outlook is Bleak for Federal Aid to Help Colleges Repair Their Decaying Science Bulletins."

Chronicle for Higher Education, August 2, 1989, "Once 5 Billion for Renovations." Bush's Nominee for Science Advisor says "small" projects will be his top priority.

Chronicle for Higher Education, February 15, 1989, "Points of View," Heilbron and Kevles, by "failing to discuss the 'civics' of science and technolgy, history textbooks distort the past and endanger the future."

AAHE Bulletin, September 1989: "The Next Academic Revolution," David Reisman, "On The Next Generation of the Professoriate," by Russ Edgerton.

The Chronicle of Higher Education, May 31, 1989, FIfty-One Institutions that will get huge institute grants.

National Science Foundation, Program announcement and guidelines for Research Experiences for Undergraduates, December 1, 1987.

American Association for the Advancement of Science: "Education in the Sciences."

AAAS Science Education Directory, 1989.

Science Technology and Human Values published quarterly by the Mass. Institute of Technology, President and Fellows of Harvard College.

American Association for the Advancement of Sciences
Science Education News: Committee on Conduct of Science, National Academy of Sciences, "On Being a Scientist," 1989.

FEASIBILITY OF DEVELOPING ADEQUATE NATURAL SCIENCE PROGRAMS IN A CHURCH-RELATED SCHOOL

Dr. J. Richard Chase

Dr. J. Richard Chase, President of Wheaton College since 1982, was President of Biola College, La Mirada, California. Dr. Chase earned a Bachelor in Theology (Biola), B.A. and M.A. degrees (Pepperdine) and a PhD in Rhetoric and Public Address (Cornell). Dr. Chase was listed among the 100 most effective college presidents in America in a nationwide survey reported in the Chronicle of Higher Education.

INTRODUCTORY PROFILE OF WHEATON COLLEGE

The suggestions advanced in this paper are based on the experiences of Wheaton College (Illinois). This College is normally categorized as a national liberal arts college, with over 70% of its students coming from outside of Illinois. (All statistics are from academic year 1988/89 unless otherwise noted.) Its history of 130 years and current character place it within the context of church-related institutions. However, the College has never been controlled nor officially related to any church body. It is protestant and evangelical. It draws from a wide range of Christian communities, including both independent churches and mainline denominations. Though protestant in history and affirmation, the College attracts a handful of Catholic students.

The College limits undergraduate enrollment to approximately 2200 students. Some 144 students are majoring in music in our Conservatory and the remaining 2056 undergraduates are in the School of Arts and Sciences. Two-hundred and ninety-five students are majoring in our natural science programs, with an additional 124 freshmen intending to declare one of these areas as a major. If the freshman class is added, we list 419 natural science majors.

Our science enrollment (with freshmen included) is as follows: Biology 172, Chemistry 83, Geology 3, Mathematics/Computer Science 85, and Physics 76.

We are selective in our admissions. The 1988 SAT scores for incoming freshmen averaged 1150 (verbal 554, Math 596). Wheaton enrolled a total of 82 National Merit Finalists in 1988/89.

The College has a history of strong science programs, accomplished with limited resources. In the Franklin & Marshall studies on Baccalaureate-Origins of Doctorate Recipients from Four-year Colleges, Wheaton ranked 37th out of the top 337 colleges listed for the period 1920-1984 for all doctorates in all the sciences. It ranked 12th out of the top 339 when all academic disciplines were considered. Over the past 25 years, one out of four of our graduates in the natural sciences has gone on to complete a doctoral program in science.

Wheaton College is also a member of "The Undergraduate Science Group." The decline in science majors among this group of 48 liberal arts colleges is less than a quarter of the decline among colleges and universities generally. In 1980 this small cluster of colleges granted 54 out of every thousand bachelors' degrees in science granted in the United States.

Currently 26.5 FTE faculty (all with doctorates in the natural sciences) are assigned to the Wheaton College Science Departments, and their combined departmental operating budgets total $1,429,594. This does not include library acquisitions, special equipment purchases, refurbishing, maintenance, and overhead.

The College also owns and operates a fifty-acre Science Station in the Black Hills of South Dakota. Facilities for lodging, food service, recreation, and academic work are suitable for up to 60 students and staff. Summer studies there are conducted in general biology, botany, ecology, geology, zoology, and astronomy.

OBSTACLES CONFRONTED IN THE DEVELOPMENT OF SCIENCE AT A CHURCH-RELATED COLLEGE

In meeting the demands for a reasonable educational experience in science, church-related colleges confront several obstacles.

Science is expensive. Even apart from the cost of laboratories and the escalating cost of scientific equipment, the natural sciences are high cost centers. At Wheaton, for example, our four Science Departments rank 1, 2, 4 & 5, in departmental cost per student. To that may be added the high cost of scientific journals and monographs that are included in the library budget.

Interest in the natural sciences has been declining in the United States. This decline in numbers is a national phenomenon that is tragically accompanied by a decline in science and mathematics proficiency. ETS Developments (Volume XXXIV, Number 4, Spring 1989) reports on the results of an international assessment of math and science for thirteen-year-olds in five countries and four Canadian provinces. Three of the Canadian provinces were split into English and French-speaking categories, so there were twelve groups. The United States was last in Math and ninth in science. Lawrence A. Uzzell, Science Editor for The Wall Street Journal, addressed this same theme in the Wednesday, October, 1989, issue of The Wall Street Journal. He writes,

> The international Association for the Evaluation of Education Achievement reports that in 1982 the average Japanese student outscored the top 5% of U.S. students enrolled in college-prep math courses. In chemistry and physics, advanced science students in U.S. high schools performed worse than their counterparts in almost all countries studied. In biology they ranked dead last, behind such nations as Singapore and Thailand.

The general decline in college and university science enrollment will ultimately create a serious shortage of science teachers at all levels. Church-related colleges will need attractive programs in the sciences if they hope to recruit and retain excellent faculty.

Church/science issues continue to exert an influence on evangelical colleges. This is a centuries-old conflict. In the face of Third Century B.C. Greek genius that determined the earth was round (within 195 miles of its actual circumference) and that it turned on its axis and orbited the sun, the church persisted for centuries in suppressing those who accepted such notions.

Today's battlefield ranges from theories of the origins of our world to gene sequencing. For example, some critics within the evangelical community encourage their constituencies to repudiate evangelical colleges that refuse to support a 24-hour six-day time frame for the creation of the universe. And most have been caught in the crossfire on the abortion issue.

In the face of such obstacles as the costliness of science programs, a decline in enrollment, and pressures from the Christian public, church-related colleges must reassert their commitment to excellent programs in the natural sciences. For several reasons, strong science programs have never been more urgently needed than they are today.

THE CASE FOR STRONG SCIENCE PROGRAMS IN THE NATURAL SCIENCES

Science is the engine that drives business. It is the basis of modern medicine and provides the background information for many of today's ethical choices. Tomorrow's college graduate will be confronted with a bewildering array of options provided by the ever expanding technology of biomedical practices, DNA technologies and environmental crises. Our graduates will eventually administer such technologies, make laws and regulations regarding such practices, conduct research, and teach the next generation of scientists, citizens, and parents.

Above all, a church-related institution that believes in God will truncate student's understanding of the very nature of God when the doing and understanding of science are neglected. Much is relative in our world, but a fertile area in which to explore absolutes and to understand an important aspect of the character of God is through interacting with His creation.

Further, the technologies of biomedical practices have already advanced beyond the average college graduate's ability to develop a reasoned response to the new choices that confront humankind. Pulling the plug on a seemingly lifeless child while holding hospital staff at bay with a gun is at once bizarre, shocking, and understandable. There is a crisis in thought and education at both the individual and national policy level. Educators have a major task before them. Those who believe in God and teach in church-related institutions need to be knowledgeable and active participants.

DEVELOPING ADEQUATE SCIENCE PROGRAMS

Institutional commitment is the very heart of the development of science programs. It is a matter of priorities. Adequate programs can be developed, for example, if science programs are as important to a College as a successful athletic program or an attractive student center. If funds are limited (as they usually are), the sciences should still receive their full share if the institution is to be faithful to both the liberal arts and the school's Christian values.

Priority must mean reasonable action, and I believe it starts with a strong general education requirement in the natural sciences. All college graduates should know what a scientist does and should have sufficient laboratory experience to see first-hand how nature works. Much of life will be unintelligible to a graduate who misses this experience. In any age, and particularly in this age, illiteracy in the ways of scientific inquiry nullify the claim that a person is liberally educated.

The priority to teach science to all students and to develop a few strong programs in the natural sciences will necessarily call for other priorities. These include the recruitment of qualified and creative faculty who have the appropriate doctorates. Terminal research degrees normally assure us that the prospective faculty member has completed an extensive research project under the supervision of competent scientists. Such experience is essential in the teaching of the natural sciences at the collegiate level.

Such faculty need acceptable laboratories and modern analytical or recording equipment for the teaching of the natural sciences. In addition, adequate budgets must be provided for supplies, repairs, replacements, and the media and library resources for each science discipline represented in the curriculum.

Even with competent faculty and adequate teaching resources, the task of developing adequate science programs has just begun. Students need to be attracted to the program. Recruiting high school or community college students through scholarships based on both need and merit is only part of the task. With the minimal interest now seen in the natural sciences in such schools, adequate enrollment is not likely from this student pool.

Most liberal arts colleges have a large pool of freshmen and sophomores who have not declared majors. These students can be attracted to take additional science courses as electives and many can be encouraged to major in a natural science program. Here are courses of action that have helped us: stimulating teaching, effective advising, seminars that demonstrate the important role science must play in contemporary issues of concern to students, contact with professionals through the extensive use of guest speakers at forums and in class, field trips, museum visits, visits to the research laboratories of industry, visits to research university laboratories, and presentation of career options. Interdisciplinary approaches to science and the development of innovative curriculum have proved especially effective in attracting students.

Once attracted to science, students need to be encouraged and nurtured. This calls for student research opportunities where the excitement of discovery can be fostered. Often these can be developed locally, but we have found that there are excellent summer research opportunities for students across the country. In addition, we have developed internships both here and abroad. Wheaton has developed a program that places students in a third world setting for a semester or more. Our Human Needs and Global Resources (HNGR) program annually places some 20 students overseas. Biology has had the highest number of students enrolled since the program started about a decade ago.

Above all, it is essential that the natural sciences have the momentum and attractiveness that come when faculty and students are excited about what science can contribute to the improvement of our world. The faculty provide models for students by being dedicated to discovery, and the improvement of our environment and the quality of life, and by displaying an enthusiasm for the life of a scientist. Such faculty attract students and build the reputation of a college's natural science program.

Two major avenues for fulfilling priorities are resources and innovation. Resources can be found and committed. Most institutions, even very small ones, have learned that funds allocated for the writing of grants will produce a substantial net gain within a couple of years -- often within the first year. Even releasing a professor from one course for proposal writing returns an excellent profit. These are great days for such solicitation, since many foundations are committed to strengthen the teaching of science and to the encouragement of scientists in their personal research projects.

The enthusiasm and cooperation of faculty are essential. The development of science is a team project. A fair portion of Wheaton's success with foundations has come from leads, contacts, and proposal writing by the faculty. Even if the institution has an office dedicated to foundation solicitation, it will be ineffective without considerable assistance from the science faculty. Faculty who argue that they are not in the fund-raising business have a distorted view of how funds are raised. In short, faculty orientation must be an integral part of fund raising and some release time for faculty who are proficient in the development of grants will also prove beneficial.

Business and industry can also prove helpful in the provision of equipment. In my nineteen years as a college president, good pieces of equipment have come from industry research laboratories, hospitals, and sister universities that moved up to a higher level of sophistication. These contacts depend upon such continuing relationships as cooperative summer research projects in which both the college and industry benefit, and the normal contacts of the president and other college personnel.

Campus creativity can also produce funds for priorities. At Wheaton all year-end surplus funds are allocated to one time capital expenses. In recent years these have included laboratory renovation and special equipment purchases for the natural sciences.

The growing sophistication of equipment for the biological and biomedical and physical sciences needs to be faced realistically with both priorities and specific courses of action. Many campuses have booster clubs for athletic teams, "friends of the library," and similar interest groups. The natural sciences can also develop such relationships. We recently inaugurated a mini-campaign for our Chemistry Department that will draw on the loyalty of chemistry graduates.

Such graduates are now serving as physicians, teachers, corporate executives, and researchers. A representative group of such alumni now serve as a steering committee for this campaign.

Innovation is the growth industry of academic development. Innovation in curriculum and research experiences in the natural sciences can: a) provide the insights and procedures of science to a wider segment of our student bodies; b) help attract new majors; c) expand research opportunities for advanced students, and d) provide opportunities for both professional growth and contributions to science by faculty.

Joan Rodgers, a science writer and public affairs specialist now associated with the Johns Hopkins Medical Institutions, notes that "studies show that 40 percent of the adult public wants to learn more about science" (Currents, January, 1988, p. 24). If the general education requirements in science are viewed as opportunities to excite students about the significance and marvel of science, education will be enhanced and science enrollments will increase.

Many colleges are finding ways to strengthen their programs, attract students, and provide new challenges for faculty. For example, at

Wheaton we now offer a general education course that is truly interdisciplinary rather than just multidisciplinary. The course, "Majestic Nature," emphasizes discovery and involves various pedagogies to the virtual exclusion of the lecture method. Eight faculty have been directly involved in planning and/or teaching this course.

We are also developing a Brain Science program that will offer an interdisciplinary major in neuro-science. It will embrace psychology, biology, chemistry, linguistics, computer science and philosophy. It will acquaint the student with issues of mind and matter and the Christian response to a totally deterministic view of the mind.

Innovation can also enrich the generally limited research experiences of the average liberal arts college faculty member. Wheaton's location in the western suburbs of Chicago provides us with excellent off-campus resources and support. If we were 500 miles from such resources, however, I would consider a summer science program in a science-rich metropolitan center as of equal importance to a European study center for the study of literature and history.

Selected affiliations that enrich our science program include both consortial arrangements and special research opportunities for both faculty and students.

Consortial arrangements of Wheaton College include the following:

<u>Associated Colleges of the Chicago Area</u>

This affiliation provides stimulation for professors who may find few colleagues on their own campus with similar interests, as well as expanded educational opportunities for students. Cooperative courses, colloquia and a spring symposium where students share reports on research projects are regular features.

<u>Great Lakes Cluster Pew Science Program</u>

Five colleges and Northwestern University comprise this cluster. The Pew grant is designed to enhance educational opportunities at each school and attract more students into the sciences. Freshmen science majors can apply for an eight-week "Pew Scholars Program" for the following summer. Five "Scholars" chosen from each school and distributed among all of the natural science disciplines will work and learn together the principles of scientific research. This is a forerunner to the "Pew Research Fellows" program, which is a summer research experience with a faculty member at one of the cluster schools. The "Fellows" must have finished their sophomore or junior year. Both programs award a stipend and provide free housing.

Christian College Consortium and the Christian College Coalition.

These two affiliations provide faculty enrichment programs that enhance the teaching of the natural sciences.

Representative research opportunities are provided through arrangements with:

Amoco
Argonne Laboratory
University of Kentucky
Loyola University
Northern Illinois University
Ohio State University

Research strengthens teaching, and joint student-faculty research is the essence of quality science instruction. At a small liberal arts college the best faculty should be involved in both instruction and research projects for freshmen as well as honor seniors. Attracting and retaining such faculty calls for priorities, funds and innovation. Equally crucial is a college's ability to attract quality students capable of serious work in the sciences. Such students add an essential dimension to class discussion and experimentation and help retain outstanding faculty.

Liberal arts education will be impoverished if quality science instruction declines in our church-related schools. The signs of demise are all about us. They include lack of interest in the sciences among high-school students and a scarcity of competent faculty. At a recent conference in San Antonio, Texas, the President Elect of the American Chemical Society expressed his conviction that a large portion of the liberal arts schools will have to close down their Chemistry and Physics Departments in the next fifteen years for lack of good equipment and competent faculty.

It is my hope that this conference will encourage both faculty and administrators to renew their commitment to excellence in the natural sciences within the church-related college. It is more than just a concern for a balanced curriculum in the liberal arts, or even the proper education of our students in a technologically sophisticated world. It is, rather, a matter of educational integrity. The natural sciences are fundamental to the development of a realistic world view. Our understanding of life itself rests in part upon scientific knowledge. Our ability to change and improve life in this universe is the ultimate business of science. And, above all, our knowledge of God -- the reason for our institutional church-relatedness -- rests upon a proper understanding of His creation and its basic laws.

Excellence in science is not an option -- it is a necessity for a church-related liberal arts college.

WHY CHURCH-RELATED INSTITUTIONS SHOULD BE INVOLVED IN SCIENCE/TECHNOLOGY EDUCATION

S. Rosemary Connell, csj

Rosemary Connell, csj is Co-ordinator of Social Justice for the Saint Louis Province of the CSJ's. She brings to this position a background in bioethics, biology and education. She has a doctorate in biology from the University of Notre Dame and is a long-time member of ITEST.

While it is not necessary to be a believer in God to be a scientist, to be a complete person, one needs to have developed some of the wonder and questioning that characterize scientists. The oft-quoted statement of Irenaeus: "The glory of God is man (and woman) fully alive," implies that all human gifts and qualities be nurtured and developed. The pre-school child has the wonder and curiosity of the scientist. What happens to this child in school? Is this part of his/her human potential developed? If not, why not? What can be done to develop the wonder and curiosity of the next generation?

Why should church-related institutions train scientists and technologists? These schools have an edge on transmitting values and they have the capability to educate and form integrated, spiritual graduates. The scientific world, as much as the world of business, needs the presence of such individuals. Only in this way will there be leaven in the scientific community.

In most church-related institutions faculty have some advantages, over their peers in state schools. They have a great deal of latitude in developing courses and curricula. They also have true academic freedom. They can present values related to science and technology. They can openly discuss both opposing scientific views and opposing moral views. They can help students develop the skills of critical thinking in relation to science and its applications. Graduates who have had this kind of education should be able to see the possible dangers in certain aspects of research and to question how and why they are done.

While The Decree on the Apostolate of the Laity is addressed specifically to Roman Catholic Christians, it is not limited or limiting. Paragraph 5 states:

> Christ's redemptive work, while essentially concerned with the salvation of men, includes also the renewal of the whole temporal order. Hence the mission of the Church is not only to bring the message and grace of Christ to men but also to penetrate and perfect the temporal order with the spirit of the Gospel. In fulfilling this mission of the Church, the Christian laity exercise their apostolate both in the Church and in the world, in both the spiritual and the temporal orders. These orders, although distinct, are so connected in the singular plan of God that he himself intends to raise up the whole world again in Christ and to make it a new creation,

> initially on earth and completely on the last day. In both orders the layman, being simultaneously a believer and a citizen, should be continuously led by the same Christian conscience.

Among the "citizens" referred to above are many specialists. The increase in scientific knowledge and in its applications in this century has resulted in a larger percentage of citizens who are "expert" scientists and technologists. Science and technology permeate almost every aspect of our lives. We need to have those who are believers, citizens, and scientists in this world.

How are church-related institutions going to carry out this commitment, if it does not extend from the beginning to the end of formal education?

We not only need the believer scientists in the laboratories, but we need those who are believers, scientists, educators in our institutions. Church-related universities need to have strong graduate programs in the sciences and technologies both for the research and the development of young faculty. At the undergraduate level, colleges need to do the same thing. The faculty at this level usually have the added obligation to interest, excite, and instruct the non-science major (the believer-citizen).

Majors don't usually become interested in science as college freshmen. The wonder and curiosity of the small child and his/her interest in the world must be nurtured from pre-school through high-school. Therefore, the training of science-educators has to be part of the mission of some institutions.

As I was beginning to work on this paper, I spent some time reading catalogues of church-related institutions. Specifically I looked at the institutional philosophy and/or mission statement. There is great variety, but there is also much sameness! The quotations presented here are typical and apply to the whole student body. They show a verbal commitment to scientific and technological education:

> "to develop humanistic, scientific, and computer literacy" (Chaminade, Roman Catholic)

> "to develop critical awareness of the impact of science, technology, economic, literacy, political and social scientific developments on society" (Lindenwood, Presbyterian)

"to develop a strong understanding of the physical world" (William Penn, Quaker Christian)

"to show that there is no dichotomy between faith and ideas" (Valpariso, Lutheran).

To continue to have departments in the sciences and in technology is increasingly more expensive. If it is a priority, there will be a way found to continue and even increase institutional commitment to the sciences. As a group, or as individuals, ITEST members may be able to influence the trustees, administrators, and financial officers of colleges and universities to give an edge to science and technology.

No institution can be everything to everyone. Creative collaborative efforts may be a partial answer to the practical aspects of science education. Collaboration may also broaden the influence of church-related institutions.

If we cannot continue and/or increase our efforts, the gap between science and religion will continue to widen and the disunity continue to grow.

As a hopeful note, I would like to include the following opinion on religion and space technology.

The article, "Religion and Space Technology," on the following page is reprinted with permission, from *__The Futurist__*, *published by the World Future Society, 4916 Saint Elmo Avenue, Bethesda, Maryland 20814.*

Religion and Space Technology

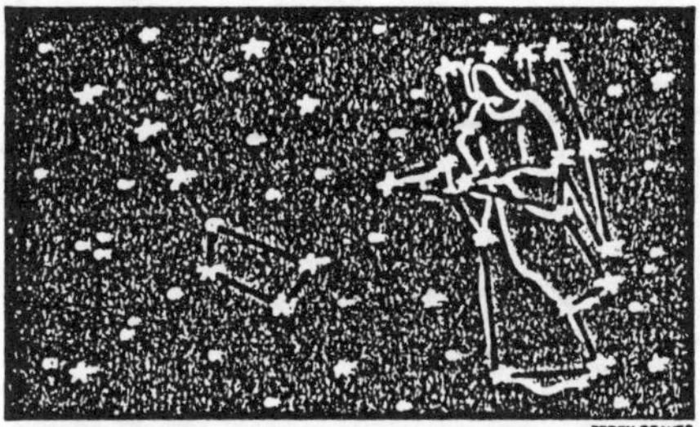

TERRY GRAVES

Man has always looked to the heavens for salvation. Where politics and religion have failed to achieve brotherhood, we look to space technology to provide an answer, as with the proposed joint U.S.–Soviet mission to Mars. Space technology, at least in the field of satellite communications, has probably done more to unite the world than many thousands of political and religious leaders could ever do.

The religious implications of the Space Age are awesome. Already, theories of "ancient astronauts" are challenging our theology. One proposed space technology, terraforming, would transform planets to make them viable for mankind. For example, Mars's polar icecaps could be melted to create oceans and an atmosphere capable of sustaining human life. Such terraforming projects would make us nothing less than co-workers with God in the work of creation.

How will terraforming influence religion? If we can congratulate the child who aspires to be like his father, might we not also take pride when mankind, born in God's image, tries to emulate the Creator? Clearly, our technology and our religion are at a crossroads. While the medical field now wrestles with the religious implications of euthanasia, reproductive technologies, and birth control, our "playing God" in space may create future religious controversy.

Will our conquest of space lead the world astray from God? I would suggest that our newfound powers are not leading us apart from God, but rather toward the day when we become a new legion of "angels," doing the work of our Creator while still in awe of the divine intelligence that brought forth the cosmos out of chaos.

Space has become the new setting for religious experience, even in recent fiction. While church attendance dwindles, people line up in droves at movie theaters to see the celestials (i.e., angels) of *2001: A Space Odyssey*, *2010*, and *Close Encounters of the Third Kind* and the Messiahs from heaven in the films *E.T.: The Extra-Terrestrial* and *Superman*.

These "religious" space films parallel—and in some cases were influenced by — the dawn of our Space Age. The appeal of *Star Trek* is its optimistic view of a coming brotherhood of man (i.e., Kingdom of God). Author Robert Short, in his book *The Gospel from Outer Space* (1983), points out that in the *Star Wars* saga "many of the teachings that Ben Kenobi and Yoda give to Luke about 'the Force' sound as if they could have been taken directly from the teachings of Jesus." Are space-related films replacing the spiritual inspiration traditionally found in the church? It would appear so.

Will the exodus of man into space be incorporated into some Scripture of the future? Are we too close to our own great accomplishments in space to understand their true religious significance? Is space the Holy Land of tomorrow?

Some space enthusiasts consider themselves disciples of a new era in human history. The new frontier promises to be an uplifting experience in more ways than one. Perhaps noted visionary Barbara Marx Hubbard said it best:

> One school of futurist thinking sees mankind on the verge of a tremendous leap forward — a kind of leap into the cosmos, reminiscent of the emergence of the first amphibians onto land in primeval times. People of this school of futurist thinking have what might be described as a religious yearning for the future and for the transformation of man and his civilization into something of cosmic greatness.

For too long, the image of the space activist has been that of a technocrat at odds with anything seemingly religious in nature. But this is not the case. Let no one doubt the spirituality that empowers the space movement. In the name of our Maker, we shall pierce the darkness of space and bring forth light.

— Mitchell Gordon

About the Author

Mitchell Gordon is a writer and a founding member of the Philadelphia chapter of the World Future Society. His address is 928 Clinton Street, Philadelphia, Pennsylvania 19107.

Future View, a regular feature in THE FUTURIST, is an editorial page giving various writers' opinions about the trends and likely events that will influence the future. Readers are invited to respond to these editorials or to submit their own to be considered for publication in THE FUTURIST. Send to: Managing Editor, THE FUTURIST, 4916 Saint Elmo Avenue, Bethesda, Maryland 20814.

SCIENCE AND TECHNOLOGY IN JESUIT EDUCATION*

Fr. Robert A. Brungs, S.J.

* *This paper is reprinted with permission from Jesuit Higher Education, edited by Rolando E. Bonachea, Duquesne University Press, 1989, p 192.*

Fr. Robert Brungs, S.J. is currently Adjunct Associate Professor of Physics at Saint Louis University and a consultant to the National Conference of Catholic Bishops' Committee on Science and Human Values. He is a co-founder and Director of ITEST.

INTRODUCTION

There are, as we have heard during this Colloquium, almost as many aspects of Jesuit education as there are people and institutions involved in it. If we are to talk reasonably about the place of science and technology in Jesuit education, we should offer a rationale for its being there at all. It is possible that there may be some repetition between my approach and what has already been said earlier in these proceedings. I would be truly consoled if there were some repetitions, since that would indicate that I am not standing here alone in all my idiosyncratic glory!

I wish to confine myself more or less to Catholic aspects of Jesuit education -- its Church relationships -- while, of course, not denying in any way its civil obligations and its strictly intellectual (and, therefore, human) obligations. This is done for purposes of simplification and personal preference, not for purposes of ideology.

THE NEED

Christianity is a faith that is necessarily and solidly based on the belief that the Son of God became man in the womb of the Virgin Mary. He became, as St. Paul tells us, one like us in all things except sin. He became so much a part of the nature and the history of the world that St. Luke can date the beginning of his ministry among us with a listing of those in power in Palestine at the time: "In the 15th year of Tiberius Caesar's reign, when Pontius Pilate was governor of Judaea..." More, we firmly believe that after his death and resurrection he ascended bodily into heaven, retaining his full humanity in glory. Thereby, he instituted a new state of bodily life, one to which we are called and destined.

As Catholics we live in a world which we believe to be sacramental, a world in which "material" things are seen to be of "spiritual" value, to have an everlasting destiny in God. We live in a world where, we believe, bread and wine become the Body and Blood of Christ, where water is a substance that washes us clean of the sin into which we are born and is the material agent (indispensably material) of our introduction into the life and love of the Blessed Trinity. In short, God in Christ has so deeply and permanently penetrated the created world in his body that part of the universe has become a part of him. Thus in him and in us, through him and through us, the physical world itself is somehow redeemed. We are all familiar with St. Paul's triumphant cry of joy that: "creation still retains the hope of being freed, like us, from its slavery to decadence, to enjoy the same freedom and glory as the Children of God."

This statement of St. Paul is echoed in Vatican II's statement in Gaudium et Spes, no. 34:

> Throughout the course of the centuries, people have labored to better the circumstances of their lives through a monumental amount of individual and collective effort. To believers this point is settled: considered in itself, such human activity accords with God's will. For mankind, created to God's image, received a mandate to subject to itself the earth and all that it contains, and to govern the world with justice and holiness, a mandate to relate itself and the totality of things to Him who was to be acknowledged as the Lord and Creator of all. Thus, by the subjection of all things to human beings, the name of God would be wonderful in all the earth. . . .
>
> Thus, far from thinking that works produced by human talent and energy are in opposition to God's power, and that the rational creature exists as a kind of rival to the Creator, Christians are convinced that the triumphs of the human race are a sign of God's greatness and the flowering of His own mysterious design. For the greater human power becomes, the farther our individual and community responsibility extends. Hence it is clear that human beings are not deterred by the Christian message from building up the world, or impelled to neglect the welfare of their fellows. They are, rather, more stringently bound to do these very things.

So the world, this beautiful blue and white planet in what still appears to us to be an otherwise sterile universe, is the arena for our service and our worship. The Council, in that passage, tells us many things about the place of science and technology in Catholic consciousness. Therefore, it should say something about their place in Jesuit education. Science (as a method of intellectual search whose conclusions are mathematically consistent, measurable, and verifiable through experiment) is a still increasingly effective way of human laboring to better the circumstances of our lives. Science and technology have become twins in our effort at understanding the structures of creation and at turning our planetary environment into a world apt for human betterment.

The Council tells us that science and technology (among other things) are a sign of God's greatness and a sign of the flowering of His own mysterious design. As such they should be seen as a part of the human worship of the Creator, especially so for us Christians, rooted as we are in the world by the body and blood of the Lord. If the pursuit of knowledge of the world and the attempts to alter it to make it a place more apt to human living are parts of our Christian worship, then they must be part of our intellectual and spiritual patrimony. What better place and what better mode is there for this understanding and changing than Christian institutions of higher learning, including Jesuit institutions. As Christians, we must live in the world penetrated and transformed by the life and death of Christ. We must love that world for its own sake as well as because of God's further will for it. The understanding of it as well as love for it must be a conscious part of Christian education.

Within the span of years since the beginning of Jesuit education to the present we have gone:

1) from the telescopic discovery of the moons of Jupiter to close-up (relatively speaking) photographs of those same moons;

2) from the beginnings of understanding of the vascular system to bypass surgery, arterial replacement, and heart transplants;

3) from gunpowder to thermonuclear bombs;

4) from the abacus to computers;

5) from primitive understanding of the reproductive system, through the discovery of the ovum, to in vitro fertilization;

6) from zero to recombinant DNA;

7) from alchemy to the multitudinous products of chemistry without which our society would no longer function;

8) etc., etc., etc.

There is really no way to compare the times when Jesuit education began with the present times. Much of that difference is directly the result of science and the technology that has grown from it. This is true of the products of our everyday lives (cars, refrigerators, TV's, etc.) as well as the more exotic products like space probes, bacteria producing human insulin, "test-tube babies," etc. Educated people ought to be aware of how such things have come about and how they are to be put together. This is certainly a part of all education, Jesuit higher education included.

Also, in a society where science and technology are so central, people must be educated to quantitative appreciation, to a sense of scale. If I may impose on you, I'd like to quote from a friend of mine at Penn State -- Rustum Roy. He was commenting on the failure even of educated people to develop a sense of quantity:

> "I was involved with Three Mile Island. And the rubbish you had to put up with was so extreme. Take my students. . . 30 seniors at Penn State. I got back to Penn State from Harrisburg.
>
> They said: "We're afraid."
>
> "What are you afraid of?"
>
> "We're afraid we'll die of radiation."
>
> "How much radiation are you going to die of? How much radiation was there at Harrisburg?"
>
> "We don't know, but it sounds pretty big."
>
> "How's it going to get up here?" They weren't sure. I asked how radiation travels. Nobody had the foggiest idea. Little creepy-crawlies? They had no idea. How much radiation? Someone recalled reading a big number -- 1120. I asked what the unit was. It was 1120 picocuries. Sure sounds like a big number! So, I said to them: "We were talking about a nuclear war the other day. We were talking about megacuries. Which is bigger, megacuries or picocuries?"
>
> Remember these are seniors at Penn State. We had a vote on this since that's the way to get the truth in our democracy. Some of them allowed as how megacuries were smaller than picocuries.

> Twenty three of the 30 students didn't understand 18 orders of magnitude. . . . How many of you know what 18 orders of magnitude is? Well, I could compare the diameter of a human hair to the distance to the sun. Then you get a little feel of how bad a mistake we can make. People simply have no feel, no scale, no sense of quantification."

In a society where quantification means so much, it is discouraging to hear that a sense of scale is that badly lacking. How would such a question be answered in any Jesuit college or university? Would our students do any better? Yet, many of the issues facing society and Church -- issues like nuclear power, nuclear war, acid rain, etc., etc., depend on a sense of scale. Statistics -- as the recent election campaign showed -- are now the grist for public discourse. How many of our students (or ourselves) have an adequate feel for statistics?

Yet, as fantastic as the products of science and technology have become, as powerful as the techniques of science are, as great is the need for a quantitative sense -- these are not primary reasons why the study of science and technology should be central to Jesuit higher education. As greatly as science and technology have altered the landscape of our lives, so greatly has it raised new questions or changed the status of all of the old questions raised over the centuries. Unless philosophy and theology come to cope with these new questions and with the revised questions of the past, they will become simply vacuous.

Perhaps the perennially central religious quest is the search for unity. It assumes several different forms: the unity within God, God's unity with his creation, the unities that occur within the creation. These form the basis of many of the great philosophical and theological questions of the ages. Science of itself cannot help us much with the search for an understanding of the unity within God. Only indirectly can it help us understand God's unity with his creation. But it is of major importance in our recognition of unities among creatures. Where has the knowledge about such unities come from over the last several centuries? We have learned an enormous amount about the unities within creation <u>from the sciences.</u>

In 1687 Isaac Newton published the <u>Principia</u>, in which he showed that the motion of celestial <u>and</u> terrestrial bodies was describable by the same equations. This was the final demise of Aristotelian spheres. Perhaps from our superior perch on the tree of knowledge we may yawn a bit when we hear it. But in its own day it represented a profoundly deeper understanding of a basic unity in the cosmos.

Approximately a hundred and twenty five years ago, Darwin, in his Origin of Species, maintained the unity of living systems at the level of the species, an idea overshadowed by the creation-evolution debate. Now, within the last decade scientists have discovered a much more profound unity in creation. Writing in Science in 1980 ("Recombinant DNA Revisited," Vol. 209, No. 4463, 19 Sept., 1980, p. 1317) Maxine Singer stated:

> We have learned that genes are fungible; animal genes function perfectly well within bacteria and bacterial genes within animal cells, confirming the unity of nature.

Thus, in our own day, in the aftermath of Watson and Crick's identification of the double helix, and as a result of the extraordinarily rapid and significant development in recombinant DNA research, we are becoming aware of the unity of all living systems at the level of amino acids. This development represents one of the greatest possible advances in the understanding of the unities with which God has constituted his universe. I personally find it difficult even to imagine a deeper physical unity. The discoveries of such unities within creation can be the springboard for a much more mature theology, a more profound philosophy, a more appropriate legal system, etc., if only we would seriously reflect on what science has already taught us.

Father Walter Ong has stated that the central intellectual and emotional problem in the Church's realization of her mission in the world today (and Jesuit education as a part of that mission) is that we have no cosmology. In a private letter to me he wrote, "We have had none (a cosmology) since the Aristotelian spheres and all that went with them were shown not to be there. The lack of a cosmology affects Christology, ecclesiology, and just about everything else in evangelization, including especially any real planning for the real future. For metaphysics, you obviously need a physics." The same is true of an anthropology; we can't have an authentic anthropology without a biology. Science has been a tremendously successful development; we can learn many things from it that are invaluable for progress in theology, philosophy, law, etc. These are among things that Jesuit institutions of higher education are in existence to promote. If there is to be anything like a research and development operation in the Church, it must come from Catholic (including Jesuit) universities and colleges. It is something that must motivate our efforts.

Biological science is now the center of interest in science, in development, in heavy funding -- both governmental and industrial. I shall go further and say that it is at the forefront of human intellectual progress. It may well eventuate that the greatest intellectual watershed of the 20th century was the identification of the structure of deoxyribonucleic acid, DNA. This crucial scientific, technological, and industrial revolution is seen in such things as "test-tube" babies, recombinant DNA, neuroscientific advances, as well as other biological developments which have already had a significant impact on the society and the Church. The spectrum of scientific and technological advance (the biological, chemical, physical, cybernetic, etc.) will have an even greater effect, especially in the areas of personal dignity, personal freedom and the "integrity" of the human body. Twice before in human history our scientific and technological genius has so radically redirected the course of human life as to merit from historians of culture the title of Revolution, namely, the Agricultural and Industrial Revolutions. A third scientific-technological revolution is already well begun. Its capacity to redirect the histories of peoples is vastly greater than that of either of its predecessors. Biological industrialization has begun -- on a very significant scale.

We have a great need for a much more positive approach to and appreciation of scientific advance. We in the university community need to be aware of where we are and of what is happening. In about 30 years the life sciences, under a very significant impulse from physics, have moved from an observational posture, through an intense and extraordinarily rapid analytic phase, to a synthetic capability. The life sciences have now become experimental sciences linked to technological and industrial capability. The late Charles Frankel has summed up the power and revolutionary character of these new techniques: "Biomedicine has eliminated the insouciance with which most people have embraced technological progress. It forces consideration not simply of techniques and instrumentalities but of ends and purposes."

This should in its own right be a mandate for the place of science and technology in Jesuit higher education. Science and technology -- especially now bioscience and biotechnology -- are significant (and perhaps the most significant) engines for changing the course of human history. To be weak in science is, these days, simply to be divorced from the real world. There may have been a time when this was not true, but that time passed 50 years ago. Without a deep commitment to scientific understanding and appreciation, Jesuit higher education is fatally weakened. Without it that education is of significantly degraded value to society and to the Church in the realm of what we can loosely call "research and development." More, if we do not offer significant instructional opportunities (the-transmission-of-knowledge part of education) to our students, we are not preparing either a religious laity nor citizens competent to contribute to the cultural life of the Church and of the nation.

Still more, unless we dare be prophetic in our approach to education, we fail to fulfill our mandate as Catholics. Transmission of knowledge is necessary to Jesuit education but it is not sufficient to it. Dare we be prophetic? If we don't, we should quit. If we do, we should be realistically aware of the quality of a prophet's life. Do we have the courage?

THE HISTORY

Does the historical place of science in Jesuit education inspire confidence? I think the place of science and technology in Jesuit education, if visually depicted, would resemble nothing so much as a painter's drop cloth. There is a significant amount of paint on the cloth, but it does not present an easily identifiable pattern. Because I have not been able to discover any real order in our approach to science, I plan to treat that history anecdotally.

After I accepted this assignment some seven or eight months ago, I looked up several Jesuit scientists of my generation and that generation immediately ahead of me. I figured that their experience would be a mirror on the place of science and technology in Jesuit higher education. That was and is my modest assumption here. I wanted, then, to check their reactions on the assumption that those reactions would be a significant commentary on the place of science in Jesuit education, say, for the last half century in the United States.

When I began my graduate studies in physics here at Saint Louis University thirty years ago, the older Jesuits, especially those in the sciences, used to speak of a priest who clearly belonged in anyone's pantheon of legendary eccentrics. The lore was that this man (a physicist) had written either a paper or a series of papers (that point was never very clear) on physics. The paper was never permitted to be published because it was considered to be irreconcilable with the then "official" philosophical doctrines. Theories proposed in that paper, the story continued, won a Nobel Prize for someone else years later. I can't say for sure whether or not this story was true. If all the stories we heard in those days about our athletic ability had been true, then almost all of us had been All-Americans. Nonetheless, what is important to this discussion is that no one felt that this sort of thing could not happen. It would have been no cause for surprise.

Another interesting chapter in the lore concerned Father Teodore Wulf. In 1936 the Nobel Prize went to a student of Father Wulf, Victor Hess, for work on cosmic rays. Father Wulf was a pioneer in such work; he invented the early cosmic ray detectors. But after World War I he was sent to teach the philosophers at Valkenberg, and relinquished the cosmic ray work. To be scrupulously fair I do not know that there were not other factors at work in the decision to send him to Valkenberg. Father Wulf had been a divisional chaplain in the German army during World War I. He may have been, as we say now, "burnt out."

Anyway, beginning after World War II, times and personalities conspired to make something new under the sun. A number of Jesuit superiors sent increasingly larger numbers of Jesuits into graduate studies in science. For a while it looked as if the parousia had arrived. There was major commitment of Jesuit manpower to science. But many of those trained at the time have a suspicion that, in terms of Jesuit education, they were never any more than a highly trained labor pool, obviating the necessity of paying high salaries to non-Jesuit professors. Others felt that it was in response to the availability of federal money in science. Still, let's take the high road and assume that it was done out of the highest educational motives. Even in that case, the love of science for its own sake never really permeated the spirit of Jesuit education. Science, it is my opinion, never really occupied a central place in Jesuit education.

I have given these anecdotes not to suggest that we ought to send large numbers of Jesuits into science again nor to say that all of the blame for the demise of science and technology in our universities and colleges is to be laid at the feet of university administrators. Cultural factors were at work as well. The decline in the granting of graduate degrees in physics matches very closely the decline in religious vocations -- a very curious correlation. Financial factors were clearly involved. Finally, many of us who were brought along in the halcyon days have not stayed in the science in which we were trained. I myself am a perfect example of the syndrome that "old physicists never die, they simply become philosophers (or theologians)."

Yet, seen subjectively, many of the people with whom I talked, were aware of an intellectual priority in Jesuit higher education: theology and/or philosophy was first, depending on whether you were talking to a theologian or philosopher. Then there were the classics followed by English, maybe next by history, and then finally by the trade school courses like science, engineering, law, et. The sciences seem to have been an aside to the essence of Jesuit education. Ours were liberal arts colleges and universities; seemingly there was little place for science and technology.

Over the years, several Jesuit schools had very highly regarded programs in astronomy and in seismology. Various reasons were given for this: some felt that astronomy was popular when Jesuits started their educational apostolate; some thought that we were not able to re-establish our efforts in physics and chemistry when the Society was restored after its suppression; several pointed out that biology was eschewed because of a deep-seated malaise over questions of human origins. So, too, anthropology was basically ignored as dangerous.

Then, too, the Ratio Studiorum, at least as it was interpreted to us, was certainly orientated to the 'liberal arts' which were so defined as to exclude science from an integral role. I am of the opinion, the validity of which I shall leave to you to decide, that in Jesuit education the theoretical was to be preferred to the practical, to the technological. The impression was given that Greek was better than Latin, pure mathematics better than applied mathematics. ontology more dignified than ethics, etc. There seemed to be a set of preferences, if not formal priorities, which promoted the more theoretical over the more experimental. This also had the advantage of avoiding the raising of disturbing questions which called for a revision of thought or behavior.

My intention is certainly not to denigrate either the people involved nor the system itself. If my informal survey is accurate, then Jesuit education put rather little stress on modern science or technology. These were never a <u>central</u> concern in U.S. Jesuit education. We must steal a slogan from elsewhere: we were the "people last hired and first fired." So it has seemed to eventuate. The Golden Years (roughly 1945-1970) seem to have been an anomaly.

SUMMARY

There can be no doubt that the fruits of modern science are not really a part of the Church's patrimony. At best the Church's conceptual life is finally Darwinian. It can not be said to be Einsteinian, Heisenbergian or Watson-Crick. The Church's failure here is mainly the failure of Catholic colleges and universities, and, reductively Jesuit institutions.

Theology is by nature involved with vast quantities of knowledge, all of which is radically beyond its control. It is not a research discipline, as that terminology is generally understood. It does not generate its own data as many other disciplines do. It derives its basic information from sources other than itself. Science and technology are absolutely basic to this process. But what is true of individuals is most likely true of institutions as well. The individual who learns a discipline as a tool for another discipline rarely learns it as well as one who approaches it in its own right, for its own sake -- things like talent being roughly equal. So, too, I think, our institutions must promote science and technology in its own right, because it is an acceptable, appropriate, necessary intellectual enterprise.

If we are to be a serious intellectual force in our communities, in the nation, in the Church, we will need excellent science programs, rather than continuing the retrenchment that has been occurring. Not all science (even research science) is necessarily expensive beyond our reach. We could pick and choose; we don't need bevatrons.

Let me conclude by urging a growth in our commitment to both research and teaching in science and technology. Until we do, how can we call ourselves universities? Until science and technology are a significant component of the intellectual air we breathe on our campuses the Church will not be able to have an intellectual presence in the contemporary world. Moreover the stakes presented by that contemporary world are probably the highest with which the Church has been presented.

I believe that an objective appraisal of the issues facing our society and the Church will reveal the need for Catholic institutions of higher education to be deeply involved in scientific and technological advance as well as in critical evaluation of the meaning of this advance. If the Church as a whole is going to begin to think in categories appropriate to the issues raised by contemporary science and technology, it will have to begin on campuses like this one. If theology is to come alive again, it will have to learn to handle the vast, revolutionary new concepts that have arisen in the last half century. If philosophy (at least in its cosmological aspects) is to speak to the contemporary world, it cannot ignore the advances in physics. If law is going to be appropriate, it must be able to handle technologies like in vitro fertilization with its attendant issues like surrogate mothers, frozen embryos, etc.

Our institutional currency depends on our ability to incorporate science and technology into our curricular imagination. If we do not, our educational approach will be simply quaint. Yet we can always look to the imagination of our educational leaders to spur their schools to leadership in at least the less expensive aspects of science and technology.

The society we live in needs it. The Church needs it. If we are true to the spirit of Jesuit educational life, we shall provide it -- because that is our vocation.

SCIENCE/TECHNOLOGY EDUCATION: AN ADMINISTRATIVE PRECEPTION

Dr. James Bundschuh

Dr. James Bundschuh is a physical chemist and Dean of the College of Arts and Sciences at Saint Louis University. Before joining the University three years ago, he served as Dean of the School of Science and Humanities at Purdue University's campus in Fort Wayne, Indiana. Prior to that he chaired the Chemistry Department at Western Illinois University. He is the recipient of many grants from the National Science Foundation, the Department of Energy, and other agencies. He has conducted research at two national laboratories and was a visiting professor for a year at the University of Stuttgart in Germany. He is active in the American Chemical Society, the St. Louis Research Council, Central States Universities and the Council of Colleges of Arts and Sciences.

I believe the liberal arts component of my undergraduate education sustained me during my academic career helping me to think critically and to understand my scientific objectives as they pertain to society and a greater good. Therefore, I am an advocate of a broad, challenging liberal arts and sciences education that includes language, development of writing skills, and substantial attention to ethics and values.

Throughout the years I have heard many references made to C.P. Snow's two cultures, "Literary intellectuals at one pole -- at the other scientists, and as the most representative, the physical scientists. Between the two a gulf of mutual incomprehension -- sometimes (particularly among the young) hostility and dislike, but most of all lack of understanding. They have a curious distorted image of one another." Several years ago, a colleague attempted to persuade me that it was simply this cultural difference that prevented humanities and science faculty from cooperating and reaching consensus on a curriculum matter. However, I would liken such behavior as befitting the man who lost his keys in the bushes at night but persisted in looking for them a half block away under a light post because he could see better. Too often the man's behavior typifies how we search for the keys to a meaningful curriculum. We look only in the areas we know well and neglect or merely tolerate contributions from disciplines that are not close to our own.

On June 7, 1989 Father Peter-Hans Kolvenbach, Superior General of the Society of Jesus, addressed approximately 750 Jesuits and 150 laypersons attending "Assembly '89: Jesuit Ministry in Higher Education" at Georgetown University. In his speech, Father Kolvenbach contended that "it is a pity that an interdisciplinary approach, the only significant way to heal the fracture of knowledge, is still considered a luxury reserved to occasional staff seminars or a few doctoral programs. Of course, an interdisciplinary approach is not without problems: it runs the risk of simply overloading students, of teaching them relativism, of inadmissable violation of the methodology of individual disciplines. But a love of the whole truth, a love of the integral human situation can help us to overcome even these potential problems."

In the matter of general education, or what is referred to as the "core curriculum" at Saint Louis University, scientists at church-related colleges and universities should be especially concerned and knowledgeable about the content and curriculum requirements of other disciplines. They should reinforce their science courses with pertinent subject matter from the humanities and social sciences, and in so doing, contribute effectively to a truly integrated curriculum. Furthermore, science teachers should minimize their reliance on the multiple choice method of testing and require that students express themselves coherently and convincingly when solving problems or responding to essay questions.

At Saint Louis University, we have been working to construct a document that clearly defines what we are and how we go about teaching values. The following is an excerpt from the result of those labors, the recently approved Mission Statement. "The University's undergraduate curriculum makes use of the resources of the humanities, social sciences, natural sciences, and technology in a unified effort to challenge students to make appropriate use of what each area has to offer in enabling them to understand themselves, their world, and God, to prepare intellectually and professionally for the career of their choice, and to make critically informed moral judgments." Although it is somewhat disquieting to me that "hard sciences" were singled out, Father Kolvenbach emphasized at Georgetown the importance of interdisciplinary cooperation in teaching values. "It is my belief that awareness exists that there is no aspect of education, not even the so-called hard sciences, which is neutral. All teaching imparts values, and these values can be such as to promote justice, or work, whether partially or entirely, at cross purposes to the mission of the Society."

In addition to serious commitments to values and to integrating science into the required curricula at church-related colleges and universities, there must be a real understanding of the unique needs of the sciences with respect to facilities and equipment. One of my favorite anecdotes is contained in a passage from Ronald W. Clark's book, "Einstein, the Life and Times." In this passage Clark describes Albert Einstein and his wife Elsa's visit to California in 1931. "He was driven up the long circuitous road which winds out of Pasadena and then back to the top of the Sierra Madre, from one of whose summits the Mount Wilson Observatory looks down upon the town. Here Elsa, when told that the giant telescope was required for establishing the structure of the universe, is claimed to have made a reply that may be apocryphal but is in the true Elsa style: 'Well, well, my husband does that on the back of an old envelope."

Using this story I liken Einstein to the scientist from a church-related university visiting his well-equipped counterpart at a state-supported university. The value of Einstein's contributions to science is indisputable, and Elsa's attitude is that good science can be done on the "back of an old envelope." Indeed, I have detected this attitude in more than one administrator from a church-related school.

Often the equipment needs of graduate and undergraduate science programs are dismissed by declaring that it is impossible for a private university lacking state support to provide funds for such behemoths as supercomputers and high energy accelerators. The truth of the matter is that most universities are linked to supercomputers via efficient networks and that high energy physics programs depend upon the facilities at national laboratories to perform experiments. In fact it is scientific equipment costing between ten and a hundred thousand dollars that is most seriously lacking at church-related schools. It is particularly ironic that this is the price range of new sidewalks, building facades, and other minor campus improvements that rise to the top of many lists of priorities. I emphasize emphatically that I believe it is very important that a college or university maintain its appearance. However, I want to make the point that even though scientific equipment and campus improvements have similar price tags, modern science cannot be performed on the back of old envelopes.

Snow, C.P., The Two Cultures and the Scientific Revolution, Cambridge University Press, New York (1961), p. 4.

The text of Father Kolvenbach's address is printed in Origins, Vol. 19 (June 22, 1989), pp. 81-87.

Clark, Ronald W., Einstein, the Life and Times, the World Publishing Company, New York (1971), p. 434.

THE IDEAL AND REALITY OF SCIENCE EDUCATION IN CATHOLIC COLLEGES AND UNIVERSITIES

Fr. Thaddeus J. Burch, S.J.

Fr. Thaddeus Burch, S.J., is currently Dean of the Graduate School at Marquette University. He was formerly Chairman of the Physics Department. Fr. Burch has a PhD in physics with a specialization in Solid State physics.

The ideal of science education in Catholic schools depends on three factors. The reality depends on how these factors are implemented in a given institution, department, or course. The types of institutions, their goals, their faculties, and their finances will play important roles in determining this reality.

> First, the sciences are among the Liberal Arts and Sciences. They are thus a part of a liberal education. Education, especially today, is incomplete without some knowledge and appreciation of the accomplishments of science and the methods used by its various branches. In addition, almost all colleges and universities will elect to educate professional scientists at the bachelor's level. Some will also offer programs at the master's and doctor's level.
>
> Second, the sciences and technology are both the occasion of and the solutions for many of our current social and political problems. Thus some understanding of these subjects is important in the education of a responsible citizen.
>
> Third, the sciences and technology inevitably interact with theology, philosophy, and religion. A confident and intelligent believer must understand these interactions.

The first two of these factors should be common to every type and system of education. The third is specific to the goals of religious schools and scholars. Further, all scientists must confront the interaction of science with philosophy, theology, and religion at least in their personal lives, as will most other people because of the popularization of scientific discoveries and concepts. Institutions will often take implicit or explicit stands about these interactions through their policies.

First some definitions and ground rules. By science and technology I mean the investigation and exploitation of nature guided by a set of insights which came out of the middle ages and began to have significant success in the 16th and 17th centuries. The writings of Nicholas of Cusa and Roger Bacon are among the early attempts to describe and organize some of these ideas. Important among these insights was the firm belief in a creator. A mind, infinite but much like our own, created intelligently and purposely. Our minds can, therefore, discover, describe, and understand the creator's plan, the rules by which nature operates. More technically, these insights deal with the use of experimentally verified data, and with the use of models to explain this data. Models are used to organize thought and also as expressions and forms of thought. New rules gradually developed about what constitutes a good model, and how models and their parts are to be tested, judged and evaluated.

My description will use physics primarily as the example of science. The other scientific disciplines experienced similar applications of these insights in ways appropriate to their subject matters. It should be noted that all disciplines including philosophy and theology have also incorporated many of these ideas in their recent development and thus have become "scientific". In all cases, that which is studied through disciplined observation, experiment, and model building tells the investigator the method by which it is to be successfully studied. Sometimes intuition and scientific taste are as important as logic. My ideas are based on relatively restricted understandings, some would probably say caricatures, of the sciences, other disciplines, and religion. Some would probably judge that the use of model in the religious arena is completely inappropriate.

In order to be a Catholic I must answer four questions which science does not address:

> First. Did the physical universe just happen or did something exist for ever?
>
> Second. Is this universe merely matter guided by a combination of its innate laws and chance, or is this something an eternal intelligent being designed?
>
> Third. Did this intelligent eternal being intervene personally in my world through creation, revelation, and redemption?
>
> Fourth. Is this revelation contained in the Judeo-Christian tradition and its scriptures, and is the redemptive intervention in the person of Jesus Christ and through His Church, the Roman Catholic Church?

Every human has to answer a similar set of questions either explicitly or implicitly. The atheist or agnostic will answer these questions quite differently. The answer to the fourth question will determine one's confessional commitment. The answers to these questions provides each of us with the model by which we understand the world and our place in it. This model provides the understanding by which we live and worship. Its purpose is to organize and make intelligible all of reality. This all inclusiveness is a property of the models used by philosophers and theologians of an earlier day and as well as of those called natural philosophers until after the middle ages. These are very different from the models used by modern science.

It should be noted that practitioners of the more speculative branches of science, such as cosmology, will answer or come close to answering the first two questions.

In the social and political areas as well certain questions must be answered. These answers set our social and political priorities. Thus they provide each one of us with the over-all framework or model on which our relationships with and actions towards others, towards social structures, and towards the state are based and are made intelligible. The answers to these questions gives us a model similar to the religious model but again very different from those used in science.

The scientific models of ancient civilizations, especially Greece, which carried over into the Middle Ages, tried to give organization to the material universe or a large portion of it. The astronomical model based on crystalline spheres, and the model based on earth, air, fire, and water, are similar to the religious models in their all-inclusiveness and in their lack of attention to precise details, of the religious model. In the same way they are dissimilar to the scientific models of modern science.

The religious model and other models similar to it are:

> All inclusive - Its postulates or starting truths must organize all of reality.
>
> Limited knowledge of major truths. Because the human mind is limited we must learn of the divine through analogy and revelation. The assents to some of the truths are based on faith rather than human reason and observation.
> Major truths are not changeable. Therefore discovery is not anticipated except on the basis of the already known.
>
> Details are relatively unimportant. Inaccuracy at the level of details can be tolerated. Details may be changed and are worked out as the model grows in perfection.

Urgent - The model must be put together in time for me to act. That is, in order for me to live and die by it.

Test of truth - The test of truth is revelation and human reason.

Personal commitment - A personal commitment to the model itself is necessary.

The models of modern science, however, have much different requirements:

Details are all important. The models must be accurate quantitatively and explain minute details. The necessity to explain details supercedes the organization of a larger collection of data.

All inclusive - Although a universal model is the ultimate goal of the science this goal must await the inclusion of all details.

The model is changeable. Scientific knowledge is in principle tentative. As knowledge of detail advances through experiment and the relationships between the data are understood the models can be corrected to have broader application or improved accuracy. They can also be displaced by more accurate, more useful, more powerful, or simpler models. New data or insights may attack the model at the level of its fundamental postulates and thus may overturn the model completely.

Discovery is expected - The purpose of experimentation and scientific investigation is discovery. The body of scientific knowledge is constantly expanding.

The model is quantitative and mathematical. Since the model is mathematical those relationships which are described by mathematical operations in an equation become the most important. Even though the model is accurate certain data may be excluded or the model may be true only with in an imaginary limit. (The undergraduate is never completely comfortable with the elementary applications of the insights of Galileo and their later formulation in Newton's Laws of Motion because of the way friction is neglected.) Further these models are subject to the rules of mathematical logic. Thus no set of postulates can explain all reality. There are an infinite number of models which can explain any set of data. Some will argue that the contact of the model with reality is an isomorphism and not an identity.

Test of truth - The test of truth is the ability to explain and predict natural phenomena.

Commitment - The scientist's primary commitment is to an ever evolving process of discovery, not to the current models.

Scientific models differ in almost every important respect from the models used in religion, society, and many other disciplines. Scientific thought and method is governed by different rules and insights. The scientific models seek to describe and understand the world around us. Questions like: how is this best described? what are the relationships between the parts? how can this knowledge be used to build a technology or manipulate nature? are important. The religious and social models and those of the liberal disciplines, in so far as they try to address certain concerns, also produce models. These models seek to make one's place in the world intelligible and meaningful. The questions Where do I fit in? and How do I live in this world? are important.

These models are complementary. That is different views of the same reality for different purposes. Those of us who have some skill in the use of two or more of these models have the unique ability and thus an obligation to address certain problems. Our role is very much the same whether we are working in the school, with social and political concerns, or with the Church. A few comments about the three factors with which this paper began are in order.

First, science is one of the major accomplishments or creations of the human mind along with literature, art, architecture, philosophy, theology, etc. In recent centuries science has earned both great success and great prestige. The material dimension and much of the intellectual dimension of our civilization have been shaped by science. (Almost all other disciplines have to some extent incorporated scientific methodology and techniques where appropriate.) An education which passes over this method of thought and investigation is not humanistic or liberal. Scientific education is the teaching of scientific models, their use, and their meaning.

The science educator faces two very different groups of students: those seeking to meet a general education or core requirement and those preparing for a career in a scientific or technical field.

Many in the first group, and it should be stressed not all of them, come to the class room very poorly prepared for even the most elementary college level science. They are from elementary and secondary schools in which science courses were either unavailable or easily avoided. They lack rudimentary exposure to scientific thought and its vocabulary and have little or no mathematics. They are convinced that they cannot succeed at science and thus are prepared to dislike, fear, and distrust it. At times these students have unreasonably high expectations of what others can do for them through science and technology. They are apt to attribute to a corrupt suppression of knowledge the inability of science and technology to meet these unreasonable expectations through immediate solutions of currently pressing problems. Much of the work in these classes is remedial. Yet, at the same time, these students must be brought to a rather sophisticated level of understanding, comfort with, and trust of scientific models of thought.

Perhaps most distressing in these students is the inability to understand a quantitative argument. To them, things like radioactivity, carcinogens, pollution, and safety are either off or on. They see and feel no difference between a million and a millionth. Unfortunately, all current environmental problems and many social and moral problems have important quantitative components. The quantitative information keeps changing, making rethinking of the problems and their solutions necessary. An example: About twenty five years ago an expensive analysis done by an outside chemist was reported to one part in a thousand. One trusted it to one part in a hundred. Today it is relatively easy to measure the same thing to one part in a trillion.

These core curriculum students are in danger of never obtaining sufficient mastery of a scientific model to understand scientific accomplishments or the integration of science with the social or religious models.

Students preparing for degrees in science and engineering often have the opposite problem. They are fascinated by the scientific models appropriate to their disciplines. They graduate a highly trained scientists and engineers. Unfortunately, a combination of their own lack of interest or lack of integration in their core requirement courses leaves these young professionals with very unsophisticated social and religious models. Their ability to integrate their science with citizenship and religion for themselves and for others is, therefore, severely limited.

Second, some integration of science with social and political models is necessary for the citizen. The environmentalist, politician, or citizen concerned about and seeking action to correct the greenhouse effect, or acid rain, are often not happy with the accurate scientific answers to their questions. This answer is often that not enough is known to describe the extent of the problem or to predict the outcome of proposed solutions. Thus it is necessary to await further investigation before a course of action can be recommended. Further, some scientists when addressing these problems, will confuse or perhaps merge their scientific and social models. This example illustrates the importance of non-scientists having familiarity with the scientific approach and scientists realizing that they are speaking to people operating out of different models. Only in this way can tension be avoided among those seeking the truth from different perspectives. This example might enable us to understand some of the less fortunate interactions of science with theology and religion.

The federal, state, and local governments are forcing integration of the scientific and social models through regulation. For example, colleges and universities must have highly developed federally approved policies, and the organizational structure for enforcing these policies, to be eligible for federal research funding or to avoid substantial penalty. Some areas are: radiation safety, hazardous waste, biological hazards, animal care, human subjects, misconduct in scholarship, and soon conflict of interest in research.

Third the ideal interaction of science with some parts of philosophy and theology and with religion is one of complementarity. All of these methods of thought or belief look at the same truth from different points of view. The statements of the different disciplines on topics like: The origin of the universe, the origin and meaning of the human person, the human mind, human society and organization are quite different. This is because these statements must meet very different criteria, and serve different purposes. In short the statements will be made in the context of very different models. Complementarity is recognizable only when thinkers are clear about the models they are using. Complementarity is lost when one allows the different models to become mixed. That is when one tries to use the scientific model to answer a religious question or vice versa. In addition some of the investigations and many of the applications raise moral questions. That is, we must decide how these investigations and their applications fit into the models which define our places in the universe and society.

History and the present teach a clear lesson. The ideas which form important parts of the scientific models also become important in social, philosophical, theological, and religious thought. Without a strong professional presence in and understanding of science the Church will abnegate the right to and the possibility of participating in the discussions about the integration of science, society and religion. The Church needs an arm of scientific education and scholarship. This arm can only be the Catholic colleges and universities.

Finally, for those of us who have some knowledge of both the scientific, social and religious models, the task in the three areas of education, citizenship, and service to the Church are much the same. In all three areas we face constituencies who either do not understand science or who are highly trained scientists often with little religious background or interest. We have a great potential for bringing about understanding by explaining the complementarity of the different modes of thought and their resulting models. Since most of those who service the church have a humanistic education it is incumbent on us to explain the scientific model and the complementarity of scientific knowledge with what they know and believe. At the same only we are the only ones who can help scientists understand the Church and its particular mode of thought.

IN WHAT WAY CAN SCIENCE/TECHNOLOGY EDUCATION ENRICH THE MORE GENERAL LIBERAL ARTS EMPHASIS OF MANY CHURCH-RELATED SCHOOLS?

S. Mary Virginia Orna, OSU
S. Angelice Seibert, OSU

Sister Mary Virginia Orna, OSU is Professor and Chair of the Division of Natural Sciences and Mathematics at the College of New Rochelle. She received her PhD in analytic chemistry at Fordham University. She is a 1984 recipient of the Chemical Manufacturers' Association Catalyst Award for excellence in college chemistry teaching. She is presently Principal Investigator for "Chemsource," a major effort in chemistry teacher preparation and enhancement, sponsored by NSF in cooperation with the Educational Division of the American Chemistry Society.

Dr. Angelice Seibert, O.S.U., Ph.D. (biochemistry); Professor, Ursuline College, Louisville, KY; President, Ursuline College; Fulbright-Hays Lecturer, University of Ireland, Galway; Presentor, International Conference, "Education in Health Sciences," The Hague, Netherlands; Editorial Board, Journal of Allied Health; Visiting Prof., Smith College, Northampton, MA; Chairperson, Division of Allied Health Professions, Jefferson Community College, Louisville; Trustee: College of New Rochelle, NY and Bellarmine College, KY; President, Ursuline Sisters, Louisville; Visiting Scholar, Pope John Medical/Moral Research Center, Braintree, MA; Presently: Bioethics Consultant and Associate Director, Ursuline Campus Office of Advancement. Member of ITEST.

Education in science and technology has always been carried on within the context of the liberal arts curriculum of colleges and universities which specialize in educating their students in the liberal arts. Indeed, it is the context of the liberal arts that endows the science and technology embedded in this matrix with the possibility of discovering the human potentialities of scientific findings.

Some years ago, the National Education Association, recognizing the fact that "the values and modes of thought which underlie science and technology also are becoming pervasive in the world," recommended that schools should promote the "understanding of the values on which science everywhere is based." It also noted that "the values of science are the most complete expression of one of the deepest of humane values - the belief in human dignity."[1] More recently, an editorial in Perspectives in Biology and Medicine [2] attributed to the new biology a central role in the liberal arts education of the future. It asserted that biological knowledge and the attitude generated from it will profoundly affect our thoughts and concepts of person and consequently of the direction that society will take.

Such statements should be of deep concern to us as scientists and educators interested in the ways that science can enrich our liberal arts curriculum. We, as science educators, face the challenge of bringing to our scientific thought, which is such a force in human life,[3] those human values which acknowledge the dignity and destiny in God of all persons. We believe that the human values by which we promote the scientific and technological advances today will determine the kind of society we will have tomorrow. For what we choose to believe and to teach about the value of human life will have social consequences.[4]

Church-related schools, with stated missions to educate their students in such a way as to honor the humanity of each individual as a creature of God, are particularly well-equipped to narrow the gap that presently exists in academia between scientific "truth" and human values. As Pope John Paul II has observed, "science develops best when its concepts and conclusions are integrated into the broader human culture and its concerns for ultimate meaning and value."[5] Likewise, the humanities are enriched by the understanding and appreciation of our universe as a whole with which the scientific disciplines endow us. This dynamic interchange between the sciences and humanities can encourage the drive toward a unity which resists homogenization and relishes diversity, and can reveal those limitations which support the integrity of both disciplines.

This dynamic interchange can take place in the liberal arts school both within and outside of the regular course curriculum. It can take place between and among science majors and non-science majors. It can consist of exposure, thinking, reading, discussion and internalization which may eventually lead to practice.

The National Science Teachers' Association has divided the goals of science education into four general headings for purposes of discussion:

I) Science for meeting personal needs. A person broadly educated in the sciences should be prepared to (a) cope with an increasingly technological world and (b) use science and technology to enhance the quality of life.

II) Science for resolving current societal issues. While the issues may not necessarily be resolved completely, science education must have as its goal the development of a broad pool of citizens who are interested and functionally literate in science and its applications in society.[6] Daniel Yankelovich has expressed great concern with the "absence of an effective science presence in the public debate on which successful democracy in our age depends."[7] Even more pertinently, a goal of quality science teaching is to help prepare students to make the tough decisions they will have to make as the citizens of the future.[8]

III) Science for assisting with career choices. Education in the sciences can give students an appreciation of the nature and scope of the wide variety of science/technology related careers and other careers which are strongly impacted by developments in science and technology. For example, students can be introduced to other aspects of the interrelationship of science and the humanities through the interests and research of their professors and mentors.[9,10,11]

IV) Science for preparing for further study. The study of science on the undergraduate level can prepare a student to enter a variety of professional and academic pathways.

Goals I and II, in the liberal arts college context, can be applied to science and non-science majors alike, while those labeled III and IV are more appropriately applied to the science major.

One effective way of meeting goals I and II is through STS (Science, Technology and Society) education. The syllabus (attached) for a course,

"Science and Society," which is taught by a chemistry professor at the College of New Rochelle is one such example of this type of education. The stated objective of this course is to provide an understanding of the principles underlying current scientific topics of interest with the hoped-for results of acquiring the ability to contribute thoughtfully to the current debates about scientific problems and come to some rational positions concerning their disposition.

Another curricular way of meeting goals I and II for science majors is to engage them in formal independent study or seminar study on issues of societal importance. For example, one junior chemistry major at the College of New Rochelle chose an independent study project on Robert Oppenheimer as a victim of McCarthyism (Spring, 1989). Many different societal issues came to light in this study; the student gave a full report to faculty and students at the annual Honors Colloquium at the end of the semester, thus generating a wide audience for debate and questions.

An extracurricular way of meeting goals I and II is through organized informal discussion such as the "Ethics Forum," an informal group of faculty, students, staff and alumni which meets on occasional Saturday mornings at the College of New Rochelle. Topics range from Biomedical Ethics to Business Ethics, but the biomedical area has had broad coverage during this past academic year. The format consists of a brief presentation of an issue by an invited expert, accompanied by copies of references and handouts of pertinent papers on the topic. About an hour and a half of discussion follows. Typically, 18 to 24 persons attend these sessions.

The preceding examples by no means exhaust the possibilities of meeting goals I and II. Indeed, some science faculty at church-related liberal arts colleges might even question the limitations of the stated goals above. In fact, it is our belief that much broader goals for science education in the liberal arts context should be formulated. These goals should be based upon the philosophical quest for truth, beauty and goodness.

With respect to truth, if science has become our god, it must be removed from the altar. It is Joseph Pitt's contention that scientific inquiry is an ongoing activity in which the so-called truths of the past are constantly being revised and rejected in the light of new theories and discoveries. Hence, no finished product of science can be enshrined as Truth.[12] The liberal arts context can emphasize the nature of science as a process constantly moving in the direction of Truth.

With respect to beauty, A. Truman Schwartz, in his paper, "Science: The Greatest of the Humanities?"[13] extols the virtues of science as contributing to a greater understanding of beauty, brotherhood and belonging. He also asks us not to forget that science, of its very nature, is ambiguous; that science mirrors the tension between the specific and general, the concrete and abstract; that a deep knowledge and appreciation of science ultimately leads to a deep knowledge and appreciation of ourselves as human beings.

With respect to goodness (in the moral sense), theologian Kevin O'Rourke questions whether we should not have something more to say concerning values relative to the new biotechnology of the medical sciences.[14] It is also encouraging to find such groups as the Women Chemists Committee of the American Chemical Society sponsoring a symposium on <u>Ethics and the Future of Chemistry</u>, during which they considered such topics as fraud in the chemistry laboratory, ethical behavior in academia, and ethics and chemical education.[15]

Finally, with respect to goodness (in the broad sense), Susan Snyder[8] makes two very important recommendations in the teaching of science which would be most applicable in sciences majors' courses: (a) an examination of scientific knowledge in its historical context in order to discover how the information came to be accepted by the scientific community and (b) the need to study the inherent values of science: respect for evidence, demand for precision and verification, questioning of all things, and consideration of unstated assumptions and premises.

We think that goals III and IV should be broadened to reflect the search for truth, beauty and goodness inherent in scientific endeavor. We also think that it is possible to incorporate these broader goals into the science majors' curriculum both formally and informally. Much ongoing discussion is needed in order to formulate specific recommendations.

In formulating these recommendations, we should keep in mind that religion and theology play a role which can be highlighted by church-related educational institutions: "The human quest for understanding requires us to draw on a diversity of different sources. Science is not merely a means to technical control or accurate prediction; religion is not just a matter of moral action or private converse between the individual and God. Each contributes to our understanding of the complex world in which we are set. The quest for understanding is thus necessarily a collaborative one in which the autonomy of the constituents must be respected."[16]

REFERENCES

1. Corey, Arthur F., et al. "Education and the Spirit of Science," Study commissioned by the Educational Policies Commission of the National Education Association and the American Association of School Administrators, Washington, D.C., 1966.

2. Kort, Fred, "A New Perspective for Biology: Its Central Role in the Liberal Arts Education of the Future," Perspectives in Biology and Medicine, Vol. 29 (4) (1986) pp. 489-492.

3. Cassidy, Harold G., "Scientific Thought: A Force in Human Life," American Scientist, Vol. 58 (5) (1970) pp. 476-478.

4. Seibert, M. Angelice, and Jacob, Martha Ann, "Human Values and Biotechnology," Momentum, February (1976) pp. 5-12.

5. John Paul II, "Letter to Father George V. Coyne, June 1, 1988," L'Osservatore Romano, Oct. 26, 1988.

6. National Association for Science, Technology and Society News, Vol. 2 (February, 1989), p. 2.

7. Yankelovich, Daniel, "Science and the Public Process: Why the Gap Must Close," Issues in Science and Technology, Fall (1984) pp. 6-12.

8. Snyder, Susan P., "Ethics and Values in the Precollege Science Curriculum," in Science, Engineering and Ethics: State-of-the-Art and Future Directions, Mark S. Frankel (Ed.) (Washington, D.C.: American Association for the Advancement of Science, 1988), p. 14.

9. Orna, M.V., Lang, P.L., Katon, J.E., Mathews, T.F. and Nelson, R.S., "Applications of Infrared Microspectroscopy to Art Historical Questions about Medieval Manuscripts," Archaeological Chemistry IV, Ralph O. Allen, (Ed.) (Washington, D.C.: American Chemical Society, 1989), pp.

265-288.

10. Orna, M.V., Cybernetics, Society and the Church (Dayton: CEBCO/Pflaum, 1969).

11. Seibert, M. Angelice, "Catholic Healthcare Identity Revisited," Ethics Medics - A Catholic Perspective on Moral Issues in Health and the Life Sciences. Vol. 14 (4) (1989) pp. 1-2.

12. Pitt, Joseph C., "The Myth of Science Education," Studies in Philosophy and Education (in press).

13. Schwartz, A. Truman, "Science: The Greatest of the Humanities?" Bulletin of Science, Technology and Society, Vol. 8 (1988), pp. 167-171.

14. O'Rourke, Kevin D., "New Science and Modern Technology: Have We Nothing to Say?" Dolentium Hominum, Vol. 5 (1987) pp. 44-54.

15. "Ethics and the Future of Chemistry," Professional Ethics Report, Vol. II (1989), p. 7 (Newsletter of the AAAS Committee on Scientific Freedom and Responsibility Professional Society and Ethics Groups).

16. McMullin, Ernan, "A Common Quest for Understanding," America, Vol. 160 (Feb. 11, 1989), p. 104.

APPENDIX

COR 051
SCIENCE AND SOCIETY
FALL 1988

DR. THOMAS VENANZI
OFFICE: SCIENCE 305
OFFICE HOURS: TU. 1-2, W. 2-3, TH. 4-5

I. INTRODUCTION: OBJECTIVE AND OUTCOMES

Science and Society is a course designed for non-science majors. Its object is to provide an understanding of the principles underlying current scientific topics of interest. Each of the topics chosen crucially affects not only the way we live but also the future of our society. In the course, we will emphasize the mastery of the principles rather than the relevance of the topics.

The course does not assume an extensive background in any of the topics we will discuss. The necessary scientific background will be provided within the context of the issue under discussion. For example, in the process of dealing with topics concerning the environment, the use of nuclear weapons and power, the computer explosion, drugs and the brain, and genetic research, basic principles dealing with the behavior of gases and acid-base behavior, nuclear reactions and electromagnetic radiation, electronics as a way of simulating logical processes, and the molecular basis of biological processes will be discussed.

Hopefully, as a result of our work during the semester, you will acquire certain competencies, such as, (1) the ability to understand and handle basic scientific concepts, (2) the ability to deal with simple quantitative measures, and (3) the ability to form scientific arguments. Furthermore, by the end of the course, it is hoped that each of you will be able to contribute thoughtfully to the current debates about the scientific problems which are discussed in our society. It is of utmost importance that each of us have the necessary scientific knowledge to explore the issue, understand it, and come to some rational position concerning its disposition. As we work together to explore each of these issues, it can only be hoped that the questions can be discussed in a comprehensive manner and, more importantly, new questions will emerge.

II. COURSE STRUCTURE

There are basically three levels of participation in the course: in-class participation, outside reading, library assignments, and semester projects.

(A) In-class Participation

In-class activities will include formal lectures, discussions, experiments and simulation exercises. Active participation is expected from all students; we have much to learn from each other. Class attendance and participation will count 20% of your final grade. More than two absences during the semester must be explained to the instructor.

(B) Reading Assignments and Commentaries

The in-class experience will be far more rewarding if all of us make an effort to come to class prepared. As you can see on the class schedule we will cover seven topics, all with a set of readings. The readings, which are drawn from Science, Scientific American, and Discover, among others, will be distributed before each of the units. A Reading List is attached to the syllabus. For five of the topics a commentary will be assigned which will be due on the date indicated. For each of the commentaries we will provide a set of questions which you may use as a guide. Your commentaries will vary in length because the readings for certain topics are longer than others. As a minimum, two hand-written pages are suggested. The commentaries will count 40% of your final grade.

(C) Semester Projects

In December each of you will present a poster session to the class. The mechanics of the "poster session" will be explained in detail during the semester and a list of possible topics will be provided. However, you may certainly choose your own topic. In this regard, it is strongly encouraged that you read the Science Times each Tuesday for a possible topic for your presentation. The poster session will count 20% of your final grade. In addition, during the examination period a final examination, counting 20% of your grade, will be given. Both the poster session and the final examination will be used to evaluate your ability to handle scientific concepts and construct scientific arguments related to current scientific issues of interest to society.

(D) Grading Summary

Class Participation	20%
Commentaries	40%
In-Class Poster Session	20%
Final Examination	20%

III COURSE SYLLABUS

DATES	TOPIC	COMMENTARY DUE DATE
Sept. 8	Introduction	
Sept. 13	Unit 1: The Reporting of Science: Is Depression Hereditary?	
Sept. 20,22,27,29, Oct. 4	Unit 2: Genetic Research & Genetic Engineering	Oct. 13
Oct. 6,11,13	Unit 3: Drugs & the Brain	Oct. 27
Oct. 18,20,25	Unit 4: Nuclear Weapons	Nov. 15
Oct. 27, Nov. 1,3	Unit 5: Nuclear Power	
Nov. 8,10,15,17,22	Unit 6: The Environment: (a) Greenhouse Effect (b) Acid Rain (c) Depletion of the Ozone Layer	Dec. 1
Nov. 29, Dec. 1,6,8	Unit 7: The Computer Explosion	
Dec. 13,15	In-Class Poster Sessions	Dec. 15

READING LIST

GENERAL TEXT

M.M. Jones, D.O. Johnston, J.T. Netterville, J.L. Wood, and M.D. Joesten, Chemistry and Society, Fifth Edition, Saunders Publishing, 1987. The material for the lectures, especially for Units 4, 5, and 6 will be drawn from this text.

UNIT 1

"Searching for Depression Genes," L. Wingerson, Discover 1982, p. 60.

"Manic-Depression: Is It Inherited?", G. Kolata, Science 232, 575 (1986).

UNIT 2

"The Genetic Code," F.H.C. Crick, Sci. American 208, 66 (1962).

UNIT 3

"Drugs and the Brain," S. Snyder, Scientific American Library, 1986, Chapter 1 and Chapter 4, pp 91-100.

UNITS 4 AND 5

"Nuclear Winter," A. Ehrlich, Bull. of Atom. Sci. April 1984, p. S1.

UNIT 6

"Greenhouse Warming Still Coming," R.A. Kerr, Science 232, 573 (1988).

"The Challenge of Acid Rain," V.A. Mohnen, Sci. American 259, 30 (1988).

"Antarctic Ozone Hole: Complex Picture Emerges," P.S. Zurer. Chem. Eng. News Nov. 2, 1987, p. 22.

"Ozone Hole Bodes Ill for the Globe," R.A. Kerr, Science 241, 785 (1988).

UNIT 7

The Sachertorte Algorithm, J. Shore, Penguin Books, 1986.

THE ROLE AND IMPORTANCE OF RESEARCH AND PUBLICATION IN CHURCH-RELATED SCHOOLS

Fr. James Skehan, S.J.

Fr. James Skehan, S.J. is the Director of the Weston Observatory at Boston College. Fr. Skehan received his PhD in geology and geophysics at Harvard University. He is deeply involved in faith/science work, being a member of Cosmos and Creation in Baltimore and the Task Force for Cultural Exchange between Faith and Science of the Episcopal Diocese of Massachusetts as well as ITEST.

INTRODUCTION

A quick glance at the question implied by the title of this paper may prompt the response, "what difference can there be between research and publication at a church-related and any other school?" My position is that there should not be any difference in the quality of research and there is not necessarily any difference in the motivating force that prompts an individual faculty member at either type school to engage in research and to communicate its results in published form. However, I believe that there is a bonus that may be reaped by the scholar for whom religious values provide an additional reward or motivation. Further, my experience leads me to think that not all such scholars are members of faculty of church-related schools by any means. However, the presumption is that a large number of those at church-related schools are there not only because of the quality of the institution but because they regard as important the value-laden religious atmosphere of the institution and the freedom to worship according to their religion within the academic oasis. Thus, in addition to considerations of research and publication as generally understood, I will address those additionally enriching aspects of the topic that are related to human nature ("natural religions" if you wish) and to the overtly religious dimensions as well.

WHAT IS AND IS NOT RESEARCH AND PUBLICATION?

Research and publication may mean diverse things in different contexts. In the context of our present discussion of Church-related schools and education, I wish to use the terms in two different senses but will try to clearly differentiate them. Research, in terms of scholarly investigation, I take to mean original studies by which the scholar carries out a project or program of research in such a way as to contribute new data, interpretations, models or theories in the particular field. Scholarly publication, in that context, is generally taken to refer to those writings that have been submitted by the author to the editor of a recognized journal or book publishing house, who then enlists peer review to establish that such manuscripts meet at least minimum standards of quality, before being accepted for publication. Review papers, that summarize the state of knowledge in a given field, may be regarded as scholarly if they demonstrate that the author has a breadth of expertise and knowledge sufficient to provide a balanced and insightful review of research developments in the field. In my own field of the geosciences there are a large number of prestigious journals and publishing houses, of which Tectonophysics and the Geological Society of America are respectively but two.

A second usage of the term research and publication may refer to studies that are published with little or no peer review. The research so published may range from excellent to poor, but the element of quality control is either lightly exercised or is more or less absent. Such a publication in my field is the annual volume of Field Trip Guides to various parts of New England published by the New England Intercollegiate Geological Conference (NEIGC) for use by professional geologists and students in field trips held on a particular weekend each fall. These papers have proved to be some of the most useful published materials on the geology of the region available, although not subject to rigorous peer review. Peer review is most useful in general, but is commonly a time-consuming process. The lack of peer review process allows the annual guidebook of "telephone-book" size to appear in a timely fashion.

In addition to research and publication that involve original contributions to knowledge, there is another spectrum of contributions that are the product of study, expertise and diligence whose main function and value is other than the development of new contributions to knowledge. Such contributions as textbooks, laboratory manuals, teaching aids, book reviews, public education materials, writings for newsletters, collaboration with the media in presenting educational materials and the like, all have an important role to play in the total educational enterprise. However, it is important for our discussion that a clear distinction be made between original research and resulting publication and other important educational activities in Church-related schools.

SCHOLARSHIP IN NON-CHURCH-RELATED SCHOOLS

Scholarship in church-related schools in North America has improved notably over the past 30 to 40 years. Nevertheless, in the recent Carnegie Foundation survey of research universities in the United States, only one church-related school, Yeshiva University, appears among the ranking institutions. I believe that the Carnegie criteria to judge which are the leading universities are misleading because the requirements for inclusion are that the institution receive at least $33.5 million in federal support and award at least 50 Ph.D degrees. Those criteria strongly favor institutions having medical schools, engineering schools and/or those having science departments having a substantial commitment to defense-related research. Nevertheless a large number of the institutions of Table 1 would be included on a list based on academic quality irrespective of the level of funding and the numbers of Ph.D degrees.

TABLE 1 LEADING RESEARCH UNIVERSITIES

Boston University	U of California, San Diego
Calif Inst of Technology	U of California, San Francisco
Carnegie Mellon University	University of Chicago
Case Western Reserve Univ	University of Cincinnati
Colorado State University	U of Colorado, Boulder
Columbia University	University of Connecticut
Cornell University	University of Florida
Duke University	University of Georgia
Georgia Inst of Technology	University of Hawaii, Manoa
Harvard University	U of Illinois, Chicago
Howard University	U of Illinois, Urbana-Champaign
Indiana U at Bloomington	University of Iowa
Johns Hopkins University	University of Kentucky
Louisiana State University	U of Maryland, College Park
Mass Inst of Technology	University of Miami
Michigan State University	U of Michigan, Ann Arbor
New Mexico State Univ	U of Minnesota-Twin Cities
New York University	U of Missouri, Columbia
North Carolina State Univ	University of New Mexico
Northwestern University	U of N Carolina, Chapel Hill
Ohio State University	University of Pennsylvania
Oregon State University	University of Pittsburgh
Pennsylvania State Univ	University of Rochester
Princeton University	U of Southern California
Purdue University	U of Tennessee, Knoxville
Rockefeller University	U of Texas, Austin
Rutgers University	University of Utah
Stanford University	University of Virginia
State University of New York Stony Brook	University of Washington
Texas A&M University	U of Wisconsin, Madison
University of Arizona	Virginia Polytechnic Inst and State University
U of California, Berkeley	Vanderbilt University
U of California, Davis	Washington University
U of California, Irvine	Yale University
U of California, Los Angeles	Yeshiva University

Note: These institutions are classified as Research Universities I by the Carnegie Foundation for the Advancement of Teaching. Most offer a full range of baccalaureate programs, are committed to graduate education through the doctoral degree, and give a high priority to research . Each receives at least $33.5-million in federal support and awards at least 50 Ph.D degrees annually.

Source: Carnegie Foundation for the Advancement of Teaching.
Source: Chronicle of Higher Education, Sept. 6, 1989

Moreover, to achieve the distinction of a Stanford or a Cal Tech is not an undertaking lightly entered into or a goal that is achieved by chance. It requires that the leadership of the institution over a prolonged period of time establish academic excellence as a priority of the highest magnitude, and that the institution be prepared to recruit faculty members, graduate students and post-doctoral fellows of such caliber and motivation as to distinguish themselves in research and publication. Granted all of these factors, a serious question remains as to why it is that those communities of scholars who populate the "best" schools are some of the brightest, most articulate, most productive, and most highly motivated academicians? I believe that each of these scholars have several notable features in common: they are preeminent in their mastery of their field and are dedicated, enthused, and perhaps consumed by their search for answers and their desire to communicate their results to their peers. Additionally they are blessed if during most of their career they serve under enlightened academic leadership that supports their research to anywhere near the highest possible extent.

Recently, I attended a symposium at Harvard University honoring my thesis advisor on the occasion of his retirement. One of his former students prefaced his Symposium paper with a tribute to this well-known and much honored faculty member in a statement that was right to the point and one that characterized that life of scholarship. The speaker, a former student and a distinguished researcher in his own right, while acknowledging that other speakers had correctly identified many endearing and important facets, felt that the most important characteristic of our professor's career was his integrity! Everyone in the audience, recognizing the great depth of perception and the accuracy of this appraisal, gave him a standing ovation! I maintain that in addition to great native intelligence and special educational opportunities, the factor common to all the truly great scholars is integrity or authenticity.

SCHOLARS IN A WORLD OF SCHOLARS

A fundamental way in which to view the scholarship of faculty in church-related schools is to recognize basically that the academic reputation of the individual and of the department rests chiefly on the quality and quantity of research and publication, on the achievement of graduate and undergraduate alumni/ae of the department and on the quality of the post-doctoral fellows who are attracted. In this respect, the scholar in the church-related school has the same opportunities and the same responsibilities as regards the academic discipline as any other scholar from any other college and university.

OBSTACLES TO RESEARCH AND PUBLICATION

Reflection on the related questions of why there is only one church-related institution among the Leading Research Universities (Table 1), and why there is such a relatively small, although growing, number of truly distinguished scholars in church-related schools suggests that the issue is not only complex but that the situation is improving. From the time of the founding of the Academy that became Georgetown University in 1789 and the restoration of the Jesuit Order in North America in 1810, much of the academic effort of Church-related institutions went into undergraduate programs that rightly were given a high priority. To keep this topic in perspective one must remember that it was only in the 1870's that East Coast universities began to introduce graduate lecture courses. And in the Midwest graduate programs were introduced after the turn of the century as follows: U. of Indiana, 1904; U. of Illinois, 1905; Washington U., 1922; St. Louis U., 1925; U. of Missouri, 1928; and Louisiana State U., 1931. Boston College initiated its Graduate school in 1924 (Fitzgerald, 1986). In the 1930's the Jesuit General, writing to superiors urged them to develop graduate schools in their institutions comparable to the best in the United States. In 1932, for example, a total of 131 doctorates were given by Catholic Institutions of which 66 were conferred by Jesuit Schools. By 1933 33 Catholic universities were offering graduate degrees. Serious attention to graduate programs and to the academic preparation of faculty to staff these programs came slowly and took place sporadically before 1930. It is safe to say generally that teaching schedules were unusually heavy and not uncommonly remain so, at least as compared to those of faculty in institutions listed in Table 1. Financial resources were also a limiting factor then as now.

SCHOLARSHIP, A SPECIAL VOCATION FOR THE CHRISTIAN

Howard Gray, S.J., in his keynote address to the Jesuit Honor Society, Alpha Sigma Nu, convention at Georgetown last October, described scholarship as "a privileged pilgrimage toward truth for those who are called to use their gifts in the world of ideas." On the occasion of the bicentennial of Jesuit education in the United States, he said additionally, "The world is formed, interpreted and led by ideas. The talented

Christian, who can bring his or her competence into the secular world of ideas has a special vocation today." He went on to say that no greater duty falls on Jesuits today than promotion of scholarship, but he was at pains to suggest that something more could be done on a university level "as an integral part of Christian formation "to create a climate beyond academic competence for professional success that will help both Jesuits and lay colleagues who hunger and thirst "to serve not just one another but others."

SCHOLARSHIP AND THE AUTHENTIC SCHOLAR - A LINK TO MYSTICISM?

I suggest that one of the most important aspects of scholarship, whether in a church-related or non-church-related school is intimately linked not only to native intelligence but especially to personal integrity and authenticity, a complex quality that Bernard Lonergan, S.J. has suggested is the characteristic shared in common by the scientist, by other scholars and the mystic. Egan (1982, p.109) in writing about A Future Mystical Theology points out that Lonergan, by correlating the basic insights of St. Thomas Aquinas with contemporary physics and mathematics, has "disclosed what theology and the secular sciences have in common, namely fidelity to the basic dynamism of the mind to be attentive, intelligent, reasonable, and responsible. Both theology and science, therefore, have a mystical basis." For Lonergan, their very dynamics "raise the question of ultimate truth, value, and authenticity." Egan (p.110) further points out that mystical theology "can find in Lonergan's theological method, based on the inherently mystical dynamism of the mind, one of the best ways to correlated critically and comprehensively religion, science and culture."

Thus, it appears that pursued to its logical conclusion, Lonergan's statement would hold that the authentic scholar, whether or not professing a religious motivation for carrying out his/her studies, operates in an atmosphere of integrity and love, "flowing from a self grasped by God's unconditional love, and a self structured by judgement and decision. Through surrender to the transcendental precepts, the basic dynamism of the human spirit to be attentive, be intelligent, be reasonable, be responsible, and be in love, human authenticity arises (Egan, 1982, p.114)." Thus, one may conclude, on the basis of Lonergan's insights in this matter, that the true scholar is a person of integrity and authenticity, and for that reason the scholarly activity has much in common with mysticism since it is responsive to the transcendental precepts.

Lonergan approaches the topic from a somewhat different perspective from that of Teilhard de Chardin, S.J. An important byproduct of all research and publication carried out with integrity, a feature that Lonergan (1958, p.349) explicitly attends to is that there is a personal transformation that takes place in the researcher over and above the discovery of new information. In the process of attaining truth, the scholar achieves personal self-transcendence in truthfulness. Even though one truthful statement does not make one trustworthy, nevertheless, habitual scholarly pursuit of truth deepens and confirms one in truthfulness he contends.

> "Pure desire to know. . .is the absorption of investigation, the joy of discovery, the assurance of judgement, the modesty of limited knowledge. It is the relentless serenity, the unhurried determination, the imperturbable drive to question following appositely on question in the genesis of truth" (Lonergan, 1958, 349).

Thus the process of research and publication has the capacity on a continuing basis to deepen the scholar's personal integrity or truthfulness.

But beyond the transcendental notion of truth, Lonergan (1972, p.34-35) introduces the transcendental notion of value which he defines as "what is intended in questions for deliberation, just as the intelligible is what is intended in questions for intelligence, and just as truth and being are what are intended in questions for reflection." Lonergan further notes that "the transcendental notions are the dynamism which promotes the subject to full consciousness" beyond cognitional to the existential. Consequently Lonergan concludes that in any activity, that involves self-transcendence, such as research and publication, the scholar can become a principle "of benevolence and beneficence, capable of genuine collaboration and of true love. . .by reaching the sustained self-transcendence of the virtuous man that one becomes a good judge not on this or that human act, but on the whole range of human goodness."

Certainly, overt fostering of these fundamental human values is germane to the goals of church-related colleges and universities. The opportunity for the scholar and student in an environment that is calculated not only to foster such values but to stimulate a reflection on them should be a strong feature of church-related schools.

TEILHARD DE CHARDIN'S MYSTICAL DIMENSION OF SCHOLARSHIP

It must be admitted that the mystical dimension of scholarship up to the present has hardly been an overarching preoccupation of the faculty of church-related institutions. However, that is not to say that it should not be an increasingly strong motivating factor, if one takes seriously the thought and spirituality of Teilhard de Chardin, S.J. Teilhard developed a mysticism of knowing, quite different from the mysticism of unknowing of many before him, particularly as knowing relates to scientific discovery. His view may be summarized in his statement from The Phenomenon of Man, "Religion and science are the two conjugated faces or phases of one and the same complete act of knowledge." King (1981, p.vii) says he believes the real significance of Teilhard is in his "exuberant claim that in the very act of scientifically achieving, he knew God. Teilhard began writing a theology of process and many of his readers came to see as he had seen; for when human knowledge is in process, God is found in the act of knowing."

Teilhard gained many of his insights from the letters of St. Paul. In particular Teilhard linked the role of co-redeeming or co-creation of the universe to the work of the sons (and daughters) of God. Paul speaks of all creation groaning. . . . To explain this passage C. H. Dodd (1957 p. 33-34), in his study The Meaning of Paul for Today cites the poem Everyman, by Edith Anne Stewart claiming that it presents beautifully a thought akin to that of St. Paul, and certainly closely related to Teilhard's view of the matter (King, 1981, p.vii-viii).

All things search until they find
God through the gateway of thy mind

Highest star and humblest clod
Turn home through thee to God.

When thou rejoicest in the rose
Blissful from earth to heaven she goes;

Upon thy blosom summer seas
Escape from their captivities;

Within thy sleep the sightless eyes
Of night revisage Paradise:

In thy soft awe yon mountain high
To his creator draweth nigh;

This lonely tarn reflecting thee,
Returneth to eternity;

And thus in thee the circuit vast
Is rounded and complete at last,

And at last, through thee revealed
To God, what time and space concealed.

TEILHARD DE CHARDIN'S SYNTHESIS

For Teilhard de Chardin, research plays a most important role in building up the Kingdom of Christ. He approaches the subject from the general point of view of geology, since that was his field of expertise. His line of thought goes much as follows. The outer crust of the Earth is made up of the layer called the lithosphere and is composed of rock. The hydrosphere is intimately associated with and is superimposed on the lithosphere, consisting as it does of water within the outer part of the Earth and on its surface. The biosphere has developed on the lithosphere and hydrosphere and is made up of the great variety of life forms that have evolved therefrom. An additional Earth-encircling layer, the atmosphere, is the gaseous sphere of air and clouds that provides our weather and interacts with the other spheres in many ways.

Teilhard has pointed out that with the advent of mankind on the Earth, an entirely new phenomenon has taken place. Unlike the other animals which know, mankind knows that he knows -- there is reflection. Teilhard recognizes that there has been produced and continues apace the development of products of the mind and heart that are forming a world-encircling, organic-psychic sphere that he refers to as "the thinking Earth" and he calls it the Noosphere." He says "we must enlarge our approach to encompass the formation, taking place before our eyes and arising out of this factor of hominisation, of a particular biological entity such as has never before existed on earth-the growth, outside and above the biosphere, of an added planetary layer, an envelope of thinking substance, to which, for the sake of convenience and symmetry, I have given the name of the Noosphere." (de Chardin, 1964, p.157). The term, noosphere, is from the Greek word, mind, and refers to the terrestrial sphere of thinking substance.

In this connection Teilhard draws our attention to the phenomenon of research that he regards as characteristic of the present age, an urge, a need to seek understanding, discovery and invention. He points out with great delight and awe that in past generations there were only a handful of researchers, but toward the end of his life in 1955 "In fields embracing every aspect of physical matter, life, and thought, the research-workers are to be numbered in hundreds of thousands, and they no longer work in isolation but in teams endowed with penetrative powers that it seems nothing can withstand." (de Chardin, 1964, p.173).

He provides a further insight into research as he continues, "Research, which until yesterday was a luxury pursuit, is in process of becoming a major, indeed the principal function of humanity. . . . As in the case of all the organisms preceding it, but on an immense scale, humanity is in process of 'cerebralising' itself. And our proper biological course, in making use of what we call our leisure, is to devote it to a new kind of work on a higher plane: that is to say, to a general and concerted effort of vision. The Noosphere, in short, is a stupendous thinking machine." (de Chardin, 1964, p.173). Thus it is by our participation in research and in various activities that foster research that each one of us participates in building up the Noosphere. Teilhard continues his vision of humanity's role: "Humanity . . . is building its composite brain beneath our eyes." (de Chardin 1964, p. 178). Thus, in Teilhard's view, by participating in the work of research and publication we participate in the mystical work of "re-creation" of the Earth and universe. It is this view, that Teilhard derives from the writings of St. Paul, that convinces him that until the masterplan by which the Earth and the universe were created is rediscovered, Christ can not assume His full role as King of the Universe. Thus, in his view, mankind's role of rediscovery by means of scholarship is one of the important keys to insure and hasten the coming of the Kingdom!

SCHOLARSHIP IN THEOLOGY, PHILOSOPHY AND THE NATURAL SCIENCES

In a lengthy message to Rev. George V. Coyne, S.J., Director of the Vatican Observatory, His Holiness, Pope John Paul II refers to the publication of the volume, Physics, Philosophy and Theology: A Common Quest for Understanding, as affording the Pontiff the opportunity to thank the astronomer for efforts devoted to "a subject of such paramount importance." The Pope goes on to say that the theme of the conference is a crucial one for the contemporary world and because of its importance he wishes "to address some issues which the interactions among natural science, philosophy, and theology present to the Church and to human society in general."

The entire fourteen pages of the papal message is a welcome treatment of several aspects of my topic, and deserves careful reading and reflection by anyone concerned with scholarly activities in church--related schools. Among other statements, His Holiness goes on to speak about these relationships and interactions as follows:

> "By encouraging openness between the Church and the scientific communities, we are not envisioning a disciplinary unity between theology and science like that which exists within a given scientific field or within theology proper. As dialogue and common searching continue, there will be growth towards mutual understanding and a gradual uncovering of common concerns which will provide the basis for further research and discussion. . . .
>
> "We might ask whether or not we are ready for this crucial endeavor. Is the community of world religions, including the Church, ready to enter into a more thorough-going dialogue with the scientific community, a dialogue in which the integrity of both religion and science is supported and the advance of

each is fostered? Is the scientific community now prepared to open itself to Christianity, and indeed to all the great world religions, working with us all to build a culture that is more humane and in that way more divine? Do we dare to risk the honesty and the courage that this task demands? We must ask ourselves whether both science and religion will contribute to the integration of human culture or to its fragmentation. It is a single choice and it confronts us all.

"Now this is a point of delicate importance, and it has to be carefully qualified. Theology is not to incorporate indifferently each new philosophical or scientific theory. As these findings become part of the intellectual culture of the time, however, theologians must understand them and test their value in bringing out from Christian belief some of the possibilities which have not yet been realized. The hylomorphism of Aristotelian natural philosophy, for example, was adopted by the medieval theologians to help them explore the nature of the sacraments and the hypostatic union. This did not mean that the Church adjudicated the truth or falsity of the Aristotelian insight, since that is not her concern. It did mean that this was one of the rich insights offered by Greek culture, that it needed to be understood and taken seriously and tested for its value in illuminating various areas of theology. Theologians might well ask, with respect to contemporary science, philosophy and the other ares of human knowing, if they have accomplished this extraordinarily difficult process as well as did these medieval masters.

"The matter is urgent. Contemporary developments in science challenge theology far more deeply than did the introduction of Aristotle into Western Europe in the thirteenth century. Yet these developments also offer to theology a potentially important resource. Just as Aristotelian philosophy, through the ministry of such great scholars as St. Thomas Aquinas, ultimately came to shape some of the most profound expressions of theological doctrine, so can we not hope that the sciences of today, along with all forms of human knowing, may invigorate and inform those parts of the theological enterprise that bear on the relation of nature, humanity and God? . . . .(John Paul 11, 1988, in Coyne, p. M1-M14.)

"Science can purify religion from error and superstition; religion can purify science from idolatry and false absolutes. Each can draw the other into a wider world, a world in which both can flourish. . . .

"Both the church and the scientific community are faced with such inescapable alternatives. We shall make our choices much better if we live in a collaborative interaction in which we are called continually to be more. Only a dynamic relationship between theology and science can reveal those limits which support the integrity of either discipline, so that theology does not profess a pseudo-science and science does not become an unconscious theology. Our knowledge of each other can lead us to be more authentically ourselves. No one can read the history of the past century and not realize that crisis is upon us both. The uses of science have on more than one occasion proven massively destructive, and the reflections on religion have too often been sterile. We need each other to be what we must be, what we are called to be."

CONCLUSION

In an address to the provincials and central government of the Society of Jesus in 1982, Pope John Paul II focused on the great importance of "the Christian penetration of the culture of the world around us" (O'Keefe, 1988, p.68). It was this concern that led his Holiness on May 20, 1982 to institute the Pontifical Council for Culture, a special permanent body for the purpose of promoting the great objectives which the Second Vatican Council proposed regarding relations between the Church and culture. The Pope said:

"Since the beginning of my pontificate, I have considered the Church's dialogue with cultures of our time to be a vital area, one in which the destiny of the world at the end of the 20th Century is at stake. Now people live a fully human life thanks to culture. Yes, the future of people depends on culture" (O'Keefe, 1988, p. 69).

One of the most important ways by which mankind today refines and unfolds his manifold spiritual and bodily qualities and thus brings "the world itself under his control is by his knowledge and labor", as

Gaudium et Spes recommends. The Pontiff goes on to further describe what he means: "Finally, it is a feature of culture that throughout the course of time man expresses, communicates, and conserves in his works great spiritual experiences and desires, so that these may be of advantage to the progress of many, even of the whole human family" (O'Keefe, 1988, p. 69).

Certainly the role of research and publication is a most vital one in developing, communicating and preserving the great experiences of the mind and heart. (O'Keefe, 1988, p. 63) has identified as "a characteristic of Jesuit Education. . . "a full blown concern to develop intellectual probity, critical intelligence, and responsible freedom." "We look to an enquiring mind because we are dealing with true education and not just training."

Daley discusses the question of how Jesuits and others make sense "of the commitment of this body of Catholic priests and their associates to an enterprise that is not, in itself, explicitly religious at all, and that necessarily occupies itself much of the time with purely secular pursuits?" Daley responds that "the continuing connection between Jesuits and humanistic or liberal studies is not fortuitous" but because of the recognition from the earliest days of the Society's existence that "the value of liberal education as a Jesuit priestly ministry" is "not simply in the possible personal influence of the teacher on his pupils but in the very content of educational enterprise (Daley, 1988, p.5)."

In the last analysis the value of research and publication seems to lie primarily in the intellectual worth of the research and publication and in the academic integrity, or in Lonergan's term, the authenticity of the scholar. Scholarship is an heuristic activity that is fundamental to human nature, to the human spirit, and when carried out with fidelity to the transcendental method, scholarship cannot fail to produce positive results in the realm of "the never ending buildup of knowledge (Gregson, 1985, p.36) that is "the natural consequence of the methodological structure of our knowing (Gregson, p. 36)." I believe that Teilhard de Chardin, S.J. would whole-heartedly have endorsed Lonergan's assessment of the qualities of one who is an authentic person. Moreover, in the spirit of Teilhard, I would add that by fidelity to these transcendental precepts, the researcher builds up the Noosphere and thus hastens the coming of the Kingdom of Christ. Teilhard believed that the committed Christian should be fully involved with the culture of the age, and that "the sons of heaven... should "compete on the human level, in conviction and hence on equal terms, with the children of the world (de Chardin, 1965, p. 65)." For Teilhard, as a priest and Jesuit, geological research was the highest and all-consuming activity of his life. At the same time his life as a scientist was suffused with and enlivened by a mystical sense of the presence of Christ in every aspect of this activity. He expresses this as follows: "Let us look at ourselves in one of those places of dominant activity and try to see how, with the help of our activity and by developing it to the full, the divine presses in upon us and seeks to enter our lives (de Chardin, 1965, p. 50).

In discussing the age old question of the value of "secular" vs "religious" activities Teilhard left us no doubt that he considered that distinction as having little meaning. He says on this point: "Nothing is more certain dogmatically, than that human action can be sanctified. 'Whatever you do,' says St. Paul, 'do it in the name of our Lord Jesus Christ'." Teilhard believed that at the same time it is written by his teacher, St. Paul, as well as in the human heart by nature that the believer "must be an example to the Gentiles in devotion to duty, in energy, and even in leadership in all the spheres opened up by man's activity." His resolution to the question is amplified further, "we can reconcile, and provide mutual nourishment for, the love of God and the healthy love of the world, a striving towards detachment and a striving towards the enrichment of our human lives" by a full involvement in human activities, the highest of which for him was research (de Chardin, 1965, p. 51-53).

REFERENCES CITED

Alpha Sigma Nu Newsletter, Spring 1989.

Carnegie Foundation for the Advancement of Teaching, 1988, Leading Research Universities, Chronicle of Higher Education, Sept. 6, 1989, p. 24.

de Chardin, S.J., P. T., 1965, The Divine Milieu, Harper Colophon Books, Harper and Row, Publishers, New York, 160p.

de Chardin, S.J., P.T., 1964, The Future of Man, Harper and Row, Publishers, New York and Evanston, 319p.

Daley, S.J., B.E., 1988, "Splendor and Wonder: Ignatian Mysticism and the Ideal of Liberal Education," p. 3 - 20, in William J. O'Brien (editor), Splendor and Wonder: Jesuit Character, Georgetown Spirit and Liberal Education, Georgetown University Press, Washington, D.C., 106p.

Dodd, C.H., 1957, The Meaning of Paul for Today, Living Ages Books, published by Meridian Books, New York, 190p.

Egan, S.J., H.D., 1982, What Are They Saying About Mysticism?, Paulist Press, 134p.

Fitzgerald, S.J., Paul, 1984, The Governance of Jesuit Colleges in the United States 1920-1970, University of Notre Dame Press, Notre Dame, Indiana, 1984, 310p.

Gregson, Vernon, 1985, "Lonergan, Spirituality, and the Meeting of Religions." College Theology Society, Studies in Religion. 2, University Press of America, Inc., Lanham, Md and London, Eng., 154p.

John Paul II, 1988, "Message to the Reverend George V. Coyne, S.J., Director of the Vatican Observatory, p. Ml - Ml4 in Physics, Philosophy, and Theology: A Common Quest for Understanding, Russell, R.J., Stoeger, S.J., W.R., and Coyne, S.J., G.V., Editors, 419p.

King, T.M., 1982, Teilhard's Mysticism of Knowing. The Seabury Press, New York, 154p.

Lonergan, S.J., Bernard J.F., 1978, Insight, A Study of Human Understanding, Harper and Row, San Francisco, 785p.

Lonergan, S.J., Bernard J.F., 1972, Method in Theology, Herder and Herder, New York, 403p.

O'Keefe, S.J., Vincent, 1988, "Jesuit Education: Myth and Reality, Context and Mission," p. 591 - 92, in William J. O'Brien (editor), Splendor and Wonder: Jesuit Character, Georgetown Spirit, and Liberal Education, Georgetown University Press, Washington, D.C., 106p.

DEVELOPMENTS IN SCIENCE/TECHNOLOGY/SOCIETY CURRICULA AT THE SECONDARY LEVEL AND HOW COLLEGES CAN CONNECT AND CONTINUE

Mrs. Marie Sherman

Marie C. Sherman received her B.S. in Chemistry from Iowa State University, Ames, Iowa, and her Master's Degree from St. Louis University. She has been Chair of the Science Department at Ursuline Academy, St. Louis, for the past 23 years and has taught physical science, chemistry, biochemistry and anatomy/physiology. Her main interest is in preparing women students for their careers and the choices they will face in a technological society. She also visits elementary schools with a chemistry show and gives frequent teacher workshops. She has received numerous awards, among them the Monsanto Award for Science Teaching.

Secondary schools, with their required courses, are really good examples of a "liberal arts core curriculum," since they usually require English, History, Mathematics, Social Studies, Science, Fine Arts, Practical Arts, Foreign Language and Physical Education, plus Religion, if the school is religion-affiliated. Most require at least one year of science and two of math, though many require 2-3 units of science and 2-3 of math, and these are certainly recommended for college-bound students. However, each topic was often taught without any connection to the others, and seldom in the context of societal implications, the effects of technology on our society, or of the ethical values involved.

STS issues obviously need to be emphasized in high school science classes because:

(1) For many students, these are the only sciences they will take.

(2) Many colleges have not arranged special courses emphasizing STS issues for non-science or science majors. Just because a student is a science major does not mean that he or she has been alerted to or forced to consider the implications of science/engineering/technology for society. In fact, just the opposite is probably true: science, computer, medicine, engineering majors are usually so deeply involved in content courses that they don't take time to think of the future effects on society of their science, their computer, their medicine or their engineering careers.

(3) Some secondary administrators and teachers pay pious lip service to the ideal of team teaching theology/science or social studies/ecology or biology/ethics. However, because of scheduling difficulties, lack of released time for the involved faculty and other nitty-gritty problems, in actual practice these efforts and courses are minuscule in number.

In the past ten years or so, a number of so-called "STS" courses have been developed in most areas of secondary science. A few of these developments are:

<u>Chemistry</u>: The American Chemical Society's ChemCom curriculum which stresses the interrelation of chemicals, the environment and society; CEPUP (Chemical Education for Public Understanding Program) from the Lawrence Hall of Science; Chemical Manufacturing Association's ChemEcology magazine; the TIE (Teachers, Industry and the Environment) program which originated with the Chemical Council of Missouri.

Biology: The Monsanto Fund has made a commitment of at least $150,000 for biotechnology education at the secondary, junior high and elementary level, starting first in St. Louis and then moving across the nation; Cold Spring Harbor has a group of scientists crossing the U.S. in a van, giving genetic engineering programs to secondary teachers, one week in each location; the University of Wisconsin has pioneered a kind of "fast plants" which can be used by elementary students in the study of genetics; the BSCS group has funded summer internships in immunology, with the pilot program having been held at Washington University this past summer.

Physics: Physics publications have emphasized in the last year such issues as the cold-fusion confusion, nuclear waste storage, super-collider expenditures, Star Wars and Space Lab plans; the recent success of the space probes to Neptune; atmospheric problems with the ozone hole and the greenhouse effect.

Medicine: All the above-mentioned sciences, plus engineering and computers/math converge upon ethics in the medical field, (and it appears to be a collision course!) with some terrible decisions facing our descendants in the years 2000 and beyond.

From the vantage point of a secondary teacher, I would also like to encourage colleges to:

(1) Develop out-reach activities for their science students and professors, to get them out into the community to explain science to Mr. and Mrs. Average and their kids in the schools and in the shopping malls; to give talks and demonstrations for Senior Citizen groups and civic clubs;

(2) Create coalitions between area scientists, engineers and mathematicians and the local college faculties, to address STS-community issues such as recycling, water pollution, biomedical ethics and biotechnology issues; involve secondary teachers in these programs.

(3) Establish formal liaisons between college faculties and their counterparts in the high schools, junior highs and elementary schools; some programs like this already exist, such as the Partnership and Bridge Programs at UMSL (University of

Missouri-St. Louis), but they need to be expanded.

(4) Encourage more women and minorities to go into science/technology careers; until we get this under-utilized portion of the population into the mainstream of modern society, we will be unable even to communicate with them on STS issues.

This paper is meant to be a rather informal and incomplete listing, so that any of the participants at the conference who are not familiar with secondary programs can get a feel for what is going on. The author notes that, for the sake of brevity, she has not included many STS programs such as the one sponsored by Rustum Roy at Penn State.

STS: A NEW OPPORTUNITY FOR THE RE-INTEGRATION OF CHRISTIAN CONCERN INTO AMERICAN ACADEMIC LIFE

Dr. Rustum Roy

Dr. Roy, Evan Pugh Professor of the Solid State and Professor of Geochemistry and Director of the Materials Research Laboratory, is the Director of the Science, Technology and Society Program at The Pennsylvania State University. Dr. Roy has served on boards and committees far too numerous to mention. One, particularly indicative of Professor Roy's interest, was service as the first chairman of the National Council of Churches' Committee on Science, Technology and the Church. In 1979 he presented the Hibbert Lectures in London on the relationship of science and technology to contemporary religious insight.

STS NEW STAR ON THE ACADEMIC HORIZON

For good or ill a new subject matter field is inexorably elbowing its way into American and world academia. The field is called in most places, Science, Technology and Society (STS); sometimes the word Values is included in the title in some combination. STS claims to be both the only necessary and sufficient education in and about science and technology which every citizen needs. Of course, it is not sufficient for professional scientists/engineers (2-5% of the population) nor for non-technical managers and leaders of our technological world (10-15%) but for the rest (80-85%) STS is the necessary and probably sufficient contact with the world of Science and Technology.

STS is unapologetically interdisciplinary, syncretist, general rather than specialized, broad rather than deep. STS stands foursquare against the dominant reductionist paradigm, borrowed from bad science, that specialization-ad-infinitum is the only way to "progress" in any field. It boldly claims that right brain rationale, and contextual understanding, visualization and conceptualization, are at least as important as left brain, isolated, linear, mathematical, more and more narrowly specialized approaches to knowledge.

In an educational world where the thinking professionals (probably more so in a small university or college) recognize that the pendulum has started to swing away from the excesses of specialization and fragmentation, the faculty have become more receptive to new integrative concepts, among which STS pre-empts the unique central space (See Fig. 1).

No wonder then that between 1500 and 2000 colleges are teaching at least one course which is clearly within STS and probably a third or a quarter are keeping up in some way on "STS" as the largest emerging field within American higher education. About 100 formal programs of one kind or another -- departments, interdisciplinary programs, undergraduate or graduate majors, minors, etc., are now in place. The unifying forces of STS-curricula have spread to the K-12 system. Many states or provinces require STS, many will introduce it over the next few years. Hundreds of schools today teach STS in the U.S., Canada, Britain, Holland, etc., and the number will be in tens of thousands in the next decade.

Now how does this situation for STS relate to the needs and special opportunities of the church-related colleges and universities?

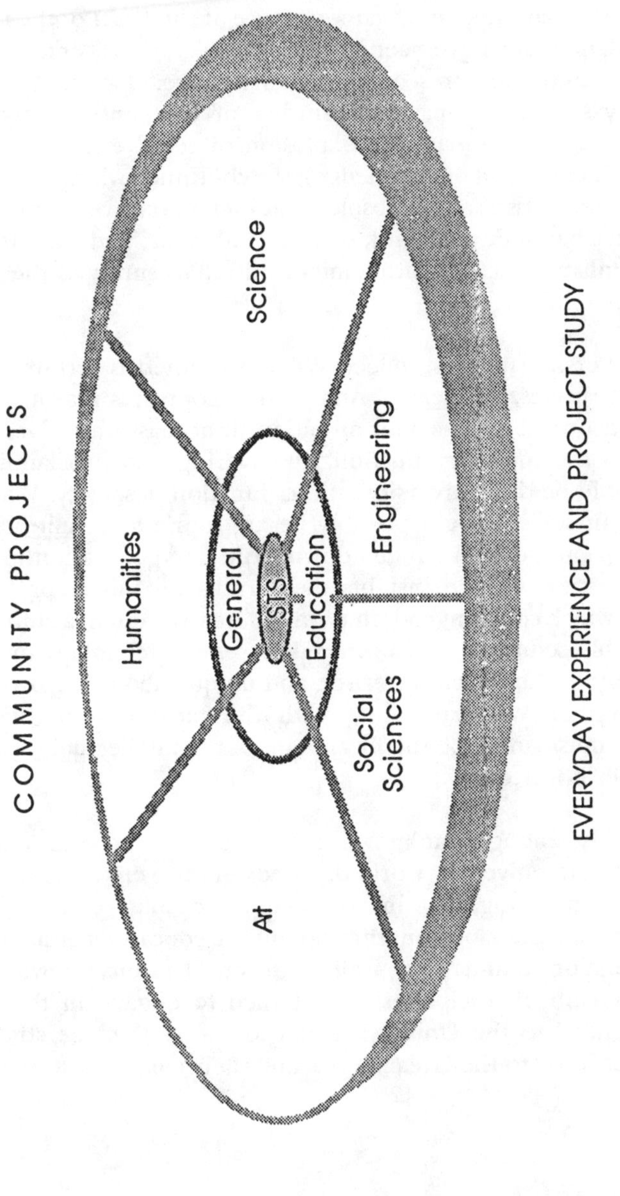
COMMUNITY PROJECTS
Humanities
Science
General
STS
Education
Engineering
Social
Sciences
At
EVERYDAY EXPERIENCE AND PROJECT STUDY

STS: ITS ROLE IN THE UNIVERSITY

STS is the reinvention of the University within the Multi-versity. Clark Kerr long ago described the transmogrification of the University into the Multi-versity. But the accuracy of this description and the impact that the reality behind the description has had on higher education has never been fully acknowledged. The fact is that the centripetal forces of "unification" of knowledge which were once at the heart of the institution called the University have been routed. The victorious centrifugal forces in the contemporary research university are: increasingly narrow disciplinary specialization; the absurdity of the continuously running research funding NO play, the explosion of relative ignorance (often mistitled the explosion of knowledge); the continued whining by the most affluent (the scientists) about obsolete equipment (last year's model) when they haven't had a day to think or reflect all year; and the institutional fundamentalism which has academics in thrall as surely as the Ayatollah controls his minions.

The multi-versity survives, indeed William Bennett is certainly accurate in saying it thrives, financially. And that, of course, is reason enough to resist any action to pay serious attention to at least one of its principal functions -- the unifying function. Discovering and proclaiming great unities should be the University's direct function in society. Which other institution in society could possibly be appropriate to unite the grand traditions of humankind handed down from one generation to the next with the latest knowledge, insights, deep truths and indeed problems and challenges which confront contemporary humans? And in a culture where the incredibly seductive and powerful forces of technology and science literally define what is characteristic and unique about our own culture, the unifying of Western values with the meanings of science and technology must surely be the focal point of the intellectual raison d'être of the modern university.

Yet strangely enough, unknown to the critics and unremarked by observers of the university world the seeds of this very synthesis we seek are already sprouting, not in the unapproachable refined air of the research universities alone but throughout the educational establishment. STS on a major campus is typically a group of faculty drawn from the widest spectrum of disciplines, determined to engage in the dialogue which is central to the University, and to assure that the students are exposed not only to the Great Books and their ideas, but to the possible connection between the Symposium and Special Relativity, and the contact between the Bible (as the religious guideline Bloom would have) and bioethics. General education, presumably, is the place where unification could be done. The spate of general education reforms is testimony to the universal awareness that, instead, on most campuses general education remains a pork barrel for the distribution of large enrollment "service" courses. For the first time, in STS, a set of integrative principles has emerged which forms an intellectual core for much of general education (see Figure 1) decisively different from the "course distribution" of a Chinese restaurant dinner. It is the genuine fusion of ideas, knowledge and values which counters the fissioning of knowledge over the last century. Moreover, this integrative style also helps, by contagion, to render more porous the walls between the higher reaches of the disciplines.

It is perhaps not an unreasonable projection to see the development of integrative general education with STS at its core as the emergence -- finally -- of the University within the multi-versity it can no longer supplant. In my view the only realistic scenario by which we can reinvent the University -- integrated, interdisciplinary, general -- alongside the other units of the multi-versity -- differentiating, disciplinary, and specialized -- is through the fledgling STS movement.

Insofar as Cardinal Newman was concerned with the "Idea" of the university, no responsible church educator can remain ignorant of or indeed engaged [sic] in this movement, precisely because it is the first time that the biggest questions, i.e., the religious questions of values, human and ultimate are raised now legitimately, indeed centrally on the campus. For the church to remain disengaged from the STS movement may sign the death warrant for any significant academic involvement for the next century. This is a uniquely suitable and legitimate entry point, there may simply be no other.

SUPPLEMENT

THE ORIGIN OF STS AND THE RETURN OF THE PRODIGAL SON

J. Robert Oppenheimer, speaking at the Bicentennial of the Princeton Theological Seminary, said 'I cannot imagine modern science without the culture of Western Europe. And the culture of Western Europe could not exist without its Judaeo-Christian roots.' Many years earlier Carl Friedrich von Weizsäcker, the world's leading scientist-theologian, in his Gifford Lectures published as the 'The History of Nature,' has developed this same theme in a more scholarly way: that modern science is rooted in the Judaeo-Christian tradition. Elsewhere I have used the 'Parable of the Prodigious (and prodigal) Son' to describe the relation of the parent Western Christian culture to its offspring, modern Science and Technology. This powerful progeny has left behind the parent's household, and rejected its constraining values as surely as the Prodigal Son indulged himself in 'riotous (i.e., unconstrained by extrinsic values) living.' The modern enterprise of Science and Technology in turn has been at great pains to establish and maintain its 'autonomy' from values -- an absurd and futile effort. Yet after the Galileo affair we, in the Church, can hardly blame S and T for being thus God-shy! Moreover we have, as yet in the Church, no loving parent accepting, welcoming and thereby earning the right to share its wisdom with this prodigious prodigal.

And yet today, something has clearly gone awry in the Technological Eden. And whatever it is, it will not be easily fixed. And slowly it has begun to sink into the Western consciousness. First came the modern prophets of the Technological Society: Einstein, Weizsäcker, Ellul, Mumford, Weisskopf who have cried out, as clearly as did Jeremiah or Hosea or Amos, against the headlong autonomous rush of Technology into everywhere at the same time at maximum speed. The problem worsens yearly. The population explosion, environmental crisis, resource shortages, the Damoclean sword of nuclear war. Today even the universities, bastions of we-tooism, we hear of it and in their scholastic tones an uncertain trumpet has sounded. Three events played major roles in laying the groundwork for the emergence of STS: Rachel Carson and the 'environmental movement'; the anomie at the root of the shortlived student revolts of the late sixties; the realization of the enormity of the threat of nuclear war. 'STS' is the response by a thoughtful minority to an analysis of where we are as a world and how we got there. Indeed, the tide has turned so far, that among those who have studied the STS issues in depth there is general agreement that, to put it with Jacques Ellul's bluntness, S and T are now out of human control. Yet all agree that somehow they must be re-integrated into Society (read Culture, Values, 'Church'), if we are to have even a chance to restore the balance of power in the Global Village.

This relatively sudden recognition all over the world of the profundity of S and T's impact upon us, this 'megatrend,' is the historical origin of the STS movement. The world of academic leadership has come to a gradual realization that the fundamental proposition that Society had control of S, and (thence of) T, was fatally flawed. Science and Technology are not merely another set of watertight disciplines on the campus. Out there in the real world there was a drama brewing, something more real than any TV spectacular, which could be titled 'Clash of the Titans -- Tradition vs Technology.' Occasional stray sniper's bullets had telegraphed the message -- a Karen Quinlan story, a Love Canal incident. Sometimes a veritable barrage told us we were in a real war, as in the Iranian revolution where a nation revolted against the 'modernization' of S and T and opted to re-submit itself to the draconian hegemony of religion. Even with the 'sanctum sanctorum,' there was trouble: 50 Nobelists and over half the members of the National Academy of Sciences urged the President of the U.S. to stop his Star Wars program even though it carried generous bribes to the science community. At least some of the 'prodigal' sons had realized their mistakes. Today 'STS' is still a movement just trying to burst out of academia. In Troeltsch's terminology it is a sect type, not a church type movement. It is a golden opportunity for an amazing array of concerned citizens to contribute to, interact with, support, network with, all others in an effort to establish a radically different balance of power between religious traditions and the technological Trojan horse seductively presented at our gates. It is a propitious time for university chaplains, whose work surely can lie astride both worlds, to enter the lists.

WHAT IS STS?

THE MEGATREND IN EDUCATION

Science, Technology and Society (STS) has become the fastest growing subject matter field in the halls of academia both in the U.S., and in Britain -- and more recently in other countries. Moreover, it has sprung up simultaneously in dozens of places: it is not organized, there is no STS-society, no government agency pushing it. Yet it grows: it is truly a megatrend.

INTEGRATIVE GENERAL EDUCATION

STS is general education for a technological society. It differs in a significant way from other components of general education in that it is the capstone rather than the foundation. STS is 'integrative' of the wide spectrum of increasingly discrete subjects and courses to which a student is exposed. It shows linkages, helps patterns to emerge, develops meanings out of the whole. For a student or adult to be functionally literate in contemporary society she or he must have acquired -- by one means or another -- the rudiments of what is included under STS. In other words, STS is the only meaningful way to describe the content of technological literacy. Indeed given the nature of the world in which one lives it would, perhaps, not be too grandiose to claim that STS is the core content of citizen education in every major country.

One does not need to document the awareness of the great difficulties which arose in the early decades of this century as the seamless robe of 'higher education' was divided even further into narrower and increasingly insular departments and disciplines. This fissiparous tendency can be linked perhaps to the reductionism inherent in 'science.' The writer has made the case elsewhere that another fundamental cause lay simply in the explosion of the amount of 'knowledge' easily available via books and journals, etc., in any one field, compared to the fixed negentropic capability of the human brain.

Whatever the cause, the fact was undeniable that to an increasing extent even the educated world was becoming bimodal. One small (1-5%) component consisting of those who understood the arcane language of science and technology and the others who were either alternately enchanted or amused by the 'output' of this minority or alarmed and bemused by the same. When C.P. Snow wrote the Two Cultures the momentum driving the divergence between the cultures was already so great, that its intellectual argument had little impact on the academic world. A much more significant work, Jacques Ellul's La Technique had waited ten years to be translated into English and it received widespread attention only when history caught up with it in the late sixties and early seventies. From the romantic paeans of praise, and downright worship of technology characterizing the mid-sixties, the developed world in five to ten years switched to recognizing Technology as the 'enemy.' What had intervened were the 'student movements' in Europe, Rachel Carson, the Vietnam war, Fritz Schumacher and Small is beautiful and towards the end the Oil Crisis, and the Limits to Growth. (See box for examples). The wave of 'anti-technology' sentiment is hardly a decade long when another swing of the pendulum seems to be in the making, new technological saviors being sold under every brand name from computer literacy to high-tech to Star Wars.

In our fragmented world, we all need some 'glue' to hold the pieces together. Today science and technology are major forces shaping our environment, workplaces, and lives. STS provides the most thoroughly developed integrative framework to enable students to understand the many factors at work in the world, and to integrate the many intellectual skills and problem-solving routines they are acquiring in their university studies.

All of the 'excellence reports' recently prepared by blue-ribbon panels of leaders in education, industry and government call attention to the need for integrative education in general, and education which integrates an understanding of science and technology with the rest of life. (See the following box for examples).

A NEW AREA OF INTERDISCIPLINARY STUDY

STS is the prototype of the new academic fields, all struggling to establish themselves in a hostile university atmosphere totally controlled by departments. STS is, of course, quintessentially interdisciplinary, attempting to link together a large fraction of all the departments on a campus. STS works towards an understanding of science and technology in the context of society.

STS brings together scientists, engineers and technologists, social scientists, humanists, and members of professional and pre-professional faculties. Through face to face discussions and tutorials, faculty members can at least make an 'honest effort' to keep up with the significance of developments outside their own fields which often have a profound relevance for their own. Humanists can gain perspectives on the whole range of technologies which they use daily -- steel, highways, sewer systems. STS helps de-mystify all the sexy names like supercomputers,

CHANGING VIEWS ON S/T

These two quotations, both by distinguished, articulate spokespersons for the American body politic, illustrate the rapidity of change in society's attitudes to S/T.

'Yesterday, most of mankind could look forward only to a life that would be 'nasty, brutish and short,' on the verge of privation in good years, starving when the harvests failed. Now wheat pours out of our ears. We swim in milk. We are threatened with vegetable and fruit surpluses and even, in some happy years, wine glut as well. Water, man's precious resource, will be captured from the oceans by desalinization; nuclear power promises unlimited energy; the rocket, unlimited speed; electronics, unlimited technical control. All the old locks of scarcity have been sprung, the prisons flung open. From the first stone tool to the cell which snaps a camera shutter on the far side of the moon, the stride of man's abundance is all but imaginable -- and yet it is here.

'This is the basic miracle of modern technology. This is why it is, in a real sense, a magic wand which gives us what we desire. Don't let us miss the miracle by underestimating this fabulous new tool. We can have what we want. This is the astonishing fact of the modern scientific and technological economy. This is the triumph we hail today. This is the new instrument of human betterment that is at our hand if we are ready to take it up.'

Gov. Adlai Stevenson, 1964

'I find that one of the great challenges of the future will be to differentiate what science and technology can do from what it cannot do. That will be the problem. Their promise is great. They can and will continue to make dramatic breakthroughs in field after field. They can continue to significantly improve the human condition but I fear that people have too much faith in their miracles and that the cornucopia of the benefits of sciences can seriously excuse, postpone and delay some public policy considerations that we must soon institute.'*

Gov. Richard Lamm of Colorado, 1977

**I disagree. I side with the small minority of distinguished scientists who believe that most <u>of the major impacts affecting the masses</u> are behind us.*

THREE METAPHORS ABOUT STS

1. STS: The Essential Glue in College Education

'Glue Not Included'

Go to your local five-and-ten-cent store and buy yourself one of those kits to build a 'model car.' Take out the plastic bits -- the wheels, panels, chassis, engine -- and spread them out on the table, and get ready to put them together. Stop! You need something else to hold the whole structure together. You forgot to read the outside label on the box. It says: 'Glue not included.'

If you have finished an American college (or high school) education you are exactly in the position just described. You have been given all the pieces: engine (math), door panels (English), fenders (social studies), windows (science), and so on. Each one a different color (neatly packaged into a course) but there was nothing to hold it together, and precious little instruction on how it all fits. The glue of making a whole (education) out of the parts (courses) is definitely not provided in the education which 99 percent of Americans receive.

So what is the missing glue in our education?

It is the study of science and technology in relation to society. STS is the new acronym for the most significant change since the war in what is taught on campus.

2. STS: The Best Topsoil for Nurturing Citizenship

The Latin root of the word education is educare (not educere) which is best translated as 'to nurture'. STS is the soil which nurtures the full variety of 'good' citizens from scientists to humanists, poets to theologians to engineers.

3. Pyramid not Flagpole

U.S. Science education has been unconscionably concerned only with reproducing scientists and engineers, neglecting the 'science education' of the 99% who support that science and engineering. The U.S. S/T enterprise finds itself like a shaky flagpole in hostile winds of a technologically illiterate society. Instead the world should be building a stable pyramid of increasingly more technically trained citizens, based, critiqued and supported by the technologically literate masses, made possible by introducing STS throughout the curriculum.

lasers and the bio-technologies. Scientists and technologists can learn STS involves insights from literally every discipline on campus, and the typical STS faculty is composed of representatives from the same wide spectrum of disciplines.

STS ON THE CAMPUS TODAY

The emergence of Science, Technology and Society as a recognizable academic unit on the campus both in America and in Europe remains a remarkable phenomenon. It was a genuine grass-roots phenomenon, nucleated in the atmosphere of crisis in the air of the student upheavals but is sustained by the deep concern and teaching overloads of faculty committed to the field. We have already noted that if anything qualifies to be called a 'megatrend' as defined by Naisbitt the emergence of STS in college education certainly does. STS as a field of pedagogy and study certainly encompasses a wider range of disciplines than any predecessor 'interdisciplinary' field. The record of U.S. higher education in coping with such interdisciplinary fields is dismal [1] and STS presents a unique case in more ways than one. It has been driven from the bottom-up with a wide base of faculty support yet it has had to try to find a place in the academic sun without any major funding aimed at a national objective (as was the case for 'Materials Science' or 'Environmental Sciences') all the while attempting to integrate knowledge across a much wider spectrum.

In 1989 we are 15 years past the point where a large percentage of these STS 'programs' -- ranging from colleges and formal departments to a group of two or three courses listed in the catalogue were put into operation. At the midpoint in this decade a Congressional committee made a survey of the status of these programs and in 1976-77 the NSF sponsored Cornell survey [2] was conducted. Since then the climate in American universities has changed rather sharply, and as a result newcomers to the STS academic marketplaces are sure to be substantially affected. In 1983, while on sabbatical at the Brookings Institution, it was decided to conduct a simple survey to determine the status of this interdisciplinary field then. This survey was limited to the United States.

THE AMERICAN SCENE

The Cornell study by Heitowit, Epstein and Steinberg showed that in round numbers some 1000 colleges give one or more courses in what we would, today, subsume under 'STS'. That number can only have gone up, and as we will describe below, STS is now reaching into the secondary

---

[1] R. Roy, 'Interdisciplinary Science on Campus -- The Elusive Dream,' Chem. and Engg. News 55 (35), 28-40 (1977).

[2] E.D. Heitowit, Epstein and Steinberg, Editors and Compilers. 'Science, Technology and Society: A Guide to the Field,' Program of Science, Technology and Society, Cornell University (1977)

schools. The Brooking survey [3] found some 50 (out of a possible total of about 60) colleges and universities which have formal academic unit specifically dealing with STS or one of its component parts. We estimate that another 100 are examining options on how to institutionalize STS on campus.

These programs break down into clusters which reflect the emphasis (or origin) of the program: genuine interdisciplinary, public policy related, humanities related. The paper [3] provides other useful information on the faculty members and disciplines in each program. From these data one could conclude that the reality of STS in the U.S. is that it is at one and the same time an umbrella term for a syncretic discipline covering a wide spectrum, while it is also used to describe smaller subsets such as science policy, history of science, etc. Thus while science policy is a part of STS, STS cannot be equated with science policy or bioethics or other subsets. Of course in many cases STS programs have grown up around early efforts in one of these areas. In other cases the presence of more narrowly focused programs may have inhibited the growth of a full-range STS program. The following five areas emerge as rational subsets of the field.

- Humanities, History, Philosophy of Science/Technology.
- Engineering/Technology/Science and Public Policy
- Environmental values, issues, policy
- STS by/for Engineers and Scientists
- Interdisciplinary STS covering the entire field.

In programs emphasizing any of the above (except the last named) the composition of the faculty reflects the emphasis and is often not interdisciplinary at all. The last set consists of the genuinely interdisciplinary faculties and these programs represent the STS experiment in general or interdisciplinary education in its present form. The MIT STS - 'College' is clearly an attempt to create an umbrella for already-existing major programs in the sub-areas of STS.

The data on the size of the programs presented are new and surprising. The largest programs serve some 1000 students per year; many

---

3 R. Roy and J. Lerner, "The Status of STS Activities at U.S. Universities," Bull. Sci. Tech. Soc. 3, 417-432 (1983).

universities offering upwards of 10-20 courses. Yet only one dozen institutions offer undergraduate and just over a dozen graduate degrees in STS. Effort levels angle downward from 15 person-years to token support for an 'office.' It is noteworthy that some of the late-comers to the field, e.g., Duke University and Virginia Tech appear among the largest programs.

Administrative issues have been probed both by recording the status and reporting channel for each program, as well as by recording whether the assignment of personnel is through the program office itself, or whether the latter only coordinates the faculty provided by various departments. We find that only six programs are full-fledged departments within a college or graduate school. In many ways these programs are the most stable since they fit the relatively rigid constraints or academic administration. On the other hand it is difficult for such programs to be truly interdisciplinary, and this is reflected in the faculty make-up. The interdisciplinary programs typically report directly to the central administration but what is gained in a more appropriate STS faculty is lost in size and control of budgets.

The power of the purse is certainly not an index of the success or value of the program. It is on the other hand, an indicator of that institution's commitment to the STS field, and probably a measure of the stability of the program on the campus.

At the time the Brookings survey was completed the subjective comments from the University academic community were not optimistic with regard to expansion and future penetration into American academic life. Since then, however, a major change has occurred in the national climate for science education and technological literacy, as noted above. It is because of this emphasis that the future of STS (as the primary vehicle for technological literacy) as a major factor in academia is assured.

NEWEST DEVELOPMENT: TECHNOLOGICAL LITERACY AND STS IN SCHOOLS

While a few U.S. universities (Penn State, Cornell, SUNY Stony Brook, Stanford) started up the STS field the British and Dutch have moved far ahead in expanding STS courses into the high schools and elementary schools. In the U.K., with its long tradition of social criticism of science, the approach grew steadily. The Science in a Social Context Project

(SISCON), an inter-university program, got underway in 1973 and set itself the admirable task of preparing teaching materials at college level, freely available to all comers. Indeed by 1980 the British had already jumped ahead in starting to introduce such materials into the high school curriculum and public examination system. Research groups in one or other aspect of STS, notably at Sussex, Edinburgh and Manchester became well established. With a time lag of a few years, similar developments spread to Australia. Canada came later but is now introducing a TV link between universities in eight provinces to maximize the return on their efforts. Europe has not been slow in making its mark: Lund in Sweden; in West Germany Ulm and Kiel, the latter producing excellent high school programs, come to mind. Holland, with its long tradition of close internal collaboration between universities and readiness to work with its neighbors has formed European Associations for STS. And there is much activity, both established and growing, elsewhere in Europe. The developing world, with very rare exceptions such as one or two individuals and groups in India, has been slow to follow and has not yet started to formalize efforts in STS. Somewhat surprisingly, there are several individuals and groups in the USSR (such as V.V. Nalimov in the Mathematics Institute of the Moscow State University) and in Eastern Europe who are writing and working in the field, but this is probably far from affecting the education of the masses. Nalimov's books [4] are of especial interest to all those concerned with religious values, which he treats more explicitly than most western authors.

THE ROUTE TO TECHNOLOGICAL LITERACY

The critical, evaluative science of STS is as significant a technological advance as any other technology. The STS experts claim that thinking clearly and systematically about science and technology today is as essential -- more essential -- to any society as biotechnology or robotics or any other catchword.

One is tempted to think of STS, then, as the content of what is so often called technological literacy.

---

[4] V.V. Nalimov, Realms of the Unconscious: The Enchanted Frontier, ISI Press, Philadelphia (1982); Faces of Science, ISI Press, Philadelphia (1981).

In the U.S. since early 1983 the crisis in 'math and science' education became the subject of intense public and administrative interest. Half-a-dozen major reports were written in 2-3 years. Without exception they advocate integrative education and some version of STS. See the following 'boxes' for quotes. From an insoluble crisis in March 1983, the media have already wrested a victory over illiteracy by 1985. Would that it were that easy!! From Reagan's literally 'zero-ing out' all expenditure in science education in the NSF, the House and then the Senate has passed a bill for $925 million for 'science education.' But will, or can, more money eradicate the problem?

Add up, if you will, the cost of all the solutions that have been proposed to curb the decline in math and science education. Dr. Gregg Edwards, formerly of the Science Education Directorate at the National Science Foundation, estimated the sum to be $150 billion. President Reagan is sure to hold back or rescind the Congress' law. Since any allocation will be a trivial portion of the $150 billion, we will clearly have to be innovative in <u>how</u> we use the new funds. Are there such new options? Unfortunately, the university world, which sets educational priorities for the country, resists genuine innovations as much as any conservative board of directors or entrenched union.

For the last 30 years, the leaders of academic science and engineering have treated the problem of technological illiteracy with what amounts to benign neglect. In recent months, however, the problem has attracted nationwide attention, and the educational community will no doubt respond to the half-billion federal dollars being dangled out there for 'science education.' The crucial question that every policy and school board or university president must ask is: science education for whom? Is this crisis merely a way of saying that we have shortages of computer scientists and electrical engineers? Or is it an epidemic affecting the entire population? For whom shall we design the cure-- the roughly one percent who become professional scientists, engineers, or doctors?

No, I submit that while this may be the group that most scientists and engineers think of first -- as we did after Sputnik -- it is not what the public and Congress have in mind. No further proof is needed of congressional intent than the 'horror stories' that have been cited in testimony to win the passage of recent bills to improve math and science education. The tellers of these stories invariably focus on the problem of

ALL RECENT NATIONAL REPORTS ON EDUCATION AT EVERY LEVEL FROM K-GRAD SCHOOL STRESS TWO THEMES: 'INTEGRATION' AND 'SOCIETAL CONNECTION'

'INVOLVEMENT IN LEARNING: REALIZING THE POTENTIAL OF AMERICAN HIGHER EDUCATION (1984).' STUDY GROUP ON CONDITIONS OF EXCELLENCE IN AMERICAN HIGHER EDUCATION

- *Liberal education requirements should be expanded and reinvigorated to ensure that students and faculty integrate knowledge from various disciplines (emphasis added).*

- *A 'principal aim' of liberal education is 'the ability to integrate what is learned in different disciplines,' and hence that reform must be based on 'collaboration among faculty from different departments,' which will 'establish specific integrative mechanisms.'*

'EDUCATING AMERICANS FOR THE TWENTY-FIRST CENTURY' (OCTOBER 1983) FINAL REPORT: NATIONAL SCIENCE BOARD COMMISSION ON PRE-COLLEGE EDUCATION IN MATHEMATICS, SCIENCE, AND TECHNOLOGY

- *(For Science in grades 7 and 8) A beginning understanding of the integration of the natural sciences, social sciences, and mathematics; familiarity in integrating technologies with experiences in the sciences (emphasis added).*

- *(Secondary Biology) Understanding biologically based personal and social problems and issues such as health, nutrition, environmental management, and human adaptation; ability to resolve problems and issues in a biosocial context involving value or ethical considerations (emphasis added).*

RECENT NATIONAL REPORTS (continued)

- *(Computer Science) General understanding of the problems and issues confronting both individuals and society as a whole in the use of computers, including social and ethical effects of computers; the ethics involved in computer automation (emphasis added).*

- *'The greater the degree to which all the Sciences and Technology can be integrated in new curricular approaches, the broader the understanding in these fields will be.'*

- *Urges educators to take advantage of the 'numerous opportunities to demonstrate the interdependence of human knowledge, and encourage students to apply the skills and concepts from one discipline in seeking solutions in the others.'*

NATIONAL SCIENCE BOARD CONFERENCE ON GOALS FOR SCIENCE AND TECHNOLOGY EDUCATION GRADES K-12 (April, 1983)

- *Science curriculum grades 9-11 will be 'structured around the interactions of science and technology with the whole society,' with instruction centered around problems that 'integrate knowledge' from engineering, physics, biology, earth science, and applied mathematics.*

- *'Integration of Science, Technology, and Applied Mathematics' throughout basic education.*

- *A curriculum 'organized around problem-solving skills, real life issues, and personal and community decision making.'*

NATIONAL SCIENCE TEACHER ASSOCIATION RECOMMENDS UNANIMOUSLY THAT

Emphasis on science-related societal issues

- *Elementary level: a minimum of percent of science instruction should be directed toward science-related societal issues.*

RECENT NATIONAL REPORTS (continued)

- *Middle/junior high school level: a minimum of 15 percent of science instruction should be directed toward science-related societal issues.*

- *Senior high school level: a minimum of 2 percent of science instruction should be directed toward science-related societal issues.*

THE NORTHEASTERN ASSOCIATION OF GRADUATE SCHOOLS, A GROUP OF 80 GRADUATE INSTITUTIONS FROM MARYLAND TO MAINE, ALSO RECOMMENDS INTERACTION, INTERDISCIPLINARITY AND STS

- *The adoption of a cohesive minor for doctoral students would stress linkages among disciplines.*

- *A new interdisciplinary seminar focusing on the process rather than the products of inquiry.*

- *A didactic short course focusing on the ethical, governmental, and legal forces that shape and influence research and scholarship (= STS).*

math and science illiteracy in the general population, and they offer alarming comparisons with other countries to drive the point home.

It is true that in sheer number of hours, the average student in the United States is exposed to one-fifth to one-third as many hours in science and math as her or his counterpart in Western Europe or Japan. Out of 17,000 school districts in this country, well over half have an inadequate staff to cover math, science and technology. And while the Soviet Union has 123,000 physics teachers, the United States has 10,000. Even more striking is the technological illiteracy of college seniors who have already had required science and math courses. According to a National Science Foundation study reported in Daedalus, Spring 1983, the vast majority of seniors still can't solve a simple word-problem after four years of college. Given the extent of this problem, we in the science and education community would betray the country if we focused once again on just creating more or 'better' scientists and engineers. The goal this time should be math and science education for all.

Those who are closest to the problem -- the nation's secondary-school science teachers -- have pointed to one solution. In a position paper adopted unanimously in 1982, the National Science Teachers Association claims that the biggest gap in high school science education is not in physics, biology or even computer manipulation -- but in the relationship of science and technology to society. Science, technology and society (STS) programs would focus, for example, on technology's relationship to the food-population seesaw, the consequences of genetic engineering, or the effect of computer automation on jobs.

Only by teaching science and technology in this context can we truly expect the American public to become interested in these subjects. By studying acid rain, not only does a citizen become informed about a major policy issue, but she (or he) learns what pH means and how bases neutralize acids. At The Pennsylvania State University, discussing the issues of nuclear war and nuclear power has helped our philosophy and English majors grasp the principles of fission in a way that their required science courses in high school and college were never able to. Science teaching has long followed the more elitist European model of teaching pure science first with very little reference to technology. We must turn this sequence around by focusing on experience and teaching technology first, science thereafter.

In implementing what amounts to a basic restructuring of science education in the United States, there are major hurdles to overcome. The first and perhaps most serious is that there is no constituency fighting for institutional reform or the dollars with which to launch STS programs at secondary schools and college campuses. While there is, for instance, an established (and powerful) physics community fighting for financial support of physics research and education, there is no entrenched group of scholars fighting in the interests of STS.

ACADEMIC POLITICS OF STS

This paper has, so far, presented the case for the importance of STS as recognized universally, and the response in the college and pre-college institutions. It also documents the sharp flattening out of the growth curve in the number of STS programs in colleges. The intellectual merits of integrative education, linking both high school and college students' learnings in science and technology to their cultural and citizen responsibilities, are widely touted as proved in our quotations. Yet in a period of financial stringency STS has not attained the status it clearly should have as an indispensable, if small, part of every student's education. Indeed, it is remarkable that not a single major institution has as yet required a single STS course of every student. Yet typically, virtually every student is required to take three or four courses in 'science' (usually a totally fragmented set of astronomy, biology, geology, etc.) which studies of science literacy show, are not retained at all. The institutional barriers to innovation are so great in a university, and the incentives for success in institutional change so miniscule, that it is not surprising to find that a new field like STS is having a hard time in the academic jungle.

'Para-educational' institutions such as the chaplaincy can therefore play a critical role in making common cause with well-thought-through changes. Indeed the Church in its 'pioneer' mode -- as the agent of change -- must learn to make common cause with the change-agents present within secular society.

The absolutely needed continuous evolution of the curriculum to meet the needs of a changing society are universally stymied by the faculty for the same simple reason that change is so often blocked in all sectors of society: the fear that change may cost those presently in charge prestige, power or even jobs. The total 'student credit hours' in any university curriculum is essentially fixed. Hence changing courses is a zero-sum game. If subject or department A gets more courses, departments B or C must lose courses, and so on. STS must make room for itself, essentially as a replacement for part of science, part of the humanities, and part of the social sciences.

STS programs on all campuses collaborate vigorously with other groups -- environmental concern, anti-nuclear war, joblessness, etc. But it is important that friendly groups work to assure the appropriate and permanent institutionalization of the STS program and its courses, otherwise the quality of the faculty and its programs will suffer. The following section will help the reader understand better what arguments can be used and the context in which students and faculty can be benefited.

WHICH STUDENTS WILL BENEFIT?

All students require assistance in integrating their learning and tailoring it to their specific goals in the vocational, social, and personal dimensions of their lives. Three types of students as they perceive themselves can see the relevance of STS.

The first type is the 'high achiever' aiming at participation in professional life, through employment in one of the major corporations or in State and Federal government. It goes without saying that such students will need a high level of scientific and technical knowledge. The addition of STS to their training will give them a special sensitivity to the social dimensions of science and technology and hence an edge in gaining leadership positions.

A second type of student has a high level of community commitment, and seeks to provide assistance and service to people in their urban/rural communities. Minority communities, among others, are often the victims of technologies, such as asbestos, lead paint, and air and water pollution. STS will prepare students with sufficient science and technology literacy and social awareness to be effective in such roles as policy analysts, community advocates, and change agents.

A third type of student has had poor experiences in mathematics and science education. They now shy away from learning about science and technology because they fear failure in this area. STS education can help to address this problem in two ways. First, it places science and technology content in learning contexts where students feel safe and comfortable, and where some basic concepts can be taught without arousing fear. Second, by relating these concepts to the social and personal concerns of these learners, STS can bring about an increase in their motivation to take the next step -- to try a course they might otherwise have avoided.

STS courses -- as we have had data for 15 years -- also serve to raise levels of awareness and responsibility for the problems now faced by people around the world. Many students place a high priority on personal goals (personal achievement in terms of income, prestigious employment, and possessions) because they cannot really see how the complex world works, especially how they could make a difference. STS education, by helping students to learn these complex factors and their interaction, and by showing how an individual can make a difference, can play an important role in effectively directing the energies of students to community and even global concerns. By doing so, it serves the goal of 'enlargement' in the best sense.

STS 'PROGRAMS': HOW ONE IS STARTED

An STS 'program' typically consists of one or more 'core' courses, and a group of courses (many already on the books) which are suitable for cross listing as STS courses. Although there are variations to suit the needs and traditions of different institutions, there is a typical pattern to an STS program.

First, a core faculty is identified. These faculty members are chosen because of their current interests and plans for teaching and research. They are selected from a wide spectrum of fields and departments in the institutions. Through some form of staff development program, these individuals share their common knowledge and their individual strengths. College- or university-wide STS seminars, often involving non-faculty, are excellent ways of getting started, and bringing in outside talent, to stimulate interest. Eventually a 'set' of STS courses will emerge on the books and then comes the difficult part: getting the administration to identify a structure, a leader, and a faculty to set the program goals.

THE SCIENCE COMMUNITY - DIVIDED LIKE GAUL INTO THREE PARTS

Let's face it, it is the very nature of science itself which has landed us in the pickle we're in -- of a nation of tourists in their native land. Reductionist science leads inexorably to narrower and narrower specialization as the totally false 'requirement' to be at the frontier in one's field. Thus scientists and engineers ignored society. What of the rest of society? Illiterate in their own mother tongue the citizens wander around on the surface of their own culture. But who should have taught them the language of S/T? Why, the scientists and technologists (and engineers), of course. But they were too busy specializing and hence they left the job to a specialty corps called science-teachers. And all this led to the fissioning of the community into three very separate blocks with very separate cultures -- scientists, engineers and teachers. Moreover, the world has a grossly incorrect view of the relationship of these three communities to each other. The enclosed box (page 155) makes that point.

SCIENCE-THEOLOGY: TECHNOLOGY-RELIGION

The distinction made at the end of the last paragraph between the communities of scientists and engineers finds an exact parallel in the religious community. Good theology does not lead to good religion any more than science leads to religion. Orthodoxy is not orthopraxis. Yet

A Threefold Cord

A threefold cord is seldom broken.

—*Ecclesiastes*

Derek de Solla Price, Yale's great historian of science, has reminded us again and again that contrary to what most scientists believe, technology almost always comes first and opens up a new field of science. As he put it, thermodynamics owes more to the steam engine than vice versa. The needs of society, the pull of the marketplace, the chance observation by the prepared mind — necessity is the mother of invention, and invention opens up new vistas of scientific understanding. Take but one example.

By anyone's account, Chester Carlson, the inventor of xerography, has affected every citizens' daily habits more than have the vast majority of scientists. The effect of this *technological* invention on *science* has been just as great: It has led to medals, to Nobel prizes, and to thousands of papers. Carlson did his research in his kitchen, after hours, according to the rules of technology, not those of science.

Yet for 40 years, the American public (and thence the world) has been told a charming story about the apple tree of science. Water it with money and it will lead, through applications, to the rosy fruits of technology. This gospel the entire national science establishment believed for decades. In my book *Lost at the Endless Frontier: American Science and Technology Adrift*, coauthored with Deborah Shapley, I have traced the record of U.S. science policy architects from Vannevar Bush, dean of MIT's engineering college and architect of the rise of U.S. wartime technology, to George Keyworth, science adviser to President Reagan. I have set forth what many policy analysts believe is a more accurate model, the "two-trees" model: Technology and science are separate but interacting trees; they are different human enterprises, run by different kinds of people, with different psychologies, goals, and satisfactions. The validity of the two-trees model can be quickly proved. The British, who have the best science-producing machine (they have won twice as many Nobel prizes per capita as we have, at a tenth of the cost), have few technological fruits to show. The Japanese, conversely, with very little "high" science, have done extraordinarily well in technology

This country's manufacturing industry is in deep trouble in its eroding technology base. I blame our national "science" (note the bias in the name itself) policy. The national science policy is, quite literally, the enemy of a prosperous U.S. economy. What can a student of science policy cite to support such a claim? Three reasons. First, we have created an absurd set of values for the young people in our universities. We have taught that doing "basic" university research is the highest manifestation of science/technology and that working in industry is a lower form of existence; that theoretical esoteric sciences are more "basic" than the engineering of a car door, a nuclear power plant, or a highway bridge. Second, through the government and public foundations, we have put utterly incredible sums of money into esoteric science of interest to a tiny group of citizens (one new particle accelerator can cost several billion dollars), whereas we have sponsored minuscule amounts of research to support the steel, automobile, or glass industries. Can you wonder about 20 percent unemployment in Johnstown? Third, we have diverted over half of our technical personnel away from our commercial health into "defense"; we have been living in a fool's paradise, oversold by those who say that more complex is better, thinking that nobody could catch up if we just ran a little faster. Yet it is a personnel shortage in science and technology that is emerging as our Achilles heel. And this thought leads one to consider another community that is part of the national science and technology picture—the science educators.

A major reassessment is due. The three communities—of engineering, of science, and of education—need each other. Only a sound education in that technology and derivative science that affects them every day will make young people into worthy citizens. Only a technology and engineering community revitalized with the vision of Yankee ingenuity and supported on an equal basis with the science community can restore U.S. industry to competitiveness. And a science seen and appreciated as our culture's cathedral building, helping to cross-fertilize technology, will be supported more honestly by a more enlightened citizenry.

—*Rustum Roy*

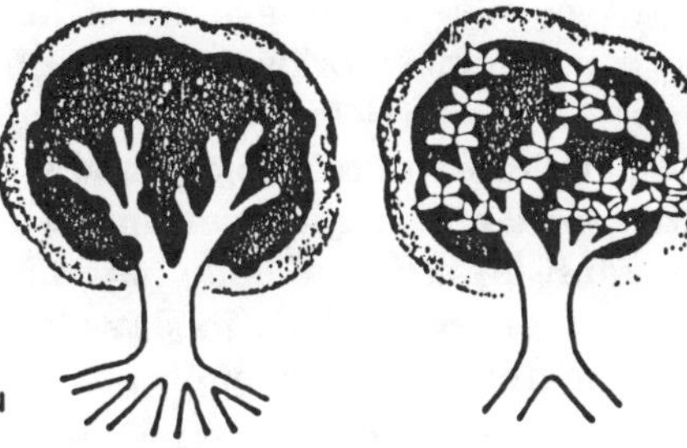

Technological Fruit Tree

Contemporary Basic Science Flowering Tree

Contrary to the belief of 99% of the public and the scientists, technological fruits (steel mills, computers, lasers) do not grow on a tree of science. Technology and science are done by different human communities--which interact more vigorously nowadays-but remain separate. The entire science-teaching community is a third separate community.

obviously in a complex world the world turns to the religious community for the guidance of the great religious traditions on what they ought to do. But acid rain issues and genetic engineering are not referred to in the Bible, Talmud or Koran. Here too the fundmentalist makes the error that I attribute to my own science community: thinking that the tree of (traditional) theology can lead to the fruit of good religion. It cannot. Theology and religion interact but are not of the same genus. What we must do -- just as the best contemporary science is one tool in making technological innovation -- is to utilize old and new theological insights to address a new religious (ethical) problem.

We have a plethora of new moral and ethical issues caused by violent change in the human situation. There will no doubt be the temptation to bring the traditional religious values to bear on the new problems, unorthodox (I introduce the term deliberately) problems. Growing up as a young Christian child in the syncretic culture of India, I often heard the smiling comment: 'If the Christians lose a cow, they search for it in the Bible.' There is too much truth in that quip and much relevance to our subject of Science, Technology and Traditional Religious Values. I am on record as interpreting and reinforcing Lord (C.P.) Snow and Robert Heilbroner as saying that the ONLY possible way to manage technology is to bring it under the hegemony of a religious worldview and the power of religious conviction. Yet the religion of a Jerry Falwell or an Ayatollah Khomeni will not do. To use the parallelism of technology and science, just as some new technology utilizes some new scientific advance whether $e = mc^2$ to build a bomb, or the transistor action to build big computer chips, so useful religion guiding orthopraxis, needs to draw on new theological insights. These, I deeply regret to say, are totally absent from the traditional theological sources -- perhaps appropriately so. But there are a very few seminal lay-theologians who have contributed enormously to this task. Whitehead is valuable and relatively well known to theologians but he lays only a foundation. All the new important work is European. Carl Friedrich von Weizsäcker[5] is the dean of the scientific theologians: his works The History of Nature and The Relevance of Science are required reading. Sir Alistair Hardy's [5] The Biology of God, Konrad Lorenz and Sir John Eccles' [5] two books, address the newer biologically-connected issues. From the social science perspective, Jacques Ellul (The Technological Society, etc., etc.) and Ivan Illich (Medical Nemesis) represent the very best examples of how Christian insight helps

---

5. These books are largely taken from the prestigious Gifford or Hibbert Lectures, where a high proportion of the selected lecturers have recently been scientists. Many are Nobel prize winners.

shape one's critique of technology at the very deepest level. Their criticisms have proved to be profound and profoundly right, precisely because they are based on the very deep insights of faith into nature and human nature.

Over the last few years I have addressed the task of developing a new evolving Christian theology which absorbs the insights of Science and Technology. My own Hibbert Lectures, published under the title Experimenting with Truth, starts with an attempt to deal with the question of 'God-language' and the images and meaning associated with the word. I summarize below the principal theses.

1. That a Christian pan-en-theist -- the Beyond in the midst of everything -- is the only conceivable meaning one can attribute to God which is consistent with our scientific-technological weltanschauung and which can form a meeting ground for all religions.

2. That the Either/Or of much Western religious thought must give way to a greater degree of Both/And.

3. That the profound role of Chance -- established as an absolute in nature -- in individual lives and society can be very creatively interpreted as 'God's' interventionist agent in human society. Everything else is done via or by human beings.

4. That Doing the Truth is an essential component of Truth.

5. I present the unique view that science and religion are related as detailed description of the parts, to the fuzzy big picture of the whole -- a matter of focus and perspective.

I cite these only to illustrate the kind of thinking in modern theology which the religious and STS communities must develop in order to be able to attack the problem of how religion addresses a technological issue. I am sure that in the next few years a sophisticated set of 'axioms' will emerge: will these be the new Creed? I only assert their absolute necessity to any fruitful dialogue between campus chaplains and the academic STS community.

WHAT IS THE RELATION OF 'SCIENCE' TO RELIGION?

The focus of Science (detail)

The detailed examination of the make-up of the nose-bridge (on someone, somewhere, it doesn't matter to science).

The personal level--Teddy Roosevelt's face.

The focus of Religion (big picture)

The big picture--of the Mount Rushmore sculpture.

In return I juxtapose my own evolving attempt at what may well be the cognate STS axioms. The list below may be regarded as one statement of the most general laws of STS. Just as Newton's laws, and the laws of thermodynamics and quantum mechanics rule the physical world, these STS 'laws' -- qualitative but laws no less -- govern the interaction of Society with the world of S and T.

In my book Experimenting with Truth from which this illustration (see above) is taken, I give a simple yet novel answer to this perennial student question. Science and religion differ in their focus on life. Science as the top picture illustrates is only, and I mean rigorously only, concerned with detail. Its method is only valid when it is reductionist, isolating and

THE SEVEN AXIOMS OF STS

1. *The SYSTEM as a concept is a description of reality: the ECOSYSTEM of nature and the TECHNOLOGICAL SYSTEM as the matrix of all modern human endeavor. Personal human values reflected in 'society', are a major force in the system, but are subject to the system's operation.*

2. *The TIME-CONSTANTS for different physical and social phenomena are fixed, but vary enormously from one another, complicating the system.*

3. *TRADE-OFFS are absolutes in all human decisions. Every technology has costs and benefits, and these are unequally distributed in space (i.e., between regions or nations) and time (e.g., between generations) and between sectors of one society.*

4. *There will be UNEXPECTED SIDE-EFFECTS to any technological change because of*
   - *(a) CHANCE*
   - *(b) The CHAOS factor in complex systems*

5. *SIMPLEXITY of concept must be held in tension with the COMPLEXITY of reality.*

6. *BEING-and-DOING or THEORY-and-PRACTICE are the ying and yang of all STS learning; experimenting with truth is unavoidable.*

7. *ALTRUISM, the cardinal ethical principle of the great traditions, is equally paramount for optimizing the technological system.*

examining in detail one tiny point. Conversely Religion is properly concerned only -- equally rigorously only -- with the whole, the big picture. Whenever religion gets involved with detail -- when does life start, prescribing dietary or detailed behavioral laws -- the picture will necessarily be out of focus.

STS AND THE CHURCH-ON-CAMPUS

The thesis I advanced in the introduction is that the nascent academic field offers a missionary opportunity for campus chaplains. Clearly even if a chaplain has an undergraduate degree in physics or philosophy he/she very soon finds that he/she does not -- indeed cannot -- participate in the professional life of the discipline. The only discipline in which a chaplain may have academic entre is religious studies, but even that is not always very welcoming.

STS is a subject matter field which is the 'technical approach' to life and society's problems which is professionally accessible to the chaplaincy. Moreover, the chaplain can -- if she or he becomes competent in STS -- bring his or her own specialization in value to the party.

STS has another attitude in common with the chaplaincy -- the bias towards acting on decisions. Here too there can be excellent two-way exchange and enrichment. The Church in the last couple of decades has been caught unprepared with 'technologically' naive policy recommendations -- simply for lack of contact with the S/T policy personnel. Even today not only the Church but the large fraction of the policy establishment fails to understand the role of R and D in determining what happens 20 years hence. R and D is the engine running the 100-car long train. Most of us hear, write and read about the tank cars full of MIC, or the Japanese cars on the piggybacked trucks, or the dining car with the shrimp from Sri-Lanka and tomatoes from Mexico, or the caboose of acid rain, all the while the engine dragging us into the future is OUT OF SIGHT. Why? Because RESEARCH POLICY is unintelligible to the lay person. In my new book Lost at the Frontier: U.S. Science and Technology Policy Adrift co-authored with Deborah Shapley, a science writer, we have tried to show -- principally in industrial policy areas, how bad R and D policy has led the U.S. to the brink of disaster.

Surely any chaplaincy worth its name should be able to relate the faith to these issues with the degree of professional competence available to the STS community. The simplexity of the gospel call to love must be interpreted into the complexity of social decisions soaked with S/T and predetermined by the R/D of the last decade. Jesus sure didn't promise anyone a rose garden or a simple gospel -- I recall something about "This ye should have done but not neglected the other also." Yes to gospel and to STS.

What can the chaplains who pay the entry fee of becoming thoroughly informed on STS contribute to the academics? Most urgently they need to call the latter to account to rethink their own values vis-a-vis their own work and profession. STS is a platform for calling such re-examination of the values of science and of the scientists as individuals. In the last box I set down my own response to this challenge: a worthy set of goals to guide world-wide science and scientists.

DISCUSSION AFTER

FATHER PANUSKA'S ADDRESS

FORD (St. Louis): Fr. Panuska, I was very impressed by your notion that the religious environment can help scientific studies and vice versa. In mentioning the religious environment promoting science, you talked about the isolation and then the stimulus from the outside. Why is it that, at least in America, no religious school, no school which has maintained its religious identity, is a first rank science school? Does the fact that scientific schools are the most secular schools in the country mean that we misjudge what good science is? Why hasn't a religious ambience produced science that is recognized in the secular world? Why don't the Catholic and other religiously affiliated universities have top scientists?

PANUSKA: I can offer a couple of observations, but not a complete answer to the question. The best scientific schools in the country are pretty much well endowed schools or state institutions with generous resources. There are no Catholic universities which have very significant endowments. That's one factor at least. It's a great handicap to us. Scranton is not a research university, but we have just received a large federal grant to take the steps we've taken. Without it, we would be struggling to maintain tuition, to maintain access, to maintain the quality we want. Science is a very expensive thing.

Also, we have not taken advantage of one of our greatest potential strengths, i. e., an interdisciplinary approach to science. We should be specialists. I don't think we've done that. So most of our schools don't have any sort of identifying hook on which we could. . . I was going to say hang ourselves. Actually, very few religiously related universities have achieved prominence in the research world, not just science. It's very much a question of resources and perhaps -- this is speculation -- for too long we were too much interested in catechesis, I think that is possible. If so, it has certainly changed and now we're trying to hold on to our identity at least as a church-related institution. And that's a struggle.

CASPERS: Another reason is that church-related schools are primarily undergraduate institutions. As such, their teaching loads are heavier. Professors in primarily research institutions teach maybe one course or half a course per year; in an undergraduate institution professors teach much more. We can't be all things to all people. We should maintain some research but we certainly can't maintain it at a level that a state school does if the professors teach only one course a year.

ORNA: I was going to make the same point that Mary Lou made. We have paid a great deal of attention to the undergraduate curriculum. The undergraduate curriculum is not, at least in our tradition, a research curriculum. The National Science Foundation has done some token work in that area by offering some grants, but it is just a token as far as I can see.

Another reason why church-related schools may not be top research schools is that we're measuring the greatness of these schools in terms of quantity. Father Skehan's paper pointed out that the schools were ranked the way they were because of the amount of money they receive from the federal government. In that grading there is no attempt to deal with the schools in a proportional way, with reference, for example, to the number of students serviced and the size of the institution. That may have a great deal to do with it.

SMOLARSKI: We're getting right to the issue here. I perceive church-related institutions as more oriented to the liberal arts. They're interested in the type of interrelation between not just the sciences but all the other liberal arts, trying to combine that and draw things from each other. We have put little emphasis on scientific research because many of our institutions, as has been pointed out, are undergraduate institutions where we do not have strong doctoral programs. There are a lot of good Christian scientists working in these large institutions. It would be a bad idea to pull these people together into the church-related institutions. We'd do a disservice to science and to the young people.

The church-related institutions should not try to become, let's say, a Stanford or a Harvard or a basically research institution. That's not what we were intended to be. I think we're there to try to integrate everything, science plus, and maybe not try to produce this very expensive research. We should do research at a basic level cooperatively with our students. We're starting to experience at Loyola-Marymount that that really works. The students are very enthusiastic about it.

Many students that are coming now seem to be extremely unprepared. They have no real notion of what science is. We have a task at the church-related institutions to get them enthused about science rather than trying to produce science on the cutting edge of scientific investigation. I feel that we have a special task not to become a research institution but to prepare people to be participants in research.

SHEAHEN: With regard to the dearth of resources in religiously affiliated schools, it's important to remember that the leading funder of research in the physical sciences in the world is none other than the Pentagon, the Defense Department. The Catholic University of America gets about $50 million a year in government contracts, some of which come from the Pentagon. If it were known that this was an important source of their revenue, I think there would be a hue and cry among at least some elements of the church membership. I think it is the case that, in general, religiously affiliated institutions do not seek out money from the Defense Department for their research.

The second thing is this chicken-and-egg effect. The people whose job in Washington it is to give out money -- we can use nasty words like bureaucrat, but they are just folks trying to work for a living and do their job -- tend to play it safe and go with the big institutions that are already well known. This means that the rich get richer and those who are not rich have to struggle and struggle.

These are two factors which have an adverse effect on research funding at the religiously affiliated universities: the defense connection and second is the long-term established pattern of funding which is included in defense.

EAGAN: I regard with trepidation this notion that we should describe the church-or religious-affiliated institution as one primarily interested in pedagogy and not research. To divorce the two in my view is intolerable. You can't have one without the other. It is a cop-out to say we should stick to our pedagogical task and forget the research. That would go against the thesis made by the keynote speaker.

I would like to ask the speaker a question. You've indicated there are research projects that could be addressed in church-related environments that might not otherwise be addressed. May we have an example, please?

PANUSKA: My point was that the broadening environment might stimulate a scientist to be more interested in a research project, not that it couldn't or wouldn't be pursued elsewhere. The environment might stimulate him or her to work on a particular project. I don't know if I can give a specific example. Perhaps it might be to bring a scientific mind to bear on the morality of certain questions, for example, related to defense, but that would not be purely scientific. It would really be the scientist moving into another area. Possibly questions relating to fertility might be stimulated from a motivation that would come from a Christian environment. I would think that a religiously related environment with an especially strong sense of social responsibility, might direct the scientist to study questions in terms of hunger, economic distribution which would be encouraged by that environment. This could and does occur in a number of non-church-related institutions, but the religiously affiliated school might provide a more congenial environment.

I want to add something with reference to this role of science in church-related institutions. Duquesne University just published a book edited by Rolando Bonachea who was the Acting President there. It related specifically to graduate education and research in a Catholic environment, primarily in a Jesuit environment. There might be some things there. I did one chapter in that book on graduate education.

SKEHAN: I agree with all the factors that have been brought up, but the history of graduate schools and when they were introduced into church-related institutions is important. For the most part, the history of graduate programs does not go back beyond about 1925, 1924. That's a relatively short history, although some of the great universities have graduate programs which go back perhaps 25 years more. There was a lack of resources and there was only a relatively small number of very well qualified scientists in our institutions for their first 25 years or so.

So there's our history, lack of resources, heavy teaching loads and a lack of equipment, until the National Science Foundation and other sources of funding or equipment and personnel were developed. But I see that in many classes in many church-related institutions the quality of research has really come to life and to fruition. At Boston College, the chemistry department has come of age, and is, I would say, head and shoulders above the rest of our science departments at Boston College, thanks in no small part to the impetus that Al Panuska gave when he was Academic Vice President. We do have a very well qualified department on a fairly broad basis. And that kind of effort is going on in many of our church-related institutions. That will in the relatively near future bring to fruition the excellence that has been developing over a long period of time.

CURRIE: Some church-related institutions are hiring some people who are more univocally focused, as contrasted to the multidimensional type whom Al Panuska mentioned. In most of our church-related institutions we put a great emphasis on the multidimensionality of things: "We're interested in students; we're interested in values." That's good, but it has distracted us from the univocal focus that the typical researcher should take. Getting more of the univocally focused people on our campuses is going to help us with the research dimension. That calls into question whether we're going to be dedicated enough to teach humanities. That sets up another dimension.

Jim Skehan made a point in his paper about the inspiration flowing from the ideas of Bernie Lonergan or Teilhard de Chardin. The thrust that should make the church-related scholar interested in research is not always there because we don't share that vision of Teilhard or Lonergan. Then we fall back on some of these other things which I think we can take to be alibis: lack of resources, doing more for students or doing all these other things. They're all true, but they can be used too easily as alibis for not pursuing the vision that Teilhard or Lonergan posed.

MCLOUGHLIN: I too was bothered by the statement about religion driving science. I don't think it happens and I think that's why you can't give good examples of it. I think that science actually drives new ways of looking at our religion. It's like the tree of knowledge in that it makes us god-like and questions us. We have new methods of consideration, new values. I really think again that science is driving religion, our approaches to religion.

PANUSKA: I don't want to see my statement exaggerated. I would never say that religion is driving science or that science is driving religion. I'm indicating that an environment, in which one single focus is challenged, creates a more imaginative mind. It is hard to give specific examples. I'll probably think of some tonight. An environment that doesn't allow one to stay in the same place broadens. That is my experience. I'm being much more general than I'm being interpreted.

COLICELLI: This is speculative, but there is some data that we should consider. When we look at the number of people going on for PhDs in chemistry, we find an inordinate number from solely undergraduate institutions. I wonder if we would find that if we looked at Oberlin and Wheaton as examples. If we looked at Catholic undergraduate colleges we may find that we are turning out larger than normal percentages of people going on into the sciences. We could probably do the same exploration for women's colleges, since many women's colleges were church-related. We know that more women from women's colleges go on to graduate degrees in, among other fields, science. Women are more likely to become scientists if they've been in a woman's college. So it's another way of looking at the question.

Perhaps in institutions where we have tried to look at all the needs of the students, at least on the undergraduate level, we may be producing a lot of scientists but just not in our institutions. We're just sending them someplace else. If we had a meeting of representatives of the 50 universities listed, they would probably all be racking their brains, wondering how they can teach Russian better. It's an interesting dilemma.

PANUSKA: In Dr. Chase's paper, we see that Wheaton College shows a large percentage of graduates going on for doctorates in science. That's a Franklin and Marshall study. We experience the same thing at the University of Scranton. We were, I think, number six in the nation in PhDs in chemistry. It's amazing.

BRUNGS: I don't know what it is about chemists, but they seem to be a strange breed in one respect. I have found much more interest in the religious area among chemists than among any of the other sciences. Chemists seem readier to work in the cross-disciplinary areas than most of the other scientists.

I want to add one factor to Charles Ford's question. Part of the reason we haven't been involved in research is that our institutions basically -- I don't want this to sound pejorative -- have tended to be more a priori institutions than a posteriori institutions. When I was coming up through graduate studies in a Jesuit university community, I certainly had the impression that theology and philosophy had all the answers. Even when I was on the faculty later, one university Jesuit asked me, every night when I was on the way to the lab, if I was going over to play with my toys. I mention this because I think it reflects an attitude. Traditionally, at least in Catholic schools we have tended to believe that we had all the answers. The knowledge coming out of research really didn't matter because we really had the true, all-embracing answers. I'm afraid that's the attitude out of which we taught. I think that's part of our problem.

ACKER: When I went to the seminary to teach all things in science -- they could only afford one scientist so I had to be the renaissance scientist -- I found exactly what Bob mentioned, namely, that philosophy and theology had the only answers. The priests never studied science and they were doing fine. They saw no reason for it. It has been a problem to convince seminarians of the value of science today. They think science is completely objective. Since they're such feeling people, they don't think scientists have any intuitive ways of attacking a problem and so on. I attended a Chautauqua Institute this summer directed by a professor from Indiana University. Believe it or not, he makes his biology students read the book Women's Ways of Knowing. It maintains that people, not just women, have different ways of knowing. Many men, as well as women -- and seminarians are high among these -- do not learn very well objectively. They've been much more subjective in learning.

Our institutions have perpetuated the idea that science is very objective. I've had quite an argument with our philosophy department that we scientists choose our theories very subjectively; we have very intuitive feelings about the science we deal with. If there's any kind of science that seminarians and, therefore, priests like, it's biology. It isn't so objective. Women will always enter biology faster than any physical sciences. I think that bears out the fact that we have a different way of approaching subjects. We have to approach them from maybe a more holistic way. It's high time we science teachers started to approach our science from an intuitive standpoint. We might reach a lot more pupils that way.

MURPHY: I'd like to follow up on what Jim Skehan was saying with regard to the relative recent history in terms of graduate education and, therefore, probably some effort toward research. In the early days, say the '20s, 30s and 40s, we had minimal resources. With those minimal resources, anyone who was doing any research probably did a pretty good job at it, but didn't have much PR. I was somewhat bothered this fall when I was looking up the discovery of synthetic rubber to prepare for a class. I did not find in two encyclopedias Nieuwland's name listed at all. I've always been bothered why Gamow gets credit for the big bang theory and Le Maître is hardly named at all.

Any of the significant research that was going on was probably overlooked because the university or the college was busy about other things; growing, developing, and without the resources it perhaps could have had. Also, women's church-related colleges particularly emphasized service. Because the emphasis was service, they really didn't pay much attention to the development of science. If any science departments developed, it was probably in spite of the system.

To follow up on what Bob said: I had a student with an A average, but with one D on her whole college transcript. That D was from the philosophy department because the philosophy instructor did not believe that any truth could come from any kind of scientific work. She wouldn't keep quiet in class and, therefore, got the D. But I feel that that sort of attitude prejudiced a good many faculties and maybe even administrations in terms of some of the developments at a time when they would have been better able to keep pace with their counterparts in other institutions.

KEEFE: I have been intrigued during Fr. Panuska's talk and responses to it. I'll pivot on something he said about an environment in which the presence of an atheist teacher might generally prompt a livelier intellectual discussion, atmosphere, and so on. We have become accustomed, I think, over a considerable period of time to the supposition that something like a postulatory atheism, to use Weber's phrase, is at least likely to provide a more objective, more antiseptic atmosphere in which less personal predilection will enter into the examination of a given question. I wonder if this is something that ought not to be looked at rather more carefully.

I submit the proposition that an atheist in science is a rather unlikely event. In the first place, historically a growth of science has been linked to the existence of Christianity. I recognize that this is a somewhat hotly debated topic, but in point of fact there has never been an experimental science -- an inquiry into the sacred truth as something discovered outside of the human mind through the historical experience -- apart from what may be called the university tradition, and that is a western tradition.

In modern scientifically oriented university and college faculties, there is, I think, a profound distrust of a close association with Christianity. The statement was made earlier whether one could reply that I'm not a Christian but I'm church-related. We are, I think, interested not in simply church-related education but in Christian education predicated upon not simply the absence of atheism but the presence of belief. Are we not awfully sensitive to heresies to which we may well be sensitive -- racism, anti-Semitism, antifeminism -- but not at all bothered by a much more profound heresy, the denial of the existence of God at all? I do not find that a beneficial input in a college faculty, and I'm not saying this in a heresy hunting sense. It does not seem to me that one can simply have that kind of postulatory atheism -- that value free commitment, that supposition that truth (scientific, humanist, or whatever) is best sought out in an absence of commitment -- in a value free atmosphere.

I'm not trying to read an advocacy for a value-free atmosphere into Fr. Panuska remarks. But I don't think that we should be bending over backwards to accept atheism on our campuses as we often do, highly sensitive to the need to free ourselves of the various enmities to minority groups from which we indeed must spare campuses. We must eliminate those kinds of human behaviors that have sullied the world in our time. But these are rooted all too often in a denial of God, not simply a denial of the rights of man but a denial of the rights of God. I think we ought to be more alert to that than we often are.

PANUSKA: I would not deliberately seek an atheist for our faculty, but I tend, as the faculty described me, to be neurotically optimistic. I keep looking for the spring element in things, and I would see the positive element of having one or two out of 300 faculty who were atheists as presenting an environment which is closer to the reality which students will meet afterwards. Though I wouldn't seek that out, overall I would prefer that type of roughness in an environment to the simplicity of a totally "pure" faith community. I think it's more maturing. But I know we differ basically in the approach to that.

KEEFE: Yes, we do. Yes.

BYERS: In a way I'm glad I'm the last speaker. I agree that we can always look for the resurrection perspective, whatever the circumstances are. I agree with Jim Skehan that things in Catholic schools may not be perfect, but they are better than they were in the last generation with respect to the science teaching. I was taught first by the Sisters of Charity and then by Jesuits and Augustinians who don't seem to be present here. None of them cared about science, none of them. In senior high school I had a physics course. Then I went to a Catholic college and I had a physics course and it was the same one. That was my entire science preparation. All the rest of my science I've managed to pick up on my own in bits and pieces. Now my children know all kinds of wonderful things that they learned in Catholic schools. So although we may not be in the forefront of research, we're doing a heck of a lot better than we were 20 years ago.

DISCUSSION

SESSION 2

FORD (NY): I was asked by Fr. Brungs to do this study in a discussion that we had about a 1988 paper of mine dealing with the future of Catholic universities and the issue of our moving into the AAU classification. I extended the results of that discussion into my scientific community at New York Medical College and I've had conversations, similar to those I've had here, on the condition of undergraduate science as well as what we receive in the graduate and the professional schools in terms of the skills and the attitudes that the students bring to us.

You can see that I view this as an educator, and my recommendations need not be repeated at this point. There are four recommendations in the paper. Basically they work off the premise that we have a wonderful challenge and opportunity in the church-related college to establish yet again in some format, which respects the character of each of our institutions, an approach to bringing the scientist, the theologian, the technologist, and the philosopher together.

This is neither the time nor place for me to give you my point of view. I have a very strong view based on having developed graduate and undergraduate programs as an administrator in several institutions. I have gone through the process of trying to pull disciplines together, trying to pull together scholars with different perspectives on the nature of reality, with different languages and different mindsets. You all know the anecdotes of what happens when you put a theologian or a physicist together or a biologist and a philosopher.

I believe Fr. Brungs mentioned playing with toys. That's a good symbolic introduction to the subject. We have to overcome both the mystery and the toy. Maybe that's the theme of our comments. We have to begin to put those two perspectives together. We have to put our cards on the table as scholars and agree to find common ground for looking at the ways in which we educate our next generation of church-related college students, graduates, future professionals, clergy and citizens to address the opportunities and problems that are generated in the rapid advances in science and technology. Someone observed that these drive theology and philosophy for our generation.

Now as to the study. I went to Peterson's Guide. I think we're all in the wrong place. We should be with Peterson's, the Chronicle, or New York Times because that's what makes money on higher education. But Peterson's Guide sold me the list of the church-related institutions that have so labeled themselves in the United States; that's 794 institutions, 1,215 departments of -- I used again discussion with my colleagues and Fr. Brungs -- biology, chemistry, physics, and natural sciences. That probably could be expanded for the next study, if there is one. It could probably take a different approach.

Being a New Yorker with a mean twist, I threw in all of the New York state institutions of higher learning that we all know were founded under religious auspices. So I have a folder here of comments and letters. Some of the letters are precious in themselves in their denial. Since there is no St. Augustine's College in New York, I can say very directly that the chairman of the biology department of St. Augustine's College in New York absolutely denies that there was ever any conceivable possible relationship to a church, a theological tenet, a parable, or a position. Didn't this man called dean down in Valhalla know that they founded in the tradition of Jefferson? How they got the name St. Augustine's, I don't know.

Denominationally, there were 28 -- I didn't put this in the report. One hundred and twenty-seven of the respondents omitted any reference. But there were 77 Catholic, 16 Baptist, 16 Presbyterian, 18 Lutheran, 26 Methodist of six varieties, four United Church of Christ, four Disciples of Christ, four Episcopalian, three Mormons, three Nazarene, three Brethren, three Calvinist, three Assemblies of God, two Religious Society of Friends, two Seventh Day Adventist, one Christian, one independent Protestant, two Churches of Christ, and one Seven Feeder Denomination. I think Seven Feeder Denomination is Loma Linda. I didn't try to summarize all of the institutions. I deliberately did not put that into the study. I indicated also that I had a very good national distribution. I think I've covered every state. But I didn't think that was important so I didn't list the numbers of New Yorkers and Minnesotans and so on.

I was disappointed by the percentage of response, 24.7. But as I said in the comments here and in my letter to Fr. Brungs, I was very pleased with the responses to the essay questions. I brought all of those with me including the letters -- and one has to have a thick hide -- including the letters that tell me -- and how many graduate deans are in the room -- we all are absolutely out of touch with reality to ask such a question. You can look at this folder if you want to. You'll find some very fascinating examples of how some of our colleges have addressed quite vigorously with good open spirits and open minds the problem of keeping philosophy, theology, science, technology related in the curriculum and therefore in all of the undergraduate educational experience.

Thus my summary of the study, the arithmetic notwithstanding, it speaks for itself for what it's worth. I see no point in debating whether people are happy with their resources or not, but I think we should talk about what the undergraduates bring to the enterprise. I deliberately highlighted the scale of the knowledge of sci/tech issues, ranging all the way from tropical rain forests through AIDS and drugs. You'll see what's closer to home gets the highest level of response.

The other very interesting point, as you saw in some of the essays and in the gamut of limited numbers, is the strong conviction that there was no room for the two views of reality to come together and that the scientists had better head in this direction and the philosophers and theologians better head in that direction. I think that that's very important and very critical to our discussion.

BUNDSCHUH: The College of Arts and Sciences at Saint Louis University is 171 years old. I'm the third non-Jesuit to be dean. I'm the first scientist ever to be dean. If I might use the words of Fr. Panuska from last night when he said that his mere presence at Emory had an effect, sometimes I feel that being a scientist as the dean at Saint Louis University has its effect. I'm going to make three points and then elaborate.

First, I don't believe in two cultures, or at least I don't believe in using two cultures as an excuse for the fact that humanities faculty and science faculty can't speak or get along or do meaningful things together. There may have been a time when that was more the case than it is now, and there are several reasons why that can't be used as a crutch in today's university.

One of them is the fact that computing has become so well used by everyone on campus. The humanities faculty jumped on computers even faster than the science faculty. Once they found out that you could put a footnote on a paper without measuring with a ruler, computing went critical. I've never seen training sessions for secretaries more effective than simply showing them how WordPerfect could perform this simple task -- simple by WordPerfect standards, but not so simple if you were typing on an old correcting IBM. Humanities faculty talk about megabytes, hard disks and storage capacity. I know theologians with the Bible on their hard disks. They access, network and they do everything that the scientists do. So there's a common language. That's something we might talk about, computer language across the curriculum.

Also, we're in an era where interdisciplinarity has become integrative.

The word interdisciplinary has been replaced by the word integrated. Everyone in this country wants to see an integrated curriculum. Interdisciplinarity has some bad connotations, particularly to the scientists, because it came to us as meaning weak or watered down. We're more likely to accept the word integrated. First of all, it sounds like calculus, doesn't it?

Secondly, it means that we don't have give up any lectures to a philosopher. It doesn't mean that we have to participate in a team and make up texts. Integrated has become a very important term in our thinking.

Saint Louis University has just created a mission statement, and here's the longest sentence you've ever heard in a mission statement. This could have been written by a German author. It's a lofty statement, but let's not turn our backs on it as scientists because it's quite meaningful if you think about it. Oftentimes we scientists have turned our backs on mission statements. As long as the mission statement doesn't say "throw the sciences out of the curriculum," we'll let the philosophers have what they want. This was written by a philosopher. I'm going to read it, so bear with me.

"The university's undergraduate curriculum makes use of the resources of humanities, social sciences, natural sciences, and technology in a unified effort to challenge students to make appropriate use of what each area has to offer, enabling them to understand themselves, their world, and God to prepare intellectually and professionally for the career of their choice and to make critically informed moral judgments." That's a mission statement in itself. I think we should take it seriously and not merely say, "Well, there's nothing offensive. Fine, it's a great mission statement."

As scientists we have to play a more active, aggressive role in curriculum and in this process that we call integrating. Integrating means that we try to understand what other people are doing, to make them understand what we're doing and try to build some sense of things across the curriculum. I'm a strong proponent of that.

I've also been inspired this past year by a speech by Fr. Peter Hans Kolvenbach, the general of the Jesuits, who spoke to us at Georgetown. I was quite moved by his talk. He talks about integration as well, but he doesn't use the word. He uses the word interdisciplinary, but what he's really talking about is what we think of as integration these days. I was a bit disturbed when he said "even the hard sciences." Even the hard sciences! I'm worried about "even the hard sciences," and I think we ought to be careful about that and not let people get by with that. The rest of the talk was magnificent, but I worry about phrases like "even the hard sciences."

Secondly, there is a administrative difference between the humanities (social sciences) and the sciences; it's one of the resources. If there's a difference between the business school and the college of arts and sciences we're willing, or at least presidents seem to be willing to accept the difference in salaries, the market driven salaries in business and the AACSB. There's a difference in the resources between humanities and the sciences. But we simply can't sit back as scientists and say, "Well, we can't do research. We can't do this because we don't have an accelerator," and all this sort of thing. We can get major pieces of equipment from the National Science Foundation. We have to try and we continue to try to do that. But I don't think we take enough advantage of the national laboratories. Argonne Labs has a high energy protron source with, I think, 70 beams with 70 different experiments going on at the same time. Fermi Lab isn't far away. You can be a high energy physicist and be at a small college. You can work out arrangements to do some of your experiments at Fermi Lab or at Argonne or wherever. Sometimes you can even get on line when you're not present. Getting on line now is much easier than getting on an airplane.

Nevertheless, sometimes presidents take more pleasure in rebuilding a sidewalk than they do in buying 20 microscopes for the biology laboratory. We have continually to make the point that indeed science requires resources. The good news is that solid state equipment stays around a lot longer. Solid state equipment is easier to use. You can store data and compare that data with dictionaries.The emphasis isn't as much on sample preparation as it was when I was a student. So some of the art has been removed. We're entering a new era with respect to equipment and instrumentation. At Saint Louis University this week we were notified by the National Science Foundation that we're going to get a 300 megahertz NMR. I did my dissertation on NMR. It's a shame because it makes anything I ever did look very trivial. I'm embarrassed to tell an undergraduate what I actually did because they can sit at a terminal now and never even see a magnet. They just push a few keys and do 20,000 times what I did over a period of four years.

The third point is a reflection on what I heard last night. My colleague

Charles Ford (St. Louis) asked why there aren't church-related schools in the top 100 research universities in the country. Let me approach an answer historically. When I first came to Saint Louis University as dean, someone gave me a tape of a movie that was made in the mid-1960s. It was narrated by Jack Buck and he talked about Saint Louis University emerging as a world class university. We had a Nobel Prize winner, Doisy, who did his work at Saint Louis University. There was every reason we would emerge as a world class university. We had 75 doctoral students in physics. We had an engineering school, we had a well known medical school and doctoral programs in all the sciences; we sustained the Jesuit tradition of being very strong in geophysics. We were also a member of Argonne Universities Association which was part of a tripartite operation that ran Argonne National Laboratories-the University of Chicago, AUAN, and AEC at that time. We were there with the Big 10 universities.

When the 1970s hit, there were tremendous budget cutbacks, particularly by the federal government. The federal grants dried up. We pulled back to our strength. That meant pulling back to our strength in the humanities. Many of the science programs were cut and the school of engineering was closed. By the late 1970s, along with many church-related universities and colleges, we began to secularize -- and I use that word very carefully. To a certain extent, we began to apologize for our church-relatedness. In the 1980s, as an institution of higher learning, we began to emerge again. We found out that our constituency didn't want to secularize Saint Louis University. They wanted a Catholic Jesuit university; that's what we are now. That's what we said in our mission statement, and that's what we hope to be in the future.

It's going to be difficult to rebuild the sciences and we will never rebuild, at least in my lifetime, a doctoral program in physics. We've always been very strong in premedicine and in undergraduate research, but it's going to be very difficult to rebuild. Maybe we shouldn't rebuild all these doctoral programs in the sciences. I merely offer you a historical perspective.

BERTRAM: There are two cultures. One of the gaps is between a theologian who announces that the next speaker will speak for five minutes and the speaker, a chemist, who transposes that by some mathematical magic I don't understand into 20 minutes. But it was worth every minute of it.

CONNELL: I come from the other Catholic institution of higher education in the St. Louis area. Only Saint Louis University and Fontbonne claim to be Catholic. I've been through a lot of the things that Dr. Bundschuh mentioned. I've been through the years of interdisciplinary teaching. I was influenced early on in my higher education, even while I was teaching in high school and going to Notre Dame summers, by the work of Teilhard. At Fontbonne in the late '60s, when Dr. Ford (NY) was part of our administration, we had a course on Teilhard with a philosopher, a theologian and myself. We had hardly gotten this course underway when we had calls from the chancery about why we were teaching this kind of a course and who was teaching it. Somehow or other, it went on and we did it for quite a few years.

The budget cuts and things that happened in the 70s cut down on what we could do. We could no longer justify having three people to teach a course. The Teilhard course went by the way. Two of us taught bioethics and then I found myself doing it alone. So I've lived through the kinds of changes that occurred.

I've also lived through the creative ideas that people like Dr. Ford got us to do. We didn't have then what I would term rather collaboration than integration, because we could not get three departments to work together. I see collaboration as the thing that could bring people together either on a campus or across campuses. Saint Louis U. may never have a physics department with 75 doctoral students, but maybe in this day and age Saint Louis U. and Washington U. can begin to do some things together because I don't think Washington U. has 75 doctoral students but they do have some. I'm talking about a local kind of situation.

I think that to some extent the two cultures still exist. I don't find it as much with the theologians and the philosophers as I find it with the people in literature and languages and even people in social studies. We must try, computers aside, to get across what science is about and why one should have at least a minimal education in science.

The other thing that I stressed pretty heavily in my paper was that we have a lot of freedom. I think that's true and it's been true for a long time. I first realized at a meeting at Southern Illinois University at Carbondale many years ago. Father Reis and I were the only two people from private institutions. It's been a while since Fr. Reis was the chairman of the department of biology at St. Louis U. But we were the only two people who had any freedom about our curriculum. Everybody else came from a public institution and they were told what they had to teach. We could create a course and do all kinds of things, with some control and also a lot of leeway.

While I was working on this paper, we were in the process of hiring a new faculty person. In one day we interviewed four people. One was anxious to move from the institution in which he teaches because he was being rather subtly persecuted in this institution. It was a very fundamentalist denomination controlling that institution. I had not experienced that before. The people I associated with were biology teachers who had gotten the liberal arts tradition in the midwest and were primarily either Catholic or Lutheran or had lost whatever religious affiliation they had once had. As Lindenwood College states: they come out of the Presbyterian tradition but they no longer have anything to do with the Presbyterian church. But this really struck me.

Another was a young man who, brought up as a Catholic and graduated from a Catholic university, had joined a fundamentalist religion. I asked: "Well, if you didn't just teach anatomy and physiology, if next year the schedule was changed and you had to teach general biology, what would you do about evolution?" He said, "I don't know," because he really is very much into creationism. Yet I know he was not taught that kind of thing as an undergraduate.

One last item! In the spring of 1988 in Liberal Education, there was a whole series of articles on creative science teaching. All but one of the schools represented were church-related liberal arts institutions. They were the ones which were arguing about and doing the creative kinds of things.

BURCH: As I was writing this paper I was impressed by the problems we face as people who know more than one model. Being scientists we tend to think and talk about models. In our schools we teach two kinds of students. We have students who take science as a core curriculum requirement, and students who are preparing to be professional scientists. In the social area we talk with people concerned with things like environmental problems. We speak with people in the church. In all three situations we are dealing with people who, on the one hand, have very little skill and knowledge about science and, on the other hand, with skilled scientists who perhaps have little dealing with the more liberal disciplines, or with co-religionists, or with those who have concerns about the environment, or with other activists and politicians. And in all these cases those of us who are familiar with more than one set of models have a tremendous opportunity and obligation to help the people on both sides.

It was mentioned last night that truth is truth. There is one truth, and we see different parts of it in various perspectives. All of the different disciplines, all the different perspectives should be complementary. They should not contradict each other. Nonetheless, they come from very different directions. I tried to concentrate on two models that were perhaps as far apart as I could get. The one set of models would be the models by which we live. It has an urgency to it, it must be complete for us to live and die. It will answer questions like the meaning of the world, its intelligibility, where we fit in it. The other is the scientific model which asks questions about the world, concentrating on how best to describe this or that, the relationships between the parts, and even how nature can be manipulated to give us a technology.

There is no reason why these things should clash. It's very difficult, however, to talk about them so that they do not clash, unless we keep our models very clear in our own mind, and unless we are able to explain the difference between the two sets of models to others.

Again let me go to extremes to describe the two types of students we face in the classroom. One is the student who is there to meet a core requirement. Though not all, they come from an elementary and a secondary school where they either did not have the opportunity to take a scientific curriculum or where they could easily avoid it. They come without the basic mathematics, the basic vocabulary, or the elementary introduction to scientific thought. Many of them have very unrealistic ideas about what someone else can do for them through science and technology. If their immediate problems are not solved right away, they are likely to attribute this to some corrupt suppression of knowledge. They are badly in need of a great deal of remedial work, if they are ever to do anything approaching a real science. At the same time, they need science on a rather high level -- that is the understanding of what a scientific model is, how a scientist uses it, what it may be reasonably expected to produce -- so that they may understand enough science in order to integrate it into their own social and religious model.

On the other hand, we are dealing with students who intend to be professional scientists. They will leave our program as very, very sophisticated technical people. For them the danger is that an inadequate or poorly integrated core curriculum will leave them with social and religious models that are far less sophisticated than their scientific model. They too will have a problem trying to integrate their science with their social concerns, philosophy or religion.

In the political arena, it is much the same. There is a group of people very concerned with, for instance, acid rain and the greenhouse effect. They are very unsatisfied with the answers they get from scientists which often honestly are: "At the present time more data is needed before we can give you an honest evaluation of the effects of what you want to do." The scientists in this area sometimes confuse their own scientific models and social models and they are not clear in interpreting for others what they are saying and where they're coming from.

I would note here that the federal government is and will enforce a certain integration between the scientific models and the models that government has of social and civil concerns. You only need to mention the various committees and various policies a university must have if it is going to get federal funds -- animal care, radiation safety, biological hazards, human subjects, misconduct, and scholarship and, very soon, conflict of interest.

In the religious arena, history has taught us that science and religion interact often unfortunately when they do not understand each other. It is clear that questions of the meaning of the human being, the human mind, the universe, of how a human should behave towards other humans or towards the world around him or her are going to be greatly influenced by science. There's a danger that the church will abdicate its right to debate these questions in a broad forum. It's our responsibility to see that this does not happen. If the church is going to have an input into science, it must be through the Catholic colleges. If other religions are going to have this input, it must be through their colleges.

This is where the church, the bishops, the clergy, and the nonscientific laity will find out about science. We can instruct. We can help prevent bad mistakes or great surprises. We have a great potential and an equally great responsibility to try to get people to understand the two different kinds of thought and the models that they come from.

SEIBERT: Since Sr. Virginia (Orna) and I wrote this as a Huntley-Brinkley attempt, we're going to try to make a presentation in that way. So we may interrupt one another. I'll begin. I have been a member of

ITEST almost from the beginning. I attended very conscientiously a conference a year until about 12 years ago. I'm back now for the first time since then. I'd like to point out the timeliness of this particular conference. I've always noted that ITEST seems to be a step ahead of many organizations, and I wanted to congratulate the planners and Fr. Brungs for calling this group together. I am delighted to have been able to be present as a kind of retired scientist.

ORNA: We've heard a lot, even in the very short time that we've been meeting, about limited resources. We've heard a lot about limited budgetary resources. What I hear coming forth from this group now is limited personnel resources.

I question whether we want to imitate the large research institutions. Or should we set a goal for this meeting and maybe for future ITEST meetings, namely, looking at our own particular goals with respect to our particular brand of science education? I do not mean that we would pursue a "lesser" science, but that we would pay attention, as we said last night, to the undergraduate curriculum, that we would pay particular attention to the research component of that undergraduate curriculum. There are some other things that we might be able to do even better than the large research institutions. For example, we could pay attention to values education; we could teach our students to wonder, teach our students the way to conduct themselves to honor the humanity of other persons.

Then the question becomes how we do this on a practical level. How do we translate these efforts into our courses and discussions? How do we permeate our curriculum with some of these goals? I would submit that we can't do it with just one course. We simply can't say, "Oh, we're going to have a science and technology and values course in order to do this." Our challenge is to see how this can permeate the entire curriculum.

I've had some limited experience in this area with my work in science and art. I have worked very closely with our art department and tried to integrate chemistry and art in the curriculum. I found, in doing this over the past ten years, that scientists across the board are very interested in doing this kind of integration, but I have not received very much response from the artistic community. We have a great deal of work to do. We have a great deal of education to undertake with respect to integrating with the humanities people on our own campuses.

I feel stretched to the limit in what I am being asked to do on my own campus. I'm confident that you have the same feeling. If you're scientists, you have to do your science. You also have to integrate and interface with many other areas on your campus. We say one thing in many instances on our own campuses and end up doing something else. I'm caught in the crunch there. Let me say, maybe with a little bit of shame, that I'm the chair of the Division of Natural Sciences and Math at the College of New Rochelle. That includes biology, chemistry, physics, math, and computer science. The biology faculty is pressing me to start a new course in the philosophy of science as a required course for biology majors. Perhaps to my shame, I'm trying to keep that at a low level because we cannot, for budgetary reasons, proliferate courses and have low enrollments.

I'm caught in these administrative binds which have to be solved in some other way; I think that's a great challenge. It's not something we can shy away from. We must try to look at this challenge and be creative about the ways we solve these problems.

Also, I'm interested in and working very closely with a new project that has just been funded by the National Science Foundation called Chemsource. Chemsource is going to be a resource for chemistry high school teachers who are underprepared or who are cross-over teachers. That makes up about 85% of the present high school chemistry teachers in the country. One of the things that we're going to try to work into this is values education. I'm going to push for this particular component in those resources. I would also predict that, if we do our job right, this resource will be used by high school teachers and by introductory college chemistry professors. Much of the curriculum or materials that are developed by the Division of Chemical Education for high school is actually cross-over material that helps one get into the college curriculum as well. I plan to try to be at the forefront of that kind of thrust and I'd be very happy to have any of you interact with me in that regard.

SEIBERT: I want to add one more point to the last one just made. Very modestly, Sister did not mention that she wrote the grant for this and was awarded a million dollar contract through the College of New Rochelle to do this work with universities all over the country.

I have been interested in the philosophy and theology of science for many years. Twenty years ago I complained that the church was far behind in doing anything about this. I've heard this complaint often. Now we are getting closer to being more with it. Some of the indications are the existence of ITEST which has been involved for a long time and the Pope John XXIII Medical Moral Research Center in Braintree, Massachusetts. I've just spent ten months there doing research in medical ethics. This particular organization, for example, sponsors a week long conference every year for the bishops from the United States, Canada, the Philippines, and the Antilles. This is a tremendous improvement to the thinking of the hierarchy of our country.

Despite the fact that many of us, including myself, think that at times our church is very conservative, I see a growth toward a common understanding. Pope John Paul II wrote to scientists in June of 1988. Some of the things that he said in that particular letter are tremendously important for us in terms of this country. Let me quote from that letter of Pope John Paul: "The significance of theology for humanity will be reflected in the theologian's ability to incorporate the findings of science." This is part of what we are trying to do here. I think the church is beginning to do more and I hope that this group can be used to help the church incorporate theology with the sciences.

I would like to mention one other indirectly related thing here. Many of you may not be familiar with it. Last year an organization came into life called the Brookland Mission. This is a mission formed by a group of women religious under a rather substantial grant from the Lilly Foundation to study the relationship of the intellectual life and the spiritual life, particularly as it concerns Roman Catholic sisters in the United States at the turn of the century. I'm proud to be a member of that Commission. I think that the study that they are doing is going to help us understand not only what has been happening in this one narrow area of women religious in intellectual life, but also in what we can do to broaden that as we go into the future.

SKEHAN: Part of the paper that I presented on the role and importance of research and publication in church-related institutions has to do with things that we are already familiar with in detail. One of the things that I've been concerned with over the years is that the sciences and scientists have felt that they don't have much to contribute that is specific to a church-related institution. As a result they have, perhaps, lacked motivation that relates to activities in a church-related institution.

As I noted in my paper, I was at a symposium honoring my thesis director at Harvard. A number of people presented accolades on behalf of his scholarship and his teaching. He had not published extensively, and this was a bit of a problem throughout his career. But his few publications were important landmarks in the field. One of the speakers, a former student and a very distinguished researcher, pointed out that other speakers had correctly identified some of his outstanding characteristics but he felt that the most important characteristic of Professor Thompson's career was his integrity.

That means something to me because of an interest in the writings of Bernard Lonergan. I can't profess to be completely conversant in detail with Lonergan's writings, but I first became interested in Lonergan's writings through Harvey Egan who teaches mystical theology at Boston College. In his little book, What Are They Saying about Mysticism?, Egan, in referring to the mysticism of the future, links Lonergan's writings to it. He indicates that scientists and mystics have much in common. He relates that to integrity, to a fidelity to the transcendental precepts, namely, to be attentive, intelligent, reasonable, responsible and in love. Lonergan points out that in order for the theologian to be a top scholar he or she must not only be skilled as an academician but also has to have integrity in his or her life. In other words, he or she must relate what he or she is personally to what is going on in his or her scholarship.

This gets into the spirituality of scientific research and the whole scientific enterprise. In many respects, it relates very closely to what Teilhard de Chardin presents in his voluminous writings. Tom King, a Jesuit professor of theology at Georgetown, has written a couple of excellent books, one of which is Teilhard's Mysticism of Knowing. The real significance of Teilhard seems to be his claim that in the very act of scientific achievement the scientist knows God. I relate that back to the concept of integrity. While this isn't something that we teach necessarily or can give courses in, nevertheless, this whole theme has been so well enunciated by Lonergan, Egan and Gregson. I would recommend to those interested in following up on this Lonergan's Spirituality and the Meeting of Religions.

The document that was mentioned by Sr. Angelice, is a message to Fr. George Coyne by his Holiness. It is reproduced in Physics, Philosophy, and Theology: A Common Quest for Understanding. His Holiness stresses quite heavily that theologians, philosophers and scientists have much to gain from each other. His particular interest in developing new theological models that come out of scientific research is exceedingly important in the modern church, just as it was in the Middle Ages. He mentions, for instance, the concept of hylomorphism and its importance to understanding the Eucharist. He urges theologians, philosophers and scientists to get together and to develop new models that can serve as vehicles for further understanding of theology.

SHERMAN: This is a heady experience for someone in a secondary school to be in your august company. Sr. Loretta (Findysz) and I are the only two here who are teaching in secondary schools. If you want to find out how it is in a boys' school, talk to her. If you want to find out how it is in a girls' school, talk to me.

There are three points I want to make in regard to the short paper that I wrote. It is not meant to be complete.

First, you're going to get students in your colleges in the next few years who will have experiences in STS (Science, Technology, Society) programs. What are you going to do about it? Some of the things involved are new chemistry curricula, such as chemistry in the community, usually called Chemcom. It emphasizes the values and the societal implications of chemistry. Also, there is a big emphasis on molecular engineering and genetic engineering now. You can't even consider that without considering its social implications.

There are a great many resources such as a thing called SIRS (Social Issues in Research) which covers all kinds of scientific issues such as earth science, life science, physical, medical, and applied science. These things are all available. They all have great values built into them. Each one of these issues has about 100 recent articles, and they're all in many high school libraries.

I also put down some suggestions since I'm not one to stand up and predict the future or criticize anybody without giving you some constructive suggestions. I made some suggestions there for how the colleges could continue to build upon what you're going to be getting in the future. The students will have some experiences, such as outreach in the communities, coalitions between industry and universities on one hand and between the universities and the high schools and/or grade schools on the other hand. That's very important. Then especially we must encourage women and minorities to go into science.

Fianlly, I subscribe to the Christopher philosophy that it's far better to light one candle than to stand around cursing the darkness, so I'll tell you some of the things that I've been involved in. One is to work with the Math Science network in St. Louis. It sponsors a large meeting every year. We invite young women who are role models in science and they meet with about 600 to 800 girls in grades 8 through 12 at an all day conference. They interact within small groups. They get to do some hands on experiments. We have very fine speakers such as young women from NASA or various places like that who come in to be our keynote speakers. This has been a very popular program here in St. Louis. It's also done many other places in the country.

I've also been involved in going out and doing chemistry shows for the grade schools. So far I have done over 80 shows. It's reached the point where I feel like a long running Broadway play. My main problem is to keep it sounding spontaneous and off the cuff. So I don't use a written script. I follow an outline and do different things. I have a whole set of overhead projections that we've made up. The first one has chemistry in the center, with a lot of different occupations radiating like the spokes on a wheel. Of course, you can't get all the various occupations in there, but I include a lot of them. I emphasize to the students that chemistry is absolutely basic to all these other sciences. I say: "If you haven't taken it in high school, kids, it's murder when you get to college." So I really push the idea that they must take some chemistry in high school. Additionally, it may be the only chance they'll have to take chemistry. So I really push that.

The last overhead says, "Chemistry is the key to understanding God's creation."

BRUNGS: Before you step down, may I ask you a question. What awards did you get in the past year?

SHERMAN: Well, the most recent one was a national award from the American Chemical Society in polymer education at the high school level. There were three national winners, and I was one of the three. It was very nice because they provided a free trip to Miami Beach for a week.

BRUNGS: I think we're in heady company.

DR. BERTRAM: That was a fitting climax I would say to that section of luminaries. Thank you for setting her up for saying that.

DISCUSSION

SESSION 3

FORD (NY): In conversations and letters, Fr. Brungs talked about a possible conference which may follow in 1990 or 1991. During the day, we ought to keep our eye on that target. Where can we go from here for the 600 or 700 church-related colleges committed to science education in one form or another? Should we have an event later that touches a larger audience of institutions? If so, how do we approach it? I think that that has to come up front, because it may help our discussion this weekend. Do we want to do that? Are we the mustard seed? Do we believe we can influence the rest of the church-related colleges? If so, how and what are the problems there?

BRUNGS: We see the opportunity fora wider meeting but we need the vision and wisdom of this group. Should we be looking beyond church-related colleges and universities to church-related schools in general, K through graduate school? Would this be too difficult to handle? Should we look to more than one meeting? Can we have success at the college and university level without accompanying success at the lower levels? We must look ahead 10 to 20 years. If this effort ends with the closing of the conference, we've wasted time, effort and money.

BERTRAM: I gather that by feasible, you're not simply asking if it is administratively feasible -- could money be raised and so on.

BRUNGS: No. Is it something that we ought to do?

BERTRAM: Something that a conference could help resolve? So far I've detected a strong consensus about doing something, less about what to do.

FORD (St. Louis): Fr. Panuska emphasized in his talk yesterday that it's God's creation that scientists are looking at. Several of the papers have touched that note of encouraging curiosity and wonder at God's creation. God's creation is urging us on in scientific investigation. In offering a sort of challenge or critique, Dan McLoughlin alluded to the story of the fruit of the tree of knowledge and of eating the fruit thereof. I refer to that same parable. We are Christians investigating this world; Adam and Eve were "Christians" whose wonder and curiosity, if that's what did it, caused them to pick the fruit off that tree. Is there, from a Biblical perspective, something tragic or dangerous or problematic in pursuing knowledge? Is it a mixed blessing?

SHEAHEN: I think probably everybody's been to management training at one time or another. There is a system in which our self-

IMAGE OF OTHERS

		HIGH		LOW
SELF IMAGE	HIGH	*Collaboration*		*Domination*
			COMPROMISE	
	LOW	*Appeasement*		*Withdrawal*

image and the image of others form these brackets or these little quadrants. (see above). If we think highly of ourselves and highly of others, you engage in collaboration with them. If we think highly of ourselves and poorly of others, we will engage in domination; poorly of ourselves and highly of others, we will engage in appeasement. If we think poorly of both ourselves and others we will withdraw. In the middle is the area of compromise.

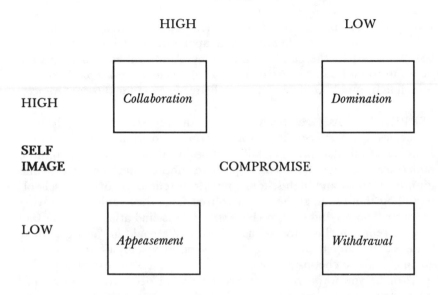

It is perhaps a prerequisite for our concerns to locate ourselves on this map relative to the secular universities. If we say, "Stanford and MIT have all that great equipment; we can't compete with them," we're putting ourselves here (low) and them here (high). If we put ourselves in the low box, we invite the other to go into the high box because we say: "Hey, you're good" -- a high image of the other, a low image of ourselves. If we apologize for our religious back-ground or our religious faith, we're going to wind up in this category (appeasement). Everybody wants to be in the collaboration box. It is certainly possible to engage in collaboration with the finest research universities; and, if you think about it, we don't have much to apologize for. If you look at what the secular humanists have achieved with the United States in the last 20 years, you see they've done a lot to put themselves in the low box. Some of their great plans and social engineering efforts have been gross flops. Every now and then you read that they're rethinking their ideas. Religiously affiliated universities and schools do not have to apologize nor be down in the low box. We can play the game on a high level and deal as equals with the major universities in research on the secular side. If we keep this kind of principle in mind, we'll have a much better agenda for this conference.

PERRINE: As I get older I become more aware how lovely little molecules are. Each one is a little greeting card from God. I've gotten some beautiful, charming crystalline kisses from God in the form of little molecules. We might have a more positive effect on our kindergarten and grammar school and high school students in religiously oriented schools by telling them that, if they want to find God, they could try studying chemistry. Some find God in chemistry, others find atheism. Some find God in religious life, others find atheism. We could go into grammar schools and high schools, saying, "if you want to be a mystic and find God, go into organic chemistry." We now say, "if you want to get a job, do this," or "if you want to solve a great national need, study chemistry." Who wants to solve urgent national needs? Many people deep down do want to find God. Many of the great scientists did that. Albert Einstein had great wonder and awe -- granted he didn't find official religion -- before God in the universe.

I don't agree with these things about the tree of knowledge being ambivalent and perhaps our getting evil out of it. If it is, it's we who create the evil in it. It's not in the knowledge itself. God made us to discover that.

ORNA: I too believe that the search for truth is not inherently evil. There is no bad in that at all. The evil occurs in our attempt to make ourselves God. That's where the problem lies. I agree with Dan that faith and religion are two different things. One can be very religious and live without faith. Yet one can live a great faith-filled life without any kind of an overt allusion to religion. I'd like to separate those two concepts.

YACKEY: I'm in biology with a strong bent toward environmental science. I'd like to mention the point of the story that God took the garden and said, "Take care of it." I'm interested in stewardship. That's the aspect in science that I brought along, namely, the stewardship and taking care of the resources. I try to get a few concepts across and some biological principles in the broader vision of stewardship. Once in a while we speak somewhat covertly of faith in that. There's that underlying core of caring for this fragile earth and resources of the earth, which I think puts the emphasis on that first part of that Biblical story.

COLICELLI: We educators have to be careful not to overwhelm people with problems. I have trouble falling asleep worrying about acid rain, the greenhouse effect and a number of other really critical issues which could possibly make life impossible. Still, my basic gut feeling is that we're going to survive. But we have to be careful when we talk to students. We have to teach them appropriate issues. Otherwise they can become numb. That's the only problem that I can foresee in terms of approaching the tree of knowledge is that we numb people. That has happened on the nuclear issues. There are a lot of people numbed by the problem. It does overwhelm.

I want to make some remarks about any upcoming conference. An interesting concept for a conference would be core curriculum, because then you pull in different people. Let me give an example of working on the core curriculum -- I give the example that I always use at my college. I'll say to the English faculty or the English faculty will say to me, "Well, we certainly don't want anyone to graduate from the College of St. Elizabeth without knowing what a sonnet is." Of course, don't be silly. And of course, I know what a sonnet is. I suspect that most of us here have more that half of our 100 and some odd credits in undergraduate education in areas other than science. This can't be said for everyone else. I always say the scientists are really the only liberally educated people in our institution. So I tell the English people that I don't want anyone graduating from the College of St. Elizabeth who doesn't know what the major air pollutants arc. Well, of course, the English faculty doesn't know what the major pollutants are. So all of a sudden, dialogue stops.

In New Jersey we have had success in global education. But we've had to educate the faculty. We've had to have them do more than talk about the problem. We've had to bring in experts to teach them. The humanities faculty doesn't know much about science. Our elementary education majors tend not to know much about science and math. They go out and create new generations of people that don't know much about science and math. Dr. Ford's (NY) study showed that we all think that people don't know science and math coming in. Somehow we have to break the cycle and we have to break it with knowledge There are programs where scientists are teaching science to the teachers. We can talk about the problem, but the bottom line is that we have to start teaching colleagues, teachers and everyone else. NSF which is becoming freer with money for this. Here we're all believers. The problem is that, if we had a conference, how would I get this English faculty to get on the plane with me to come out here. They're going to feel pretty lost.

SEIBERT: A lot of people question where genetic engineering is going and how it should be done. I agree with Mary Virginia that the scientific information we get is certainly not evil. The question is what do we do with the information. Take the splitting of the atom. There's no reason why the atom shouldn't be split. It's what we did with the splitting of the atom that certainly was immoral. The same thing could happen in genetics. We should question where we are going in recombinant DNA, as the biologists did when genetic engineering first began. "Should we really apply this? Ought we to do everything that we can do?"

EAGAN: I want to pick up on Tom Sheahen's matrix there on the board. It raises a terribly important question in terms of a plan that most of us would like to see develop in the future. To sum that matrix up, it is true we are what we pretend to be. We must be very careful about what we pretend to be. If we pretend to be fully in the matrix of research at those colleges and universities, we're going to have to make a terribly important decision as to whether or not a future conference focuses on church-related schools or institutions, or conversely colleges and universities that are church-related, because there is a fundamental distinction, I think, to be made between the educational process as such.

Legitimately we could go either way. I'm not suggesting we do one or the other, but it's an important consideration. If we pretend to go the route of becoming first rate research institutions, scientifically and technically oriented, we have to do what those other institutions do. We have to cooperate with them. I'm not sure to what extent a conference that just focuses on a whole educational or pedagogical scientific and technical educational process would lead towards that. It's a decision we're going to have to face if we take seriously that church-related colleges and universities ought to be first rate institutions where the integration of science and technology and the humanities takes place.

BARNES: It's encouraging to hear all the scientists say positive things about the relationship between science and religion. I think Elena and Ford (St. Louis) are correct about the division. I see a lot of theologians carefully isolating or quarantining science, praising it for doing its thing but trying to make sure that it cannot impinge on theology. Some philosophers of science say science is just a particular language game that is a kind of faith and a myth of its own. They say that it follows a sequence of paradigms with no real validity, and it is dependent simply on social pressure. This is a pretty powerful philosophy for a lot of theologians. Avery Dulles, a Catholic theologian, Lindbeck from another tradition, say that it's okay for people to continue with their religious beliefs untouched by science because the two are entirely different kinds of things. If we're going to have a conference on religion and science meeting at the college level, that's one of the problems that will have to be faced.

CONNELL: I want to respond to this. I think that's always been a problem. Last night someone brought up Nieuwland. There was also Zahm who wrote a book on evolution which he was asked to withdraw because the church wasn't ready yet for evolution. I really wanted to respond to Charles Ford (St. Louis). In some of the translations -- I'm not a Biblical scholar -- you still have "conquer the earth." To me, that means conquer the understanding of nature. Research will enable us to understand the physical and biological world. This is a part of what Adam and Eve were told to do. The other quote I use often, -- though I don't say it quite as Irenaeus said it -- is: "The glory of God is man and woman fully alive." If we do not use our intellectual potential to study the world around us, I don't think we can be fully alive.

FORD (NY): We use the term church-related. It struck me, in laying out the study and identifying the schools, that I automatically eliminated the Jewish community. Now my world is Jewish.

BERTRAM: You had Yeshiva in your paper, didn't you?

FORD (NY): Yes. But overall, it's really a Christian based study. At any future meeting, I certainly would like to have some of my Jewish colleagues, particularly those who are Orthodox and who are clinicians and scientists, participate in this discussion when and if it occurs in 1990 or beyond. After all, they wrestle with God by definition on a daily spiritual basis. We're wrestling with God as well. We would sell ourselves short not to have that very strong fine tradition. Where we have great commonality with the Jewish tradition, all of our discussions should be Judaeo-Christian.

Further, to expand the ecumenical perspective, I happily live near Yale and benefit from that fine university. Yale is a very Catholic university. It's a very Jewish university. It's filled with a lot of believers. If you follow its activities, some of the most exciting things come from Hillel and Newman Centers. So let's look at the Jew and the Christian in the secular university who also lives in the same universe. We might go beyond the concept, church-related.

BERTRAM: The example of Yale also brings up Michael Barnes' reference to Lindbeck, who stands on the other side of the very issue that you're talking for.

SMULDERS: So much is being said it's difficult to respond because everything brings up another thought. In southern California we started what is called a southern California colloquium on religion and science. It is made up of Jews, Moslems, Orthodox, Catholics, Christians. It's fascinating. We started with presentations by specific scientists who talk about religion and science.

I'm disturbed because I see a greater separation of the liberal arts from science. I see colleagues trying to degrade science. They don't want to listen; they block it out because they don't understand it. When this topic was announced -- I'm sorry to say this was the first time I had ever heard ITEST -- it was sent to our president. He sent it to the chairman of the religious studies department, who mailed it to the dean of the College of Science and Engineering. I looked at it because I am in charge of our science and technology program. I thought it would be a great thing since we have a core curriculum review committee. I hoped to get somebody from the liberal arts to come with me and bring back these ideas to the Dean of Liberal Arts, who is a Jesuit. He said: "Oh, another one of these. Just a waste of time, energy, effort and money." When I told him I'd pay for it, he said that no one in the college would benefit from it. That disturbs me. I admire what you are doing.

I wish I had the time to go into the high schools, since we need to instill enthusiasm for science at the high school level. But I don't think a conference is going to do it. I think we should go out and spend time. We all should go into a high school and help to get these students enthused about science. The latest issue of the American Scientist noted that the number of students interested in science is down. Young people don't want to go into science. I don't know why that is. My colleagues are afraid of science. They're afraid of graphs and statistics. I don't think it applies only to church-related institutions. Its cause is, I think, the separation between science and the arts or philosophy. The gap is becoming wider. Church-related or not, we need to educate people to realize that science is important. I loved what was said about finding God in science.

RECK: This question may betray my own lack of background in science. I'm from the humanities side, with much more experience in theology and pastoral work. It was suggested yesterday and this morning that the question basically is concern for values integral somehow to scientific research and education. If so, how does it enter in exactly, at what point? Is it something around this question of responsibility? Several people mentioned finding God in their scientific research or their scientific life. Where exactly does it enter? How can one who's teaching theology to a group of technologically inclined students hopefully get in touch or recognize this entry point? Or, on the other hand, is the problem, as several also have suggested this morning, largely one from the point of view of the humanities? There seem to be many more scientists intersted in this dialogue than people in the humanities. They either don't know the sciences or they're afraid to try to bridge the gap. Where does this concern for values enter in?

BRENNAN: Because I'm a student, among the other hats that I wear, I also wear my ignorance well. I hear people talking about education and sciences being means and ends unto themselves. I realize that part of what we're talking about here is the role of technology education by the church-related schools in order to approach science and technology. How does theology play into this whole question?

St. Louis University just had a meeting about the mission of the university. We talked about what it means, how we are going to cross disciplinary boundaries within the university. We're not talking about collaborating with other universities but just trying to get our own act together. I'm sure that there are other schools which face similar problems. We've talked about questions that we can address from many different areas. What are the pressing questions where we can draw resources from theology, from different sciences, from technology?

Someone from the humanities department suggested that a great question for us to work on together was what Henry VIII really died of.

Working in a school, surrounded by some of worse poverty that I've experienced outside of Milwaukee, I think that there are pressing questions for the solutions of which we might use our science and technology. Let's develop some means to build this kingdom of God to alleviate some of these problems and injustices. Education for many of the students at Parks, as I understand it, is not an end in itself. It's a means to a career. Many of our students typically earn $35,000 when they walk out the door with a bachelor's degree. I don't believe that we're offering that same kind of salary to people who have doctorates starting out in theology. The question is where the buck is.

The Ignatian anniversary year is coming up in 1991. A conference, bringing together people from kindergarten through graduate school through post-doctorate, may be something that would interest people outside of education. It might interest students and people in the community to see an application of some of the wonderful things we have which might help solve some of the problems society has missed. Perhaps this might draw interest from outside the immediate university and college community.

BRUNGS: Unlike Dan Perrine, I have never found anything in chemistry except dirty dishes and bad smells. Now physics is another thing! There are two areas where we can begin to work with technological students. One is Dan Perrine's notion of beauty. A good engineering work is beautiful. I'm always impressed by the beauty that the Golden Gate Bridge adds to the Golden Gate. I think the gate itself is more beautiful for having the bridge across it. More and more I'm of the opinion that we cannot worship God except in a world God created. Only in the one He did create, only in the one in which He became incarnate can we worship Him. This world is the world in which science operates. There are a lot of other operations going on that are just as important. But science is an area of enormous importance, not for value, not for things other than the fact that the world Christ became incarnate in is a world capable of producing computers and the minds to build them. It's a world that is already 15 billion years old when we came into it, give or take 2 or 3 billion years.

I work on the assumption that church-related schools are related to the church. That may not sound profound, but we really haven't talked about the church's need for science in order adequately to proclaim the Good News in the only universe that exists. In order to proclaim the Good News and in order to live it, we in Christ -- in the only world there is -- have to love, understand and manipulate the creation. I'm using manipulate in a positive sense. We reshape it. Science is an important vehicle for doing this. It's not enough to talk about ethical values. This is, I think, Michael's (Barnes) point with respect to theologians. This is not something that theology can ignore. This is not something that Christianity can ignore.

I could be wrong on this but, as far as I know, Christianity is the only major religion that started in a city. It's an earthy, urban religion, and it's centered on the creation. To worship God fully, we have to do our best to understand the world God has given us to worship in. Until we can get this stuff into our doctrinal understanding, I don't think any discussion about values is worth anything. They have to be concomitant. They have to proceed together and work on each other. We must have a scientific understanding of creation.

I remember reading one of Teilhard's letters (ca. 1910), which I haven't been able to find again, in which he wrote that the Catholic church is the world's largest organization without a research and development operation. That was written a long time ago, but I think the statement is basically true. This is what the Pope is expressing in the book that Jim Skehan mentioned, the need for commitment to scientific understanding in order to increase our understanding of what God has done.

SKEHAN: I'd like to follow up on Don Reck's point about where we insert the question of values into engineering and technology. Although it may not be a common thing in science classes to talk about values, it is becoming more common. We do look toward the implications of science and technology. Students are concerned about who they authentically are. So I think the question of integrity is very much at issue in every kind of scholarship and in every discipline. This is particularly clear with regard to science where we are trying to understand the outside world and the universe and to be in conformity with it. What is conformable to our humanity? As Lonergan says, it's the transcendental precepts, namely, attentiveness, intelligence, of being reasonable, responsible, and in love. That is a measure for Lonergan of how you match the individual to what the individual is learning and professing in the outside world. I would say the question of integrity and authenticity is possibly the place where there's a meeting point.

TRUCHAN: I have three comments which sound disparate but which are related. In terms of a future conference, we have to look seriously at another model -- and I'm not saying it's either/or -- which would deal with those who are not the converts. If we could come up with a package or several packages of workshops, we might create a very interesting application effect. I wear a number of hats in many organizations. I'm sure that would be true of everybody in this group. If we have a package of materials for organizations A, B, C, D, E, F, of different natures, we may be able to create something very interesting. That does not exclude the major conference. It could be an outcome of it. At least it would address the issue of how we could get to other audiences to convince people that this might be worthwhile. I'm thinking of STS, the work of Rustum Roy and others. That's a natural forum for us too.

We who work in church-related institutions should be people of hope in the present and the future. We seem sometimes to forget that. Yet that is one critical thing society needs. In our institutions, values must be taught in all disciplines. We're outcome oriented institutions. I teach values in microbiology. I not only teach values, I assess the values for them. If anyone is interested in doing it, I'd be glad to share it with them.

I just gave the DAS (Draw a Scientist) test. I don't know if you know how that works, but it's very revealing. I should have brought them with me. I gave it to students in a science methods class and had them give it to children. They brought them back and we evaluated them against criteria. Even first graders have very strong myths about what a scientist is or is not. They fall into two categories that are very germane to what we're saying. They are male, with a lab coat on, with lots of hair and glasses, and eccentric looking. I'm serious. We're talking imaging here. We may consider ourselves liberally educated but our colleagues consider us eccentric. We have to address that issue among ourselves. Collectively, not necessarily individually, we lack social interaction graces. I can give many examples of that. It's worthwhile seeing this test. The drawings came out into two categories. The bulk of them were the eccentric male scientist thing. The others were not human; they were strange space creatures with horns and things like that. That says something to me that portrays a strange perception of the "mystical. I did this work about four weeks ago, so I'm talking about very current data.

Finally, I'm concerned about all this multiplicity of ideas that are coming out on the floor and how we're going to focus it. I would like to suggest that we break up into small groups and try to focus it. Then one person can report it to the plenum. That might help us come to some kind of conclusion in terms of whether or not we want a major convention and what other things would be included. We could spend the next hour adding wonderful things and not be any closer to a decision.

SMOLARSKI: Last year I was at the convention of Sigma Xi, the National-International Science Research Society. The main theme was the public understanding of science. I was fascinated by the presentation of a government official for science, from Australia. He brought up some of the same points that Sister just mentioned in terms of the public perception, especially of grammar school kids. They thought that scientists do secret and very weird things. If you reflect on the popular understanding from the movies (War Games and Weird Science) you see the culture we're dealing with in English speaking countries. That's not the perception among the Koreans, Japanese or Vietnamese. They see science as a high value, whereas the Anglo Saxons do not.

We could do some housecleaning ourselves as we search for unity and collaboration between the science half and the arts half of an arts and science college. For two years I was president of the local Sigma Xi chapter at Santa Clara. I'm discouraged when maybe six scientists out of a faculty of 50 show up for a Sigma Xi lecture. If you bring in a mathematician, a few mathematicians may show up, but nobody from the other sciences. We've become so specialized within science that we can't understand other scientists. I can sympathize with the English person who doesn't want to come to a science talk, but I'm not sure why some of the other scientists might not want to come to a broader scientific talk. But that is a concern even within a small number of science departments. We don't do that good a job of collaborating among ourselves. Perhaps if we did, we could collaborate among other factors in universities.

Take the scientific research done in church-related schools or by church-related individuals. The Jesuit Studies group at Fusz (St. Louis University) published a book about an early Jesuit mathematician. I gave a copy of that to my chairman who said: "this is great, but what has happened in the last 200 years?" Have we reached the plateau Rustum Roy mentioned, namely, that there will be very few significant types of discoveries in the future? When people hear of Santa Clara, they think about the great glory days of football when we went to the Sugar Bowl and the Orange Bowl a long time ago. Scientifically, Santa Clara had a professor who made the first manned flight (by glider) before the Wright Brothers. We had a Fr. Riccard who did great things in predicting weather by analyzing sun spots. Nobody ever hears about that. They think about the glory days of football. But that was in an earlier day when perhaps more significant discoveries could have been made which may be impossible in our smaller sized schools now.

MURPHY: I feel that Don Reck's point of talking to engineering students underlies the problem of scientists and theologians talking together. How do they find God in what they're studying? We also have Elena Collicelli's point about the difficulty of talking to the English people or of getting them to talk about science. I think the route to the English people is to talk about creativity and the creative imagination. The same would be true with engineers if you would talk about discovery and innovation. Talk to them about something they're concerned about.

Let me suggest some resources that I feel can do it. I feel that with the English people one of the key things might be Michael Polanyi's article. It's a gem of an essay on creative imagination, because he focuses in part of it on how to talk to English people and vice versa. And you can use it with them because they can follow along. It's a real discovery for them to find out that the creative process is essentially the same and the discovery process is essentially a creative process. A second thing that's very helpful is a 20 minute film about why people create. It is a Saul Bass film which won several awards. It has Einstein, Hemingway and Bonner talking about how they came on their discoveries. It's all simple. The idea was simple and they didn't realize quite what it meant and so forth. Engineers could have a closer look at biographical sketches about how some of the major innovations, things of this century say, came about. They could consider, for example, Carlson and the copying process and even something as simple as, say, the coaster brake. Those are two routes to get at what is probably common ground. In other words, what is the creative process for everyone?

ACKER: I was an English major before I was a nun. After Sputnik I was sent to major in science. I have degrees in chemistry and in English. I keep telling the seminarians that science is one of the humanities. We talk about the humanities and science as if they were dichotomies. From past history, I have discovered that science has always been considered to be one of the humanities. When did it stop being one of the humanities? It's true we're not talking the same language. As an English major, I thought a log was something you burned in a fire. In the Master's program in chemistry at Notre Dame I learned what a log was in science. A field is something you plant, but to physicists fields are something else. We must do what Dr. Langdon Gilkey said, when he spoke at Hiram College this year. We have to start talking to one another.

If there is going to be a future conference, it should have a narrow focus. I don't think we can go from kindergarten on up. I have been a high school teacher for 30 years and I think it's the high school that feeds our colleges. We have to start talking to the high school teachers of all the disciplines. I think we can approach the high school teachers from the point of view of creativity if they're English teachers. Moreover, science teaches the scientific method but it's all wrong. The scientific method isn't what's in our books at all. We must reteach scientists what the scientific method is all about. The scientific method is very subjective and very creative. It's not so objective as we'd like to think.

As Sr. Leona said, ITEST could get a Chautauqua Institute. The people from Dayton know what I'm talking about because Jordan Minor at Dayton is in charge of these three day institutes given to college teachers all over the country. I've taken three of them and they've opened my eyes. We could have such an institute to consider God and science. We would get people from all disciplines in college. Why don't we get involved in a Chautauqua Institute focusing on the high school teachers. That's the way we're going to come upon God in His laboratories of creation, in many different ways. When I was an English teacher, I came upon God in poetry. So too, when I got into astronomy and into geology. I just finished a ten day river-running trip in the Grand Canyon. But God in creation there was wonderful too. We can come upon Him from all disciplines. And that's what I think ITEST ought to do.

MCGUIRE: I want to come back to the question of the core curriculum. It seems that a number of colleges, many of the colleges represented here, are engaging in a re-examination of the core. I'm wondering why. What is the driving force? Is it a question of the dominance of the humanities? Do the departments feel they need more space in the curriculum for their own majors programs? Perhaps they're looking at a reduction of core in those institutions where we have so much of our program in core. Is it a question of reshuffling when courses are taken rather than looking at the basic content of the core? Are we looking at it from the viewpoint of the student? What is the best education that this institution can give to this student in the tradition of our institution, without, perhaps, worrying too much about the turf we are protecting?

It's very difficult to change the core, because we've already locked ourselves in so much to the faculty that we already have and in the requirements that we already have. Even to shift the time when a core course is taken -- whether it's taken in the freshman year or the sophomore year, for example -- becomes extremely difficult. Take, for example, a science course for non-science students. We often tend to put that in the freshman year or, perhaps, the sophomore year. The opinion is that we need time for students to sort out what their major is going to be. Therefore, we'll let them take these general ed requirements early. But, in fact, at the developmental viewpoint of the student, that might be the worst time for the student to take the course. The student is not prepared to be able to handle the concepts of the kind you give him.

Another point! I come from chemistry, but I wonder whether or not we in the chemistry department would be willing to have a departmental policy that we incorporate in our chemistry courses, the question of values. We do that as an individual teacher in our course, but I don't know that departments would be willing to establish this kind of policy. Secondly, is the faculty prepared to do this, since many faculty now come from a program which has not gone into these particular questions themselves? I think these questions related to the core are extremely important in terms of the kind of education we're going to provide for our students. Coming from the kinds of colleges that many of us do, we seem to indicate that we are trying to educate "the whole person." But I wonder if, in terms of our core, we as the faculty are going to make the commitment and the sacrifice to give up some courses so that we can better educate our students.

MAGILL: I would like to develop comments by the three previous speakers, and add a few remarks. The core question is important in terms of focusing our attention on a future conference. But there may be a more fundamental underlying question. First, I want some clarification.

There may be an understanding, certainly among elements of the scientists, too readily associating theology as being almost synonymous with a church-related institution. It seems to me that the problems that science has in a church-related institution are about the same that theology has in terms of research and in teaching. Questions that science has in terms of identity or in terms of tradition, understanding and promoting that tradition, seem to me the very problems that theology is also struggling with. That's my first clarification, that science and theology have the same problem in a church-related institution.

Second, I gather from many of the comments not only in the papers but also in the discussion, the words paradigm, model and creative imagination are being used rather frequently; and it seems to be forming a sort of common language. It's a concern that many of us are raising. We're trying to voice the specific problem in terms of a paradigm. It should be no surprise to us in science or theology that our problems at the moment are seriously examined in various paradigms. I'm suggesting, particularly in terms of the comments made by Sr. Joan, that, as a focus for a future conference, we may want to allude particularly to paradigms as a way of doing science and of doing theology in a church-related institution. I see the question of paradigms underlying the core question.

Having said this, I would first make a specific proposal. If we have a future conference, I would suggest paradigms of theology for science in a church-related institution and paradigms of science for theology in a church-related institution as a focus. If that is worthwhile, it would probably be better to do it with the focus of specialty, remaining at a level that might be too difficult for high school teachers to deal with. ITEST might be able to make a substantial contribution to the academy in this country by promoting some paradigms as clearly delineated. This goes between theology and science in a church-related institution.

BERTRAM: Many themes have been touched upon, but I'm going to isolate two of them. One was Charles Ford's (NY) reminder that we are trying between now and adjournment time tomorrow to come to some terms with a proposal for a future conference. Under that general heading, I discerned at least three subheads.

Who should be included? Ought the participants be only the people from the sciences or ought they include our sisters and brothers from the arts and the humanities? Some thought they ought to be included. Next, how could we get them there? A second subhead under that general theme was how inclusive the personnel ought to be in terms of levels of education. Should it be K through university, or should it be more restricted? Then in the more recent remarks, there was some consideration of the substance of such a conference. What ought the themes to be, et cetera?

The second larger theme that wove in and out of the discussion -- and this is very tricky, at least for me; you're at the mercy of a theologian -- but I'd like to weave it into a kind of chain of reasoning which none of you was reckless enough to venture. It goes something like this. Step one: science is a way to know God. There were many variations on that theme. Another theme is that many people resist, yea fear, science. I'm not using any stronger language than the speakers did. Now comes an intrusion of my own. These people must sense that there is something about science that is fearsome. Whatever else it is, it may be that science knows God. The next step, also my own, is that so many people cannot be wrong. There is something fearsome about knowing God. None of you conceded that. My job is partly that of a provocateur. That brings us to a dilemma which I think many of you might share, and that is if there is something fearsome or dangerous, as Charles Ford (St. Louis) said, about knowing God, there is something at least as dangerous and fearsome about not knowing God. It's, I suppose, the dilemma between Perrine and Brungs, the dilemma between dirty dishes and bad smells on the one hand and kisses on the other. Being a husband and a father, my recollection is that every place I've ever gotten kisses is the same location where there have been bad smells and dirty dishes. Seriously, if that is a dilemma, then one of the acknowledged or unacknowledged frightening things about science is that it might just lead to the knowing of God. The other pole of the dilemma is that it is at least as dangerous not to know God. Put crudely, you are damned if you do science, you are damned if you do not.

That, then, creates a job for theologians, but not just for them, for all reflective Christians. The proposer ought to find a way to that dilemma. Here I would come back to what my colleague Robert Brungs reminded us about when he said he assumes that church-related colleges are indeed related to the church. He developed that and said that by church, he means the church of Jesus Christ in which this God is incarnate. One of the challenges remaining for us is to see if my statement of the dilemma has value to it and if Fr. Brungs' proposal meets that challenge of that dilemma. I could see a much easier way than using the Christian Gospel as a solution to the dilemma. An easier way would be to dismiss the dilemma and say that in no sense is the knowing of God dangerous.

DISCUSSION

SESSION 4

BERTRAM: As you know, Dr. Chase from Wheaton College could not be with us for the weekend. His colleague, Dr. William Wharton, will speak to us in his place.

WHARTON: I'm the science division coordinator at Wheaton. I encouraged our president to write a paper for this conference. When he had a conflict, he asked me to represent him.

We've been talking about research universities. I'd like to contrast them with our school, a small four year liberal arts Christian college. For nine years I was a faculty member at Carnegie Mellon University in Pittsburgh doing research. I probably knew more than half the nuclear physicists in the United States, Europe, and Israel who had been in the field for five years, but at my own school I probably knew only 25 % of the faculty. At Wheaton I know all the faculty and interact with them all the time.

In the science/math/computer science division, we have a Tuesday lunch for the science faculty. One person will speak on something he or she is doing. On occasion we have someone from another department -- psychology, history or theology. We also have full faculty meetings for the whole college almost every Tuesday afternoon. Some are business meetings; others are faculty development meetings. All the faculty were asked to read Steve Hawking's book, A Moment in Time. I don't know how many read it -- maybe only a quarter -- but it was good having faculty in the English department and history department who didn't know much science, discussing their perspective of this book.

We're a very strong evangelical Christian school where everyone attends a chapel three times a week. The faculty are encouraged to have the devotions during class to help integrate the course material with their Christian faith. That's very important, too.

As President Chase mentioned, we have a new course called "Majestic Nature," a freshman course for non-science majors. We encourage students who have a fear of science to take it. The degree requires eight hours in science, and we feel strongly that everyone should take a pure science lab course. We argue that STS courses should not replace a pure science course and that students shouldn't even take an STS course until they've had the pure science course.

We emphasize that anyone who studies nature and tries to understand it should consider himself or herself a scientist. We take science off its pedestal. The first few weeks we go through Del Ratzsch's Philosophy of

Science and let them see that science is subjective as well as objective. The course is twice the length of a normal four hour course. There's a lot of hands-on lab work. Last year, its first, we taught it for 11 students. When I took my section in the course, the students were open to trying new things. They weren't intimidated by science so much.

The course description says that "Majestic Nature" is an "interdisciplinary natural science course that includes perspectives from biology, chemistry, geology, mathematics and physics. This course is dedicated to helping you develop conceptual and analytical skills necessary for critical thinking in science, exploration of the nature of science, and origins and changes that occur in matter and energy. The faculty who have designed this course want you to capture the thrill, sensation, and exhilaration that emerge when science is practiced. We hope that you will learn the limits and methods of science and that you will discover what scientists are and how they solve scientific problems. Take an exciting intellectual journey into nature with faculty who have studied it for years and discovered the majesty of the universe."

Let me read a few of its six goals. "Science through its concepts and its products has been important throughout history. Aspects of science and technology pervade every area of American culture as well as that of most of the world. Since you as a Wheaton College graduate will influence our society and the world, it is important that you be trained in scientific thinking. This course is designed, therefore, to help you develop skills in scientific thinking so that you can understand and evaluate the scientific issues which you will encounter as a liberally educated citizen, people who have questioned and continue to question their place in the universe. Scientific discovery embraces the natural world and brings content and experience to what could be an abstract philosophical discussion. This course provides you with the tools to discern and understand new scientific inquiry as a method for explaining natural truths."

Another goal: "curiosity, exploration and learning are natural attributes of young people. Discovery in nature can be inspirational to your imagination and increase the sense of wonder for the universe. You will experience the pleasure and excitement which comes through studying scientifically the phenomena of nature."

Why have we done that? This course is very labor intensive. It's not always practical to offer it to a large number of people. From 11 students last year we've expanded to 25 each semester. It's harder with 25. But the students who finished the course last year were very enthusiastic. One was interested in environmental issues and is now thinking of becoming a geology major, even though he hated science before he took the course.

We have a Pew science cluster. The Pew Foundation is funding interactive activities of Wheaton College with four other colleges and Northwestern University. Most of the activities are in the area of student and faculty research. Two faculty members from each school are meeting and developing a new course similar to Majestic Nature which all schools are committed to teaching. Let me point out that most of the issues discussed don't pertain solely to a church-related school. They pertain to all schools. When we interact with a school like Northwestern, which is not church-related, we find we have practically the same goals they have.

I teach astronomy at our science station near Rapid City, South Dakota (near Mount Rushmore). We have two courses there each summer. One is a field type course for biology and geology majors; the other is for non-science majors. We advertise this as an excellent way to meet the eight hour science requirement. They meet their science requirement with a four hour course in introductory geology, and a course in environmental geology or environmental chemistry. Then they take my astronomy course. The students learn more there than back on the main campus.

Every student has to learn how to use a telescope. They have to pass a proficiency test in which they mount the telescope in an equatorial mount and tell me in advance what deep sky object (any object they can't see with their naked eye) they're going to find. They have to find it with the telescope. They're up long hours every night looking. My lectures are only about half as long as those on the main campus, although we cover the same textbook material. I de-emphasize the textbook material. I sometimes give them the same exam I usually give at the college. Every time I've done that, the lowest score out there has been higher than the normal median score. I wonder how can that happen. Maybe I get them after they've already had six hours of science. Maybe they've learned how to take science by then. The main reason may be they're concentrating on science. Also, it's the only course they're taking out there. At the college they have a major about which they're more concerned. If they get behind in their work, their science course is sacrificed. There's a lesson to be learned. Some colleges have short courses between semesters.

It might help non-science majors to take their science course when it's the only course.

At a later conference, we might discuss how church-related schools can meet the needs of the church. At Wheaton we've treated the creation-science issue. Our pastors and teachers in our elementary and secondary Christian schools are bombarded from both sides -- the creation-science movement and the non-theistic evolution movement. They've never been exposed to a position in between those two. We offered a series of lectures one night a week for eight weeks on this issue for the area pastors and science teachers from Christian secondary schools and other full-time Christian workers for whom this is important. We had faculty members from the Bible theology department and from the anthropology, geology, chemistry and physics departments. We discussed this whole issue and gave a balanced view which helped them. It is good to do things like this for the church. That's one of the things I'd like to see discussed in a later meeting.

BERTRAM: I live in St. Louis but I teach in Chicago. The reference to the Mt. Rushmore station reminded me of an old story about Chicago weather. There was this Chicago father who said one day, "Oh, how I wish the sun would shine in Chicago, not so much for my own sake -- I've seen it once."

The tack that Dr. Wharton's presentation took may suggest a line of direction for our own discussions. In the attempted summary at the end of our morning session, I tried to fix upon two themes more or less, which had to do with a possible later conference. I had caught remarks from you dealing with at least three subpoints concerning that conference. One had to do with how inclusive the participation should be. Should it include people from kindergarten through university, or only people from colleges and universities? Should it include people from the sciences or ought it to include people from the humanities, and so on? A subissue had to do with the theme of such a possible conference. Bill Wharton picked up on that toward the end of his remarks. Maybe you'd like to consider this afternoon what a likely theme would be. Whether you choose to do that or not is up to you. So far we've done a pretty thorough job of establishing that there is need. It might be a good time to take this suggestion of content seriously. You may differ as to what you think the diagnostic problems are.

What if we switched the mood of the conference and assumed that we are pretty well agreed that there are problems? What would the solutions be? A kind of gnostic approach to solutions thinks that establishing what the problem is is the solution; knowing what is wrong will automatically lead to a rectifying of the wrong. No doubt that is part of the solution. But what if we would concentrate on what we at least imagined the solutions might be? It need not be some grand cosmic proposal. It may take the form of reciting, as Dr. Wharton just did and others have done, some of the attempts made at your institutions to meet those needs.

BARNES: We might write up the successful things done at our own institutions. It would take too much time to do it here.

I'm interested in paradigms. As I listen to scientists here talking about how comfortable they are with a meeting between science and religion, I think I hear one particular paradigm. I can see four different ways that science and religion can meet.

I'll simply list them: 1) have scientists determine the outcome, to some extent at least, of specific religious doctrine. Karl Rahner recently said transubstantiation must be rethought in terms of current physics. 2) have scientists discuss fundamental anthropology, the understanding of what a human being is, what a soul is. Our current evolutionary understanding no longer defines a soul simply as an immaterial, immortal, platonic, substantial form. 3) consider the cosmological issue. I heard Dan Perrine talking on this level when he found the love of God in the lattices. When any of you find the glory of God or the grandeur of God in nature, I sense that most of you find religious meaning in your science on that kind of raw cosmic level, God was working through those things. That seems to be the basic paradigm many of you are operating from when you think about the relation between science and religion. This is a question. 4) take the skeptics, the agnostics and the atheists, who look at the range of scientific theories and say, "There's nothing intrinsically religious to that." They would say that if you find God in the lattice work or the molecules and so forth, it's not because that's intrinsic to science. That's an addition you're importing from your religious faith. It has nothing to do with science. That's on the level of the fundamental nature of what science is and whether there are religious implications to that. Those are four different paradigms, and I don't know what level any conference would be operating on if it were to talk about the relation of science and religion. It would be good to clarify which one of those four levels (or all of them) was being treated.

BERTRAM: You remembered Gerry Magill's third point about paradigms. He made conscious, explicit reference to a previous speaker, Sr. Mary Ellen Murphy, who also had suggested a paradigm that science and theology might have in common, namely, a creative imagination or discovery. Would you like to elaborate that, to find ways of being critical about it.

CROSS: I see the practical problem of how to teach science. There's always the difference between scholarship and its communication. The problem is most acute in the physical sciences. The skills, talents and activity in the humanities and in the social sciences necessary for scholarship are closer to the skills needed to communicate its results than they are in the physical sciences. Perhaps we need to recognize a possible division of function between those who do science and those who teach it. Any national conference addressing this question for the churches and church-related schools could be very helpful to educators and scientists alike by exploring how best to communicate science to students. How best can we divide the task between the scientist, doing research at the cutting edge in perhaps some very narrow area, and those who investigate and communicate the fuller and larger meaning of those scientific findings in the academy?

SHEAHEN: For students, particularly brilliant high school students who are candidates to become science majors, the opportunity for undergraduate research is extremely attractive. They know that what is in the textbooks is knowledge that somebody else already has discovered. They feel the need to do more than simply grind through it for four years. To be part of a research team and to do something more than making coffee -- maybe doing the computer programming or something having to do with the data -- is an experience that helps them feel good about science and about their role in it. Being part of a research team helps immensely to learn what science is all about and helps them find value in the science. I cast one humble vote in favor of getting undergraduate students involved in a research program.

BERTRAM: With this new direction, an earlier concern with upgrading science research and education in church-related colleges to the point where it's competitive with the top 100 is noticeably absent. That's not been a part of the concern here.

FREDRICKS: Tom, did you have in mind science majors participating in research projects or the general liberal arts student?

SHEAHEN: I think the predominant example would have to be the science majors because, if you're a non-science major, it's unlikely that you could be a significant participant in a science research program.

FREDRICKS: Can I ask that of Bill Wharton?

WHARTON: Yes, it should be for the science majors. I could give one quick example with a new science cluster initiative. We had a math and French major work for some geology professors at Northwestern this past summer. She ended up working on a lot of math codes on the computer predicting from seismic data where the epicenters of earthquakes were. She was surprised how much math there was in geology. She decided to drop her French major, and go on for a higher degree in math. That's one example of a positive experience that occurred.

BERTRAM: In church work, that's called sheep stealing and it's frowned upon.

PERRINE: I don't think more than two or three church-related colleges are ever going to hit the top hundred. It's unreasonable for the rest of us. We can fill a slot not being filled by the big research universities. Wheaton College seems to be doing well in giving kids a hands-on experience at the undergraduate level. Usually the big PhD granting schools use their undergraduates as cannon fodder. Wheaton has a large percentage of people going on for their PhDs. After listening to you, I think I'm going to become an evangelical Christian.

I was delighted to find in Dr. Chase's paper and in your remarks that you see a responsibility to help the churches. In the Catholic church or Christian churches, the church authorities are so ignorant of this huge and wonderful cosmos that they are producing a terribly wasted, atrophied notion of God. Karl Rahner said somewhere that people who think they're atheists are often profoundly in contact with God. Conversely, people who mouth notions like the Trinity are often really polytheists. Some Christians in practice have so little understanding of the true Nicene Creed that they really have three gods. There are outstanding church authorities who are anonymous atheists in the sense that their ignorance of the true God who made this universe is so vast that they're at least schismatic if not heretics. Also, could you explain what "devotions" mean in the evangelical tradition?

WHARTON: Different faculty do different things. Some faculty just spend a few minutes at the beginning of each class period. I don't do it every class period, but sometimes I take one whole class period and really go into something quite deep.

PERRINE: Do you turn a classroom into a prayer service?

WHARTON: No, no. It's a study trying to integrate our Christian beliefs with the science we're teaching.

PERRINE: Do you actually pray sometime in there?

WHARTON: Some faculty do have prepared prayers. I don't.

PERRINE: But you do discuss the integration of science and faith. In Catholic schools like mine, we've long lost the courage to do things like that. There ought to be some theology across the curriculum. There ought to be some devotion. I'd like to see a great poet who is in science write a wonderful liturgy incorporating the knowledge of science into the idea of the image of God. Let's sing about how wonderful God is.

JABLONSKI: In a church-related institution we can help our students develop a sense of their ministry as scientists. We can help develop a spirituality for scientists, so they can integrate their science experience with their image of God. We should start talking to each other about our commonality. Is there such a thing as a specific spirituality for scientists. As we've explored the issues of social justice, we've seen that the prayers, songs and poetry have spoken of spirituality concerned with social justice themes. We scientists also have images that are more kindred to our spiritual growth. Are there scripture passages that speak to us more? Are there forms of worship best suited to the work of scientists?

I was privileged to be an observer at the impressive conference at the National Center for the Laity in Chicago on preparing the next generation for leadership in the U.S. church. It was particularly geared for the post World War II folks. They've helped people in different fields -- business people, secretaries, teachers. The science document will not be done unless there's planning and support from people who say it's important. That's something we can do. The University of Dayton has one of the largest campus ministry programs in the country -- 24 people involved. But we are not successful in getting people in the same discipline to work together. It seems as if students from different fields go on the retreats sponsored by campus ministry. They talk with other students on the campus. One student in premed last year asked me how one can go on a retreat with friends and acquaintances. They've had these experiences of sharing with people they don't know, but not with people they know. A group of premed biology majors put on a retreat for science majors. Some of those experiences seemed to give them something and helped them see what they were taking from their Christian environment in education for later. Without that retreat they may not have had that support.

RECK: As valuable as campus ministry is, I think that courses on an academic level are essential if we're going to achieve this integration. Could one of the agenda items for this proposed conference be the working out of concrete possible courses that might help achieve this? Take, for instance, an introduction to theology. I've seen courses done by others and I was able to develop something along that line. Take, for example, things we've heard here, like this "majestic nature" course at Wheaton. One person could outline a bibliography and others could develop it according to their local situations. A second suggested proposal was helping undergrads get into research programs. That's a possible idea. A third mentioned something along the idea of images of God, or where one finds God in one's experience, in one's work, in one's life -- something we could call introduction to religious experience. I'm sure there would be other possibilities as well. I'm not saying the whole conference would be focused on that but maybe some sections could be, so that people could come away with five or six possible courses which would allow an integration of science and theology.

BYERS: It would be helpful to focus on how one integrates science and religion. That is a question we usually do with the Bishops' committee, namely, how one is a person of faith in an age dominated by science. That may be a particular contribution a church-related school can make. There is ignorance in the Catholic hierarchy on science. It's not a repressive ignorance or particularly negative; it's simply there. The bishops went through the education system I grew up in. They don't have much science training and their time is taken up with a thousand other things. A conference of that nature could be a positive contribution to filling in a gap which inevitably exists at the episcopal level. I think the bishops would welcome any results from a conference like that. It could help make Catholic schools find their Catholic identity and incorporate the scientific component into that.

FORD (NY): I'm going to keep finding work for Fr. Brungs. Thanks to E. L. Smith's money at New York Medical College, we began to organize the medical ethics/health ethics curriculum for both medical and graduate students. I searched out all of the sources of information and landed with the Kennedy institute at Georgetown, among others. Ed Pellegrino and staff collect syllabi or course outlines, keep them on file, and sell them for two bucks a shot. Fr. Brungs should get a Peterson's list of church-related colleges and write every appropriate person asking them to send a copy of their syllabus. You'll get one or two pages, depending on the school. Then make a library and publish the roster by title. I've gotten valuable one or two page syllabi appropriate to the field; it's a diverse and useful service to American medical and health education to be able to get that information and not reinvent courses. I'd like to see the already mentioned paradigms written up as well as the Wheaton program. That would be helpful to all of us and to those who are not here.

BRUNGS: I'll do that during the lunch break.

FORD (NY): That's the beginning of a conference. You need a data base in what's happened. That's one way to do it.

SMULDERS: If we introduce young people to research at the undergraduate level, we're too late. I judge state science fairs in California and the Los Angeles County Fair. These are for junior high school and high school students. There are 12 and 13 year olds doing real research, able to tell you what they're doing. They're excited about it. These are people who will most likely go on in science; that's where we have to focus. Otherwise, they're turned off by science because they're not participating or they're not being allowed to participate.

I also have a program called the minority biomedical research support program. It's specifically designed to get under-represented minorities involved in research. My biggest problem is that the researchers get the funding and use it to do their research. They're supposed to help educate the young people whom they end up using as dishwashers. They don't involve them in science which is the purpose of the program. I have a difficult time picking the proper researchers who can motivate and excite them.

I arbitrarily take one lecture from a general biology course and talk about life as a religious. First, they don't know what a brother is. That class gets the most comments, because they're struggling with incorporating themselves into a scientific society. Why can't a religious be a scientist? Many struggle with that. How can a believer be a scientist? I talk about that for a whole class period.

CONNELL: I want to respond to Charles Ford. It's a great idea but it's narrow because it becomes biomedical ethics, not biological ethics. That ignores all the environmental issues which interest people now. It's fine to read about some of the very esoteric kinds of biomedical things. But what are we trying to do in terms of pollution and waste? It must be broadened beyond biomedical ethics.

BRENNAN: From discussions during the break, it appears that the bang and the buck go together to some extent. Complaints that we don't have enough scientists are tied to the potential salaries of scientists when they graduate. Is there a way to find an interdisciplinary education in both theology and sciences? Is there a way that ITEST and other groups can do some of what ROTC does for the United States military? Could we somehow involve some type of student affiliates on given campuses with ITEST, creating and developing resources to fund an interdisciplinary education at our church-related schools? People here are already versed in their own fields and think the dialogue is important. But many of the undergraduates are in either the "liberal arts" or in the "hard sciences," and dialogue doesn't always occur.

FREDRICKS: I want to comment on Tony Smulder's comments. I think you said it might be too late for the research experience in the undergraduate population. That is not our experience at Marquette. Students come from high schools with a variety of training, but little or no experience with research. The students we take into research laboratories with the faculty are enthusiastic about that experience. I would not want people to be discouraged.

SMULDERS: I meant that there's a whole group of people who are never going to be exposed to science because they end up in college as liberal arts majors without a chance even to be exposed to the excitement of science. I'm all for continuing research at the undergraduate level. There are fewer people interested in science. We must begin at an earlier stage. Assistance must be given in high school and junior high school.

SHERMAN: I particularly want to reply to Br. Tony's remarks. For about 20 years we have been doing a lot of research at the high school level. Many times we have consulted with various people -- Fontbonne, University of Missouri-St. Louis, Washington University, St. Louis University, anybody we can find. We've had a lot of success interesting students in research. We've visited cement plants and water works. I have never found a scientist who has refused to let us visit him or her or has refused to send us reprints of papers. The students love it. Tony's absolutely right, there's a whole group of people who never get interested in science because nobody takes the trouble to help them. It's terribly labor intensive, time consuming, but it's a hobby of mine. Now that I'm not teaching full time, I have more time to do that type of thing. People in the church-related colleges can help by making themselves available. I know that time is the big problem, but perhaps your administrators could see it as good PR for the school to do this kind of thing, to let a student come over and share the equipment. Let them use an infrared spectrometer or something that they wouldn't possibly get in high school. We go anywhere anybody will let us use their instruments when we need it. It's been tremendously successful.

Many church-related high schools these days -- most of you are aware of this -- require many hours of student service to the community before they can graduate. Our school requires 120 hours from freshman through senior year. Some schools like St. Louis University High School require about 60 hours in the senior year. Other schools spread it out over the whole four years. It varies from school to school, but it's pretty much ingrained in the students. A lot of those students go on to church-related colleges. I'm asking you to encourage students to continue that. This makes students aware of the community and of social problems. They go out to old folks homes, work at charitable institutions, so they see some of the problems of society. They see old people hooked up to feeding tubes in nursing homes. They see the problems of handicapped children. I'm asking for my own information, if you can build on this type of thing.

BERTRAM: You leave us with a soul searching question. Elena, do you want to respond to that immediately?

COLICELLI: Two things! Our campus has a center for volunteerism which picks up on all those kinds of things. Second, every year on campus we have a seminar on a social problem. Much of the seminar involves students making reports. They research the issue -- we're doing global warming this year -- and give a series of talks on its different aspects. Yes, we're trying to follow that.

BERTRAM: Mrs. Sherman, did you have in mind to relate your experience to this proposed conference in some way?

SHERMAN: Not necessarily, except to urge people to reach out into the high schools and make your people and your facilities available to them and, if possible, encourage student research. I have worked with science fairs. It is thrilling to see these young people doing some type of science research. It takes a lot of people working together to do it. That's what I'm really urging there.

BRUNGS: About five years ago ITEST put in a proposal to a major foundation for video production equipment. After serious consideration it was turned down. The reason given was that church people don't share their resources with each other. It may sound like a strange reason not to fund a project. In terms of Marie's remark, we don't have a good track record on sharing resources and skills. When I was teaching we did not encourage high school students to use the equipment, even though it was sitting idle. Maybe we just never thought of it. It's one thing we can begin to think of. That would be a positive step forward. How about sharing lab equipment, faculty time, secretarial time? All these things are important to the success of any operation, and I don't think we've done that very well. The foundation's reaction was legitimate. We tend to hug our empires to ourselves and protect their boundaries lest somebody else get an advantage. I am amazed that we can say we are Christians while building these self-enclosed empires rather than helping each other.

BERTRAM: It follows a point Jim Skehan's has made a few times It's called love.

BRADFORD: I want to continue with Br. Tony's point. Undergraduate research is successful at Benedictine College and has been for at least 25 years. We've gotten many National Science Foundation grants to support undergraduate research. All science majors at Benedictine College are expected to enroll for a certain number of hours of undergraduate research credit. Many have the opportunity to present their work, usually at the Kansas Academy of Science. They enjoy that. Much of it has been published over the years and it has had a very positive effect on the college as a whole. The science departments at Benedictine College have produced by far the most undergraduate students going on for advanced degrees. I would be willing to guess that there probably haven't been more than five people, say, out of the philosophy department who have gone for an advanced degree in philosophy. We've had dozens and dozens of biology, chemistry and physics majors get PhDs. One of the reasons is that our science departments give the students an opportunity to do real science whereas the philosophy department does not give students the opportunity to do real philosophy.

WHARTON: Is the research done during the summer or during the year?

BRADFORD: It's all during the year. Although I haven't been on the faculty long enough to establish or start my own research yet, I am expected to do so once I get settled in.

NICHOLS: As a possible additional paradigm for the conference we might discuss what we would like our graduates -- either science or non-science graduates -- to be. What would we like our alumni to be? We might develop some way of assessing whether any of our alumni have actually changed from the time they entered our doors to the time they leave. Jesuit high schools and others are ahead of us in assessing what they would like their graduates to be and whether in fact their graduates are changed in ways that can be polled. I'm talking not only about academics, but also about social involvement, awareness of their relationship with God, with Christ, with their neighbors.

We like to have our students develop certain scientific ways of thinking and reasoning, objectivity and subjectivity, but also assessing the way scientists find their attitudes changing during these growth years -- their relationship with God, their ability to pray, their ability to find hope in the kind of world that they are learning more about. Whether one could discuss outcomes and ways of assessing outcomes that we would like to see for this category of students might be an approach for the conference.

EAGAN: It occurs to me that selection of a theme is critical. A theme that allows discourse between the scientist and religiously oriented is important. The suggestion has been made several times that we talk about a comparison of paradigms. I have difficulty with the term paradigm. Most philosophers and scientists have difficulty with it. What might be a catalyst for this vitally important discourse? I recommend the one suggested by Fr. Skehan in his account of the ceremony recognizing his mentor. The term integrity strikes me as an intensely personal, religious and scientific word. It's a term that speaks across boundaries. Although not a practicing Christian myself, I know enough of my Christian friends who understand that integrity has very deep religious connotations. Something might be done with that. It's obviously important for scientists. It's the word that allows us to understand that the scientist's activity is itself intensely personal.

Those who do graduate work in science often do not pick an institution for their development but scientists to work with. There's something that goes on among scientists that is very important and intensely personal. I don't know whether it would work, but I feel that something could be done with the idea of integrity in the sciences, in religion and in personality.

SHEAHEN: One of the interesting things about 5:00 pm on a Saturday afternoon is that the good Catholic mind naturally turns to confession. However, I think that I see something that is fundamental to the goals of any conference that we might think about here. It has to do with forgiveness. If I understand confession correctly, we not only ask God's forgiveness but we accept it within ourselves. Four hundred years ago the church made a bad blunder with Galileo. It took 100 years or so for it to become clear that Galileo was correct. In the years that have gone by, we have quietly deleted the condemnation of Galileo. But I don't think the church has ever forgiven itself or accepted God's forgiveness in the Galileo incident. There are many people, probably including a big fraction of the hierarchy, who still feel guilty and, as a result, stay aloof from science.

In Rustum Roy's contribution there's a section called "The Origin of STS and the Return of the Prodigal Son." He talks about science starting out as a part of the church but then going off as the prodigal son. It went off and did its own thing and teamed up with the secular humanist, the atheist. It wouldn't have anything to do with the church. Now, if it comes back home as the prodigal son returned, is the church, the forgiving father, ready to take it back? A prerequisite for the father must be that he forgives himself and accepts God's forgiveness. The church must accept God's forgiveness in the Galileo fiasco and put this blunder behind it. Let's accept science, a prodigal son, and celebrate what we have together and can do together and achieve a certain integrity between science and the church this way.

BERTRAM: I thought you were going to compare the church to the older brother in the parable.

PANUSKA: I have two comments. One, a lot of the suggestions have been made about themes. I think that in the selection of the theme we should stay very close to the primary purpose of ITEST, the issue base between science and theology.

I find that volunteerism is thriving on the campuses of certainly many private schools and of the state supported system. It's a major effort. At the University of Scranton we've been able to work out a cooperative effort with our sister institution -- about the only thing we've done together very seriously -- through a funded program on volunteer services. The Commonwealth of Pennsylvania through its consortium of colleges has recently begun a campus contact system which offers assistance to various colleges to encourage volunteerism. It hit me through this conference that almost all of the services considered volunteerism are socially oriented, people oriented, sometimes for the elderly, sometimes tutoring. If we could stimulate some groups to recognize research and science in a way that relates to the alleviation of human suffering, what a leavening that might be. It would be something that would influence images attitudes. It might even help solve some of the human problems. That research could be medical or physical. It could be sociological, demographic, what have you. But to have young students on the campus counting research as their volunteerism -- something they've become proud of and display on all resumes or job applications -- is something that could spread through the country with significant effect.

COLICELLI: I don't want a future conference to end up addressing undergraduate research, because that's taken care of in other places. All of our professional societies recognize how important undergraduate research is. We can read about curriculum variety in a lot of journals. We do everything we can for high school students. That's probably true of everyone in the room. We're on all these science fair committees and we love it. The science departments in small colleges are doing outreach. We must get students who are running programs, who are doing everything, and people are exhausted. We've had people do other than direct service by working on environmental commissions in local towns. Let's not reinvent the wheel.

Bill Nichols' suggestion is something we could do, an assessment that would bring in Christian values versus science. Every state sooner or later -- New Jersey seems to be sooner -- is going to be smacking us over the head on outcomes assessment. They're not going to ask the question about Christian values or church related values. Of all the themes I've heard, that's the only one we couldn't do at an American Chemical Society meeting.

On the larger issue of science and the public, there are a couple of initiatives from the National Science Foundation (NSF) on values and science and making science education available to the public. Again, I'm not sure if you want to be writing grants. It doesn't seem to me that science education is the major thrust of ITEST.

TRUCHAN: I concur with Al Panuska that we should keep, as the focus of a potential conference, the interface of religion and science and/or the integrity of science. If we focus on the first one, technically I think the second one might be assumed. One thing that is very important to me from my experience since 1972 is that, unless one talks about taking ideas and translating them into the actual teaching and assessing goals, it ends up being only a nice experience.

One of the outcomes at our institution was valuing. In all our disciplines we have to translate how we're teaching for valuing. We have created an external valuing instrument for our majors at the upper levels to make sure that, before they leave us, they come out with some kind of a value assumption and point of view. That takes an awful lot of work and reflection even to get there. It seems to be a way of getting at religion and science.

Though I agree with Elena that there are a lot of curriculum discussions, we may lure some people into a general meeting by talking about them. Then we can have some broad presentations that will focus the specialized groups who wouldn't come if they didn't see the specialization.

We have managed to do a lot of research at our institution by using industry. I say that for all of us who are in small schools. There are more than a hundred industries in the greater Milwaukee area where our students, since 1970, have spent a semester, taking the equivalent of a course, staying eight hours doing research at an industrial lab. It's a structured program. There are a lot of advantages. They have the latest equipment and do honest industrial research. It gives the students a chance to decide whether they want to stay in that work or not. It's been effective. Anyone in a city could find many tech places without much difficulty. We have a seminar on campus to make sure they're learning out in industry. It's not as if we cast them to the wolves and forget them. On returning they reflect to validate that experience. That can extend the small college opportunity for research without extending personnel. I recommend a model like that.

COLICELLI: Industry is eager to get people, and they consider them as feeders for their own plants.

TRUCHAN: Yes. They have repeatedly said that. The science students are pretty well trained by the time we send them out. Industry says that the students are wonderful because they're a stimulus in the department. It keeps the departments on their toes. It's been a plus situation back and forth. We also call in the mentors from industry to the campus for a seminar. We train them to be effective mentors. We've both learned how to clean up our acts. It's a way of effectively extending resources into industrial work or into medical colleges.

CASPERS: At the University of Detroit we have a co-op program which is a great benefit. Such a program helps the students to make career choices. We've had students change their perception of what they want to do with their degree. Often discussion can lead to ethical questions -- should they go to a company that may or may not be completely ethical. The students are not dumb. They come back and share their experiences.

We have a requirement in our core curriculum that the students have to discuss what the ethics are or the major challenges facing their area of study. They do that. The chemistry club decided that they wanted to share this experience with high school students. They put together a little traveling show. At first they had a hard time finding a high school that wanted them. When many of them talked -- with the exception of the church-related high schools -- they could not hold the students' attention.

I think our problems begin even before the high school level.

SKEHAN: Following on Bill Nichols point and several other points from Leanne Jablonski, Dan Perrine and Pat Eagan, many of us are groping for a spirituality related to scientific research and the area of science. I found something of an outlet for this in offering a 24 week retreat, called a 19th Annotation Retreat. Bill Nichols has been doing likewise in a different format at his institution. At the private level there is a need, as Bill ultimately said, to try to see what results of this spiritual development have taken place during the time in our institution. A program that relates to articulating the spirituality of scientific research is something that may be in order.

BERTRAM: Let me just lift into quick prominence something that's been talked about more than a few times. Some of you have addressed yourself to the question of what Pat Eagan called a comparative metaphor or a comparative image, one that's inclusive enough to jolt the energies both of the faith sciences and the natural sciences. Not far from that is Dan Perrine's suggestion of having the good poet who knows scientific cosmologies construct a liturgy. I even found myself wondering whether Br. Lawrence, being a Benedictine, would think of doing that. He turns out to be a molecular biologist. A few have commented on how many people in the physical sciences are also musicians and so on. Brother Lawrence happens to be an organist.

Perhaps the theme of a potential conference could take the form of exploring what inclusive images might heighten the encounter between theology and science/technology. Another requirement that some of you see is that it should be one that not only engages the imagination of, let's say, theologians on the one hand and scientists and technologists on the other, but it should also be a kind of theme that would be highly teachable to students. I say that only by way of reminding you of what you've been discussing.

DISCUSSION

SESSION 5

BARNES (GROUP 1): Our topic concerned modes of scientific and theological knowing. We came up with four aspects which we thought were major elements. First, we considered science and religion as ways of knowing. The discussion quickly revealed that science is in fact several ways of knowing, disputed even among those who do science and the philosophy of science. This is true also of theology or religion. Each side should be introduced by the other to the complexity of these ways of knowing, if we are to understand why things get so confusing. That discussion developed into subtopics concerning the nature of truth, the nature of knowledge, and eventually into objectivity and subjectivity. A second major factor then arose: the question of the place of values in theology and in science.

Most of the discussion centered on ways in which values can affect science. Here, the major issue was gender, the way in which gender orientation influences the language and making the models in science come out in a certain way. Models of dominance are used more often than models of cooperation. That's true in theology also, as you're aware. That is big enough to be another topic of how religion (or theology) and science act differently with relationship to each other.

The third topic was the models of reality that science and theology can use. For example in the sciences, physics, chemistry, and so forth have a variety of models. Also, models may change. In geology, plate tectonics is now the dominant model, but was not always such. Each of the sciences may have more than one, even conflicting, models. Theology is the same. Theology also shows different models of reality. Take the difference between eastern theology and western theology. A process theologian in the West doesn't see reality the same way as a good Thomist would see it.

A fourth and lesser point, but I suspect very important, was language. When we talk to each other across the divisions between theology and science, we'd better constantly make clear to each other how we're using words like paradigm, model and so forth. Otherwise, we'll never get very far.

PROCACCINI (GROUP 2): We discussed the interface between science and religion. I offered from my own experience a course that I had designed and continue to teach relating 20th century science to 20th century art. I have a joint appointment in biology and art history, particularly the modern period. When I began to research the course, I expected to find parallels. I did not expect to find so much convergence or so much symbiosis between them.

New research has shown that Picasso and Brach in 1907 were familiar with Einstein's 1905 paper on relativity. They made a conscious attempt in cubism to equalize the spatial-time relationships he talked about. Also, between around 1900 and 1930 there was a style of sculpture called biomorphic sculpture because of its profound allusion to the development of organic forms, particularly in multicellular organisms. The artists who espoused this style are major figures like Brancusi, Henry Moore and Barbara Hepworth. Their sculpture parallels some intense research in developmental biology in Europe then. These artists looked at the journals and studied the pictures. I never assumed that they understood all the scientific terminology, but they were moved by the process they saw unfolding in the pictures. That gave them the inspiration for their art. Very recently, the new science of chaos has engendered a whole variety of performance arts in New York City which attempt to do exactly the same kinds of things.

I found several dozen such parallels and convergences and symbiotic relationships. What startled me were the autobiographical writings of some of the scientists and artists whom I decided to study. Some of the scientists were Pasteur, Darwin, Marie Curie and Stephen Hawking; some of the artists were people like Paul Cezanne and Barbara Hepworth. I found all of them talked about being conduits through which the answers to some essential question somehow flowed. None of them took responsibility or credit for what they had done. They said that somehow something passed through them which gave them an insight into organic forms, the beginning of time or biomorphic sculpture.

The role of intuition in all of those creative acts was pronounced. I wasn't surprised to see that in the artists, but I was quite surprised to see it so dominant in the scientists also. Einstein, near the end of his life, wrote that scientists would be the priests of the 20th century. Stephen Hawking gave an interview several years ago to the New York Times. The interviewer expected that Hawking would talk about all the mathematical formulations he thinks through as he's working his way to this new grand theory. Instead, Hawking said to him, "I don't do that at all. I simply make an intuitive leap into the dark and if it seems right, if I get a feeling of rightness, I back up and try to develop the mathematical formulation to present it in a logical way." The interviewer said, "That sounds remarkably like what an artist does, the leap of intuition that enters into painting and sculpture." Hawking said, "That's exactly right. That's how I think about myself."

I showed the writings of some of the scientists and artists to some friends. I took out all the proper names and asked them to tell me who the scientists were and who the artists. They were not able to uncover the difference between the two. They saw the essential similarity.

Group 2 used this as a springboard. We decided we didn't like the word interface because it still talked about boundaries. We used the integration of one discipline and another. We also discussed intuition as a central way to bring together interrelationships between art and science or religion and science, and that the intuition occurs in a person. We briefly discussed the logic of discovery as a binding agent, particularly because of the element of uncertainty there.

SEIBERT (GROUP 3): We spent part of the time asking if there was something unique about church-related colleges. Each time we mentioned something somebody would say that that's done in state universities. We went through any number of things, engaging science and theology departments in that order. The University of Florida does this, and so on down the line. We persisted and finally came up with the conclusion that maybe we had better change the word to "characteristic" rather than "unique." The things we had discussed prior to that -- the atmosphere that permeates the institution, atmosphere translated into individual actions, having a mission statement -- all of those things would involve characteristics that should be part of a church-related institution. The institution itself should have the link to religion or faith. How should it be expressed? It's used in the institution particularly in science classes to touch on the future of the human race. The Lord and science should be discussed. One person suggested that in every church-related institution, there should be a discussion of Vatican documents and a report given to the bishop on the results of those discussions. Provide a forum for such discussions rather than just a classroom area. Communicate the results. There should be value focus in courses in the curriculum, and courses that have a value basis should be required in the core. That also applies to some non-church-related institutions.

We discussed the concept of hiring people in the institution. What kind of policies should we have and what kind of questions should we ask individuals? Many institutions have individuals teaching for them who are not of the same faith persuasion -- Catholic or Protestant or whatever. Some institutions have policies and some do not. We ended up saying that we need to strive for the ideal world. We should try to hire those who would uphold the same values as we see our church-related institution holding.

BERTRAM: It's not for me to add to your group's report, but had it occurred to you that what might be distinctive about the Christian community that it keeps asking the question what is distinctive about the Christian contribution?

SEIBERT: No, we did not discuss that. But at this point I'm not even sure that would be unique. I can remember 50 years ago one of our sisters used to come in and ask what it was that makes an Ursuline college. How are we different? We still haven't answered that.

CROSS: Four things emerged in our group about the characteristics of science education at church-related institutions: 1) they're person centered, which might make them different; 2) there's an extra freedom; 3) there is or ought to be an emphasis on science fields as service fields; 4) there's a need to counteract the negative view of science.

On the first theme, the person-centered nature of church-related institutions should make it easier to teach the difficult sciences, should encourage more tutorial instruction, should create an atmosphere in which minorities are helped to overcome any disadvantages they may have with respect to science education. This person-centered nature of educational ideals in our institutions ought also to extend to non-science majors.

The issue of freedom in education, of course, in this country means that we're free to express our religious views and the views of our churches within our institutions which is, at least, more difficult to do within the secular institutions. Dialogue is possible about the interrelationship of religious and scientific views. We're freer to relate science and religion, to examine the myths and traditions of religion from a scientific perspective, to discover that there are, as other groups have pointed out, multiple models. We noted that in all events we have limited approach to the truth both in religion and in science. We would expect in our institutions more integration between the sciences and beyond the sciences because of a more holistic view of human experience.

Then there's the third topic, namely, science fields as service fields, with a caveat: not everything that can be done should be done. We can instill a kind of risk/benefit perspective in our students with respect to the pursuit of scientific knowledge of certain kinds and its application. We can make our students sensitive to the problems of resource allocations within society. We also have a need to point up our own personal biases, to show a respect for plurality in our sciences and educate for responsible citizenship, which includes knowledge of scientific advances and possibility. We can avoid scientism (the making of science into a religion) which is a problem in some secular institutions, and recognize the contribution of science to religion and religion to science. We can emphasize the role of stewardship as a Christian ideal.

Fourth, we should work to counteract the negative view of science, pointing out to our students the vast potential for good along with the limitations of science and the possibility of misuse of science.

SHEAHEN (GROUP 5): Our topic was the faith development of scientists. We tried to find commonalities both from our own experiences and from what we think we know about scientists in general. The motivation to develop faith begins with the setting aside of old images in the search for new ones. Very often it is the case that professionals in the sciences do not keep their religious development up to the standards which they have for their professional fields. This is a serious problem which should be worked on in the church-related setting. For example, it's important that adults who are professionals in the sciences also be at an adult level in faith. I didn't hear the word clockmaker mentioned, one of the old images of God which is dismissed by scientists. The god of intimacy is more the god that scientists find. Since their science is an incomplete body of knowledge, awe and wonder are big components of the faith development of scientists.

There was widespread agreement that we need to communicate this image, the values, and so on to our young people in the educational process. It is helpful for scientists with faith to communicate with one another in small communities, in order to articulate the ways in which they engage in apostolic activity. Health care is a good example of engaging in an apostolic activity in the framework of science. This kind of reinforcement in a life of faith can be a valuable asset.

KEILHOLZ: That last point sounds like a commercial message for ITEST as a community of scientists and theologians.

VOICE: One of the other mystical aspects talked about is the experience of limit. That brings a humbling experience, realizing there is an ultimate dependence on God.

BERTRAM: May I presume to speak for all of you when I thank all of you for investing yourselves so imaginatively and resourcefully into the evening's proceedings. I want to thank those who worked as volunteers to identify these isolated questions. It's clear now that we've got more than enough to talk about tomorrow in the sessions that remain. When we do talk about them, we'll talk about them with greater focus.

DISCUSSION

SESSION 6

BRUNGS: Normally I don't do what I'm going to do now, namely, start off the session. But some people will have to be leaving before the end of the meeting. While everybody is still here, I would like to thank Al Panuska for an excellent keynote address and for his excellent interjections into the discussion. For me to say that of a former superior is great testimony. I also want to thank our essayists while they're all here. The meeting simply would not have occurred and would not have been as profitable as it is without them. I want to make a special note of Dr. Chase of Wheaton and Rustum Roy. Though they were not able to attend, they contributed a great deal to our undertaking with the excellent papers they've submitted.

I want to thank all of you. I'm always amazed at these meetings how charitable and how patient people are. I've been to meetings where this simply is not true. The one thing I like most about ITEST meetings, as distinguished, for instance, from American Physical Society meetings, is that we don't run a "prima donna of the meeting" contest. There is no oneupmanship in our meetings. It's refreshing to see people looking, if not for the right answers, at least for the right questions. One of my physics professors years ago used to come into quantum physics class every day and start by saying: "you will not get the right answer if you don't ask the right question. And even if you do get the right answer without asking the right question, you won't know you have it." That's the purpose of these meetings.

I think it's the purpose of the kind of interdisciplinary work we all seem to think we need in our schools -- to help each other come up with the right questions so that we can work toward right answers. One of the major contributions, for instance, that the science faculty can make to the theological and philosophical faculty is to talk to them and help them to pose the right question. Without the right question, we can forget about the right answer. This weekend we've been groping for the right questions. In this context I would like to launch into a little speech. The weekend has been much of what I would call algebra and I think it's time to do what I would call geometry. We've been looking at the "quark" of sci/tech education in church-related schools, and it's time to look at the environment in which the "quark" lives. What is the environment? It is both promising and threatening.

First of all, many of us are religious. Our numbers are decreasing and we're getting older. We aren't going to be around too long, certainly not in terms of the history of the world. We are not going to be replaced by other religious at least in the foreseeable future. Now, this is good.

It's far beyond the time for the laity to be moving into these areas. But there is a down side to this. Almost all of us who are religious have degrees in fields other than science, and it makes interdisciplinary work more natural for us. I have four degrees, only one in science. Losing this is going to affect the campuses, to affect this broader education that we have. The science faculties in church-related schools in the future are not going to have this by and large. There will be a price to pay for that. It's all the more essential that we look at what we are doing and try to get these kinds of initiatives started now.

In the broader context this is the world in which our schools exist. We see the "eastern empire" crumbling back into the nationalities, ethnic and religious groups from which it was forged. We see the ancient hatreds rising. The Azerbaijanis and the Armenians are fighting again. At least it seems that that empire is crumbling. We have to consider seriously whether the "western empire" is not also crumbling for much the same reasons but under a different set of circumstances. When I had John Murray in theology 30 years ago, he was even then worrying that American society and American education was excessively pluralistic. Will our society degenerate into an aggregate? I think we can see that it well might do so. That's what a "philosophy of privacy" (I am my own arbiter in all ways of what I think and what I do) leads to. That's a significant danger to our society. It's a real danger to education. We are not our own arbiters. We are not the creators and designers of reality. We must realize that we have to live in a reality that is a given.

I'm not worried about what's going on in the cosmologies. They're presenting whole new sets of data, whole new issues. But by and large, they are not going to touch our daily lives. Scientific writers are promising us a new human on the biological level. Our religious tradition promises us a new human on the eschatological level. This is going to affect our lives. It's going to affect our bodies, and that's pretty immanent to who we are. We have to approach sci/tech education in the context of these issues. They present challenge, they present menace, and they present enormous opportunity. How does the new human promised us by science relate to the eschatological new human of Christian revelation? Is there any relation beyond the two "new humans"? How can we help each new human feed upon the other and help it grow? That's a serious question facing church-related education. How can we bring these two concepts of what it means to be human, one immanent, one eschatological to point accurately to the new human promised us in Christ?

We would serve our society, science, and Christianity by looking at that question. I'm not giving an answer; I don't know an answer. Nonetheless, I think that's a valid question.

That's what I mean by context. We must do more than just teach science. We have to teach science well, as science. I don't want the physicists teaching ethics, and I don't want the ethicists teaching physics. But if we can work together on our campuses, we can work on an overarching question -- who is this new human? -- in our institutions, as a genuinely interdisciplinary focus. We can cooperate in seeking the proper questions.

Finally, I want to take this opportunity to thank Bob Bertram who routinely does a superb job as moderator of these meetings. I also want to thank Sr. Marianne for sitting out there taping the meeting and doing all the work she's doing. I want to thank Bernice Morris for 17 years of devoted labor and loyal service to ITEST. I thank them all very much.

BERTRAM: Well, folks, we've got our agenda. Thanks to the superb way in which you all as a group took that challenge last evening, we're presented with a somewhat sharper focus to our discussion than we might have had. I suggest that we keep the questions that you considered in your small group discussions last evening in our consciousness this morning. If there are very compelling reasons for your dealing with issues that are not embraced in those three, then, of course, feel free to do so. There's no need to confine ourselves to one topic at a time.

KEILHOLZ: There are two people here who had important roles in the development of my faith and my scientific training. I want to acknowledge that. Sr. Leona Truchan was my professor of biology and advisor at Alverno College in Milwaukee when I was in school there. And Sr. Rosemary Connell was my professor of biology and advisor at Fontbonne. I'm moved by that. It always seems to me that at these meetings we come back to talking about the human person, the qualities which make us human. For me, one of the most important is the ability to have relationships with other human beings.

It may be true, as Bob has pointed out, that the numbers of religious are dwindling, but I hope you will never forget that you have touched the lives of many, many people. None of us have any idea of our impact on others. For me, this is a rare opportunity to be present with two people who are not aware of what an important part they played in my life. I hope that my life is worthy of the gift that they have given me.

BERTRAM: I'm sure it adds nothing to what Peggy just said for me to come in, as the egghead, and explain that the genre in which she just now spoke is what in the history of theology is called a confessio. Remember Moliere's comedy in which the man who suddenly became rich and, therefore, was accelerated into a higher class of French society felt he had to equip himself for his new social expectations. He took dancing lessons and instruction in rhetoric. He comes home from his rhetoric lesson and says, "Guess what I learned today? All my life I have been speaking prose." Many Christians, without knowing the name for it, give testimony. The rest of you might use what Peggy has said as a trigger to ask the Brungsian question perhaps -- remember, it wasn't an answer, it was the question -- whether the sort of thing that Peggy Keilholz has benefited from under the tutelage of Sr. Leona and Sr. Rosemary might begin to qualify for what Brungs asks concerning the new human. Well, that's just a sub-question to that question.

BYERS: Bob, I'm more optimistic than you are on the religious. I don't know if they will be replaced in the same form, but I don't think the religious have died yet. When I asked for the floor yesterday, I wanted to comment on the Galileo case. As it happened, I had the latest copy of Origins with me. The Pope has made another speech on science and faith. The side bar contains a little bit of history on the Galileo affair I thought I'd read that into the record:

"Pope John Paul II's rehabilitation of Galileo began in 1979 in a speech to the Pontifical Academy of Sciences in which he used the Galileo case to illustrate his belief that there should be no irreconcilable tensions between science and faith. The following year he created a commission to restudy the Galileo trial while he continued to speak sympathetically about Galileo in speeches to scientists. The commission finally proposed in 1984 that the Holy Office judges were wrong in condemning Galileo. The findings were published in 1984 with an introduction by then Archbishop Paul Poupard who, now a Cardinal, is currently head of the Pontifical Council of Culture. Galileo's judges 'committed an objective error,' the Archbishop said in part, and related the error to the prevailing mood at the time in which science and religion were integrally linked. Galileo's views 'seemed to shake the whole theological structure' and the judges believed 'he had violated a point of Catholic doctrine.' The error is a healthy warning against confusing faith with points that can be changed by time." That's where we are with the Galileo affair. At least at the level of the Vatican that confession has been made and reconciliation hopefully can proceed.

I would like to comment on one other thing. When we were in our small group yesterday, I was reflecting on our small but not insignificant experience in the Human Values Committee with dialogue with the scientists. Although it's too pat, it helps to look at the overall situation this way. Perhaps in Galileo's time, the church was overly confident that it had the "Truth" and was not willing to listen to what Galileo was saying. It's more complex than that, but I think that is the premise. It is also true now that the matter has largely reversed itself. The scientific community believes it has the "Truth," with a capital T. Individuals will back off from that if pressed. In the atmosphere of this dialogue, the hardest thing is to get the bishops to say anything because they're almost unconsciously intimidated by the scientists and by the drumbeat of propaganda, for lack of a better word, over the last 100 years that science is the only way to truth.

There is an interesting reversal when religious people in effect ask whether they can say something in this forum? We are defensive; no, not defensive, we are shy, very, diffident. Scientists are saying, "Well, we'll listen to what you have to say." It's an interesting phenomenon and it took me by surprise and flip-flopped the images that one has of the religious establishment. The religious establishment, when it engages science, is remarkably self-conscious and unsure of itself. As we continue the planning for a conference, it's useful to bear that in mind.

KEEFE: I'd like to speak to the matter of the interface that Dave has been discussing and relate it to a few things that have been perennial problems at once in theology and in ecumenism. Generally one may suppose that the discussion of the interrelation of science and religion has certain dimensions of an ecumenical project. One of the problems that we continually run into is a very general understanding of the terms which is sufficiently ambiguous to permit statements to be made whose intelligibility suffers from that vagueness. For instance, theology and religion tend to be lumped together. And as Dave has remarked, science has a tendency to be identified simply with the truth of the material world. Let me explain what I mean. An historian writing a history of some particular period or event is governed by the data before him. His work is a synthetic effect which at his most optimistic he would not identify with the actual conditions for history which actually happened. That which actually happened is always a bit beyond the attainment of the historian.

Thus, the faith presents a challenge to a theological inquiry which is never complete. I might presume, without having any scientific training, that by analogy it may also be said that the scientist is continually questioning a reality which continues to respond to him and will not cease so to do. Thus, one does not identify history with what the historian does or physical reality with what the scientist does or the faith with what the theologian does. Yet when we see statements such as science brings us to God, it sounds to me very much like saying theology brings one to God.

There is a theological tradition which indeed hopes that to be the case. It's the tradition that moves out of Augustine, Anselm and Bonaventure, the Augustinian tradition, which intends to be a faith seeking an understanding. It operates, when it operates at all, only in prayer. There's no doubt whatever that any human inquiry so can operate. Faith is not limited simply to religious questions. It's an overall grasp and appropriation of the free truth of the concrete order in which we live. But it's very difficult to keep that in mind.

Last evening I came in during the discussion and so I missed some of it. Dr. Procaccini came out with a very insightful and provocative statement about the unity of scientific insight with artist insight, and this is precisely what the Augustinian tradition has insisted upon since Augustine first remarked about the ancient beauty he had found too late. This ancient beauty which is forever new is something we all find too late. But we continue to seek it and in the end, please God, we shall find it. We find it, however, only in terms of prayer.

For Augustine to seek the truth was to seek an ordered free unity which could only be called beauty. In contemporary theology, people such as von Balthasar, who has written a theology of aesthetics or an aesthetical theology if you prefer, realize this. This attempt sees the unity of truth as free, as something that escapes conceptualization in a sense of being always transcendent to the best that we can articulate. Our articulation is not false, but it's always an additive. What draws us on is the lure of beauty, the desire to possess an order of freedom which transcends us but which is at the same time very much our own.

There is no question that when we understand, we understand in a moment of appropriation of this beauty in a fleeting sort of fashion. It's what an artist does; it's what a scientist does; it's what anyone does when they seek to understand and after much struggle make some slight advance by which they see. The only word that can describe the unity of that insight is clarity. It is not a conceptual necessity; It can't be reduced to necessity. It has the clarity of a work of art, the clarity of beauty. When we try to articulate it, then we begin to stumble.

I would expect that Bach, whenever he wrote a fugue, ended up dissatisfied with what he had done. The few artists that I have known never seem to be entirely satisfied with their work. Writers re-write and re-re-write to make their work better. Many of them finally drive their publishers to despair. We all are dissatisfied with our work to the extent that it's not perfect. That will always confront us.

That relates to what integrity, this search for beauty, might be. If it is free, it's obviously debated. One cannot reduce it to necessity, one cannot show that it must be this way. That it is this way is gift. If one is doing theology, this is easier to understand. Theologians have a tendency to confuse this gift with a kind of voluntarism; but in the end, if one is going to do theology, one must accept the given, the gift character of the historical order. For a theologian, this is generally a doctrinal, a Biblical, a confessional tradition. For the physicist, this is the free data that comes to him through a dial, a telescope, a detector in the lab, or whatever. It comes to him as truth, as something upon which he may rely utterly. He may not understand it but the data don't lie. While his or her interpretation of them, however, is always doubtful, the data are sound.

Take this problem of the interrelation of science and religion -- religion not theology. Take science in the broad sense of the appreciation of the splendor of the material order of the world -- of majestic science of which we have been hearing. That's a good term. If we look at science and religion in this context, the great question is always going to be how to preserve the freedom of those percepts which make it all worthwhile. There is in theology always a tendency to rationalize, to reduce this free truth to an accessory. At the moment when the Augustinian tradition peaked in Bonaventure, it was recognized that one understands the material, singular, historical reality before us by an intellectual (not a sense) intuition. That is to say, the "isness" of the thing is given us not conceptually but through an existential apperception.

Hardly had that been grasped than its condition of possibility, an ongoing illumination by which the mind is freed of its own necessities, was said by Scotus and by those after him to be unnecessary. Their Aristotelian logic had by then begun to declare -- and there was a tendency to suppose -- that what is true is true because it cannot not be true. Its truth has the structure then not of freedom, not of beauty, not of rectitude, not of that integrity which is personal, but of an integrity which is impersonal, necessitarian, and determinist. This has happened in theology over and over again, and not least within the Jesuit tradition. One might think here of Suarez whose work underlies that of Descartes.

If we're going to maintain the historicity of the theological enterprise, it's only going to be done in reliance upon an historical God. For the theologian this is a doctrinal, a confessional tradition. I say this to explain why I objected to the non-doctrinal emphasis which I thought I heard in Fr. Panuska's willingness to accept a certain failure of traditional orthodoxy on a campus. I'm speaking specifically about the presence of atheism and so on. It is very clear that you cannot in any university prescribe belief. Belief is free. There is no way in which it could possibly be forced. To try to force doctrine, to try to force dogma, is clearly a waste of time. Nonetheless, a certain self-identity in an educational operation seems to me to be utterly necessary. If there is no sense of historical identity, we begin to look upon the truth we're seeking in nonhistorical terms. If we look for truth in nonhistorical terms, the community of the university then is threatened by doctrine and at the same time another kind of orthodoxy begins to replace it. There have been enough incidents of this in the past to require no particular illustration.

We must remember when we are seeking the union of truth which is scientific and truth which is religious that we are dealing with historical inquiries. Ultimately what is at issue is the very meaning of history. Is this a theological category? Can it be said that the world with which the scientist is concerned is the world that God made good? Does not the goodness of this world, its freedom, underlie the free scientific inquiry upon which the experimental method rests? I've raised that point in a number of these conferences. It is by no means a novel idea. In physics today in the persons of people like Capra, in Ernest Mach a few generations ago, there is a tendency to discover a nonhistorical truth, a tendency to look upon the world in terms that can only be called Buddhist or Hindu. This seeks a soteriology from history, a salvation from history, a tendency to find the truth in ideas only and not in the world about us. It is difficult under those circumstances to understand how an experimental inquiry, the very life blood of science itself, can take place. If we do not take the world about us as the source of our information, we're going to find it in our own pointy little heads. Then our quest becomes impersonal. We are simply seeking a pure, nonconcrete, nonhistorical truth and the search is going to dehistoricize us. We cannot do otherwise. This has been spelled out too often in the history of ideas even to be a matter of very great interest.

The notion that one fulfills one's humanity with a free spontaneity is something that came in with the Old Testament, with the old Covenant. It is verified continually in the New. It is by this kind of free commitment to a Good Creation that we image God. It is, therefore, true that a scientist who seeks the truth in this fashion cannot but seek God, because God is present in his world. It is by His presence that the world is good. Now, he may not be clearly conscious of this. I don't mean here to speak in terms of Rahner's notion of an anonymous Christianity. It's not necessary to impose Christianity on people merely because they're doing physics. Nonetheless, there is in this a certain dogmatic background, and that can be lost. This is a free inquiry. When it begins to be pursued under terms of necessity, when you begin to identify theology and religion, science and reality, then there's no longer any need to check your science by theology, if you check your theology by doctrine. This is a danger to both sides. It makes a very bad theology. I'll leave it to the scientists as to whether it makes bad science. I suspect it does.

FORD (ST. LOUIS): I give talks at high schools, and my latest topic begins with the question of Galileo. I ask them what they can tell me about Galileo. The students invariably tell me that he was suppressed for his teachings. Then I ask how many of them are aware that within the last 50 years a first rate physicist was destroyed, was killed because he advocated the Einsteinian view of relativistic physics. It's almost unknown, but the Soviet physicist, Boris Hessen, died in a Gulag 50 years ago for advocating the Einsteinian view. I wish I could give you a good reference to the story. And he was not the only one. Mark Bronshtein disappeared into the Gulag for the same reason. Nikolai Vavilov, the famous geneticist who died in the Gulag in 1943. The 20th century is the era of the destruction of science for advancing valid scientific truth.

There is a Soviet scientist whom I am studying, who also disappeared into the Gulag 50 years ago. He started as a mathematician. The title of the paper I'm writing is "The Religious Roots of Modern Soviet Mathematics." This person plays the key role. He left Moscow State University in 1904, having been perhaps one of the most brilliant math students they ever had. He then went to the Moscow Theological Academy. He was a professor there, with brilliant promise, when it was closed in 1918 after the revolution. He returned to his science and made significant and notable contributions to science in the Soviet Union. He was a naturalist, a biologist, an artist. He taught perspective drawing and wrote about iconography. He was a mathematician and a physicist. He wrote a defense of Dante on the basis of the modern relativity theory. The whole point of his life and work was to say not only is science in no way incompatible with theology but, in fact, it's just the reverse of that. And he himself was, as it were, living proof of that.

His name was Pavel Florensky. There's no name that is being urged forward more urgently today under glasnost than the name Pavel Florensky. "Science and Religion," the publication of the leading atheist society of the Soviet Union last January carried a biography of Florensky, and published the letters that he wrote showing the scientific investigations that he carried on after he had been sentenced to the Gulag. Right up to the end, he was studying permafrost while he was freezing to death in Siberia. He never gave up his scientific inquiries nor his urge to contribute to society, to advance scientific knowledge. He never wavered in this until he was finally done in. The letters are tragic, the most dramatic letters in the history of science perhaps.

In the Soviet Union the theologians -- remember the Galileo case here -- have plenty to say to science. This man went into the Gulag because, in the 1920s, the notion was that once science appears, theology will evaporate like the mist. But he was one of the leading figures in the electrification of Russia, one of the greatest achievements of the revolution. Because he went to those meetings wearing his pectoral cross and black cassock, he was eventually arrested and not allowed to continue. I offer that as an additional comment on the situation that Dave Byers described. The religious community feels itself on the defensive, but, at least in some areas, the situation is really quite the opposite.

VOICE: When was he killed?

FORD (ST. LOUIS): In 1938, probably.

VOICE: He was a Russian Orthodox priest?

FORD (ST. LOUIS): A Russian Orthodox priest. I've written a still unpublished paper on him.

BERTRAM: Take what Don Keefe said about history and the freedom in which the historical reality is given to us, and then to use Charles Ford's telling history as a case in point, ask what kind of connections you could draw between those two. That would in itself be a project in relating a historical science at least -- you didn't speak as a mathematician, you spoke as an historian -- to an effort by a theologian. I guess it would take us an hour just to find the entry point to pursue that, but I couldn't help but notice how engaged you all were as Charles Ford spoke. What Lonergan speaks to is attentiveness to the particularities, the concretenesses of the history. I can't help but think it has been something more than an accident.

PERRINE: I have a lot of sympathy with those who condemned Galileo at the time. It's hard to see how anyone but Galileo could have realized how wrong they were, because it would be difficult to extricate what was bad science in the Old Testament and what was good theology.

I was thinking of something that came up in conversation last night about the unique contribution of church-related schools to science education. I'm fairly sure that something which science never will provide us, and something which religion and world views always provide us, is the conviction that there's some meaning to life beyond death. That I think any church-related school will provide and it really enhances the argument and changes the outcome of a lot of decisions. When we have a conviction from some transcendent source that death is not an ultimate tragedy that has to be fled at any cost, we make different decisions with regard to things like people dying of cancer, or things like organ transplants. There's a million areas where there's a different behavioral and concrete outcome because of a conviction that death has some meaning, that there's a possibility of meaning and existence beyond the termination of this physical existence. That can be a very important and indispensable contribution of the church-related school which can't come up in a secular context.

EAGAN: In terms of this discussion of the importance of history and the sensitivity to it, I'm thinking how practically we might think again about how a religiously integrated or religiously oriented school could contribute to science and technology education. I think it's important if there's going to be contribution of church-related schools to science and technology education, it's important to think about the impact or effect scientific and technical development can have in a society. And that's a very dimly understood subject. In my field, there are people who try to get at the social and economic impacts of science and technology. This is a difficult subject. But there has been some progress.

Some kinds of impacts can be referred to as resource freeing. When the steam engine was first brought on line in England, it was used to pump water out of the mines. It simply replaced donkeys or horses that had driven the pumps. The English weren't doing anything new. They used the steam engine to do what they had always been doing, but it was a resource freeing effect. On the other hand, there are scientific and technical developments that enhance human capability. Someone got the idea of putting that steam engine on wheels which ran on tracks. That simply by a quantum leap increased the capability of travel on the part of the English.

Also, there are times when scientific and technical development simply redefine or define a new reality. When Galileo put those lenses in that brass tube and looked at the cosmos, human understanding of cosmology, our place in the universe, was altered significantly. In today's world, we have to think about those three possibilities. The resource freeing possibility presents little problem. I don't see anybody in a religiously oriented school having any difficulty with that. The religiously oriented have little difficulty with the enhancing effects of scientific and technical development. What seem to be driving our concerns are the impacts that really are altering the human conception of our place in the universe. Such developments as the pill, for example, simply altered the choice many Americans or many people had. Such things as amniocentesis, for better or for worse, altered people's choices in significant ways and redefined for them their possibilities and their desires.

If we're going to plan a conference to get at this question, it ought to be understood that scientific and technical development have a variety of possibilities. We ought to take that into account in determining the agenda of such a conference.

ACKER: I would like to talk about the church and Galileo. Galileo was right but for the wrong reason. The church has not been given enough credit for understanding that. Galileo used the proof from the tides. The sloshing up of the tides was proof to Galileo that the earth was indeed not the center of the universe. Ernan McMullen and Gingrich had an article in the Scientific American at least ten years ago about the Galileo affair. Galileo interchanged the major and minor premises in deduction when he saw that Venus underwent all phases. And he said that, if Venus undergoes all phases, not just crescent phases, the system was heliocentric. Galileo was called to task even at that time for interchanging the major and minor premises in deduction.

Tycho Brahe produced another system which would also have made Venus show all phases. Just because the streets are wet doesn't mean it was raining. They could be wet for a number of other reasons. The church is getting a bad rap on Galileo. When we talk to these high school students we ought to show them that the church wasn't so bad. After all, the proof for the heliocentric universe was never even discovered until about 1834 when Bessel had an instrument that was sensitive enough to know parallax. The ancients had been looking for parallax for a long time and could never find it.

Galileo was right, but he was right for the wrong reason. The church had every reason to question Galileo more thoroughly. We jumped on the bandwagon too fast about the truth of theology and scripture and everything. Galileo told the church that the Bible is to tell us how to go to heaven, not how the heavens go. He was quoting the Vatican librarian, Baronius. That is not an original statement of Galileo's.

I've looked into this a lot because of teaching at the seminary. I'm trying to teach these priests that there's more than one side to the Galileo affair. We have to be very careful as members of the church not to step on today's bandwagon about Galileo.

SEIBERT: I'd like to note one other church/science relationship in the relatively recent past. In the mid 1930s Archbishop McNicholas of Cincinnati established the Academy Divi Thomae which was a series of educational institutions. Within it he set up the school that he called the Institutum Divi Thomae. It was a graduate school offering only four graduate degrees, both masters and doctorates in science and theology. At that time only priests and religious men and women, could attend it. Later on it was opened to lay people. The Archbishop's entire idea was to invite priests in his own diocese and religious men and women to come to this to study science and theology. You had to have a background in one to get in to study the other.

I had the honor of going there for two years. We were expected to go back to our colleges and do research. As far as I know we were among the first undergraduate schools who were getting their undergraduates to do scientific research.

PANUSKA: I'm about to depart, but I thought that I should respond to Don Keefe. Don, I really do appreciate your historical perception and learning. I'm jealous of it. It's my weakness that I don't have that perception and I could learn a great deal from you. But I think that you did not understand fully my side bar observation about the possible spring element or even value in tolerating some seriously distorted voices on the church-related campus. I'm not encouraging this, but tolerating it and seeing that it can help in the total educational environment if the environment is positive enough and supportive enough. I just wanted to say that, but I think we could talk a great deal about what's involved in that.

MURPHY: I want to pick up on Sr. Angelice's comment. At least with some of the small women's colleges in New England, research was a requirement for graduation for a chemistry major. I graduated in 1950 from St. Joseph's College in Connecticut where that was a requirement. So all of us were doing this before NSF was doing any funding for undergraduate research. The research itself was done on a major requirement basis and you had to do it. Some of that work was published. Since that time, St. Joseph's College has managed to have undergraduate research grants almost as often as the rules would permit. You get it for two years and then you have to step aside for a while. I also know that Mount Holyoke had that as an undergraduate requirement as well. So I don't think it was that rare back then. I think it was rather more common but people weren't talking about it. There's a report from the National Advisory Board regarding funding from the National Science Foundation. One of the points that they made in that report is that they would like to encourage undergraduate work and have as one of its components undergraduate research and their researching faculty to do it. Undergraduate research has been around a long time. It's not universal, particularly at large universities. But the smaller colleges I think were doing this way back and probably are continuing to do it well today.

BERTRAM: Let me ask a question. Suppose you took the trends of citations that we just now got from Sr. Mary Ellen and from Sr. Angelice which I suspect are best case scenarios of church-related colleges, and then let's remember Sr. Angelice's caution last evening, not necessarily to press for what's unique about church-related colleges but the somewhat more modest question of what is characteristic of them. Would anyone venture a guess as to why in these best case church-related experiences there is that kind of encouragement for undergraduate research or the kind of research that you described in this Institute of St. Thomas. Does that have anything to do in your imagination with the fact that they were related to the church? Not unique to the church, but characteristic of the church.

CONNELL: In a way Sr. Mary Ellen answered that because she mentioned that Mount Holyoke was doing the same kind of thing. But it's my own personal opinion -- partly out of experience and also from hearing other people -- there was a movement in many colleges in the '50s and even in the '60s toward teaching and away from research, even research for science majors. I came back from Notre Dame hoping to begin research, and I did for a short while. But the big thing was, no, you have to teach so many courses; that's why you were educated. I know that there were people who finished at other institutions and went back to other colleges and it was the same kind of thing. That's when the colleges were attracting larger numbers of students and not necessarily larger numbers of faculty. So the emphasis was on teaching. It was hard to persuade an administrator who was not a scientist that research should be part of teaching.

One, a psychologist, saw no reason for that kind of thing. She was not into experimental psychology herself and the whole thing was teaching. Therefore, if you do research, do it on your own time and do dorm duty, and all the other things that were done in those days. The background and the personality of the administrator and the emphasis on teaching, particularly where we had a lot of people going out to teach -- large education departments -- all were part of this.

BERTRAM: I gather that you are saying, Rosemary, between your lines that it would have been more like a church-related college if there had been occasion for research as well as for teaching. My question is what's churchy about that?

CONNELL: I don't think it was churchy. I think we would have sent out better prepared scientists. If Mount Holyoke did it and St. Joseph's in Connecticut did it, it was because they were good colleges that had an understanding of what their students needed, not because they were church-related.

BERTRAM: But I gather church-related colleges do what good colleges do. And one of the good things to do is to do research.

CONNELL: And one of the good things to do in the '50s and '60s was to send out people prepared to teach.

MCLOUGHLIN: I think that in chemistry it's almost universal that, while it's not required to do undergraduate research in a state institution or a private institution, it is most strongly encouraged. Every institution that I have been in strongly encouraged that the undergraduates do undergraduate research, whether it's a state or a private institution. In fact, the American Chemical Society gives credit to the institutions that strongly encourage this. So I don't think that it's unique, at least in chemistry, to do undergraduate research.

CROSS: There's an up side to undergraduate research. I'm talking about that thrill of discovery that we've been giving testimony to, namely, how wonderful it is to be a scientist. The down side is that being a scientist can be terribly tedious. And I think in a church-related institution the notion of scientists as servants is an important concept, especially in the contemporary atmosphere in our country which is very egoistically oriented. I would think that, if there's anything unique about our church-related institutions, it's providing a larger perspective on the nature of a life of service than secular institutions do.

SKEHAN: I'd like to follow up on the idea of undergraduate research. I'm most familiar with Boston College. I had the privilege of founding the undergraduate geology department. The undergraduate research flowed from the need that I had to do research. Also, we were understaffed in the early days and we needed to offer some other course credits. We could do that with the undergraduate research. Another necessity that became a virtue was to expand, offer and require of our majors courses in mathematics and physics and chemistry which has been highly praised in theological circles because it was not the trend. It came partly out of necessity and partly because there were no other faculty.

Some of these things that come out of necessity can also be virtues. I'd offer that as a partial explanation in addition to the need that I had to have some associates in undergraduate research.

BERTRAM: I wonder if I could try my hand once more at what I tried rather fumblingly to do earlier. The church-related colleges, even in best case scenarios, simply do what any good college would do. It strikes me as a wonderfully Christian understanding of church-related colleges. Might it not be though that one of the strange chemistries about what's Christian is that Christians do what any good human would be doing. In that sense, Christians are not distinctive, but they do what any good human being would do for very distinctive reasons. They have reasons for doing what everybody does and the reasons they have are not those which everybody has. There is nothing more distinctive than the kind of historical givenness of God's gift to us in Christ Jesus.

That may seem to put us back at ground zero where we started this conference. In other words, the gap may seem to be unbridgeable between the faith and the reality which sciences probe. I guess what I'm fishing for is whether we can take something which good church-related colleges do and, nevertheless, attempt to make a link, provide reasons for their doing what any good college would do out of the very distinctive thing called Christian faith. Can we do this without falling into making up, manufacturing, good reasons for bad deeds? So, it's not ideology. I would think that we need not be put off by the fact that Christians are not distinctive necessarily in their institutional behavior, but they are distinctive in their reason giving. Ultimately they are. But that means drawing connections.

DISCUSSION

SESSION 7

BERTRAM: When you receive the printed transcript of the discussions of this conference, you'll be impressed at how articulate everybody was thanks to the work of the Holy Spirit and Bob Brungs who can somehow improve on us. Watch for how often in the course of the two days someone has thrown out -- you can tell them by retrospect -- rather provocative suggestions that were not taken up for further discussion. As a friend of mine would say, it felt like bird dogging into the porridge, you know, just swallowed up and never heard from again.

If we had pursued all these leads, we might have made the world a better place. I was reminded of that during the coffee break. One of you said that you had noted that an almost unchallenged term in our parlance here has been the term church-related college, as though that were some univocal given, when in fact we all know out of the other side of our heads that there are church-related colleges and there are church-related colleges. You'll remember how yesterday morning Fr. Brungs had the floor for a moment and made, as he called it, a very modest observation, that he assumed that church-related colleges are related to the church. Now, perhaps as a provocation, that was rather subtle, but I know Brungs well enough to know that he really meant to get a rise out of us.

We promptly proceeded to breeze on ahead on our merry way. That's one instance of many. I know that several of you -- I could tell by the twinkle in your eye as you spoke -- couldn't wait to get finished with your statement and then sit back and savor the response that you would get. It was never forthcoming. That's probably part of the sheer givenness of the free creator about whom Don Keefe was talking. We don't always pick up on those gifts.

ACKER: I think that one of the reasons that church-related colleges were so effective in promoting research was the vow of celibacy. I don't know how provocative that's going to be. It's related to John Cross' point about service. It takes a great deal of time to ready a student in research, especially an undergraduate. Research is brand new to them, and this takes an untold amount of time. You can give it only because you have time yourself. I speak from experience. At the risk of sounding arrogant, I've had 14 Westinghouse Science Talent Search winners in the past. I'm no longer in the church-related college where I did that work, but I did the work in a very highfalutin high school where I had to start freshmen out with research -- 14 year olds -- in order to have them reach Westinghouse caliber by the time they were seniors. You can take those tests only when you're a senior. These were all girls whom I directed from about 1959 until 1978 when my last one, before I left high school teaching, went to the international fair in San Francisco and got the biggest prize there, a trip to the Nobel Prize ceremonies in Stockholm. The service was available because I had the time. I gave my life to that. I did not have another family. This was my life. That's one reason why church-related colleges were in the forefront in the research.

BERTRAM: First, you just disproved the statement I made a moment before you spoke. One of the provocative leads that I thought had been quickly overlooked was John Cross' comment about servanthood this morning. I think he thought so too. John made another provocative comment yesterday about communication which I'm still waiting to have responded to. But right now he's batting 500. Some of you may not know that my wife and I live in St. Louis and I teach in Chicago. I spend half a week up in Chicago and half a week here, so I'm a part-time celibate. I've the best of both worlds. You've heard it said, there's nothing like being a little pregnant. Well, it's something like being a little celibate.

MURPHY: I want to add some of the reasons why I feel the church-related schools or at least schools who had a positive attitude toward research for undergraduates were fairly successful. One of the factors is size. If it's not the size, it's the human environment rather than the physical environment with its instrumentation, equipment and library resources. The human environment important here is the fact that the students and faculty knew each other and interacted closely. In other words, the students had a mentor or guide who was in fairly close contact with them. When it came to needing someone to direct their undergraduate requirement, they had someone that they could look to. Whatever the advice and whatever the direction, it was adequate. The research may not have been world shaking, but it was an authentic research experience. These factors are somewhat responsible. Even in large universities, if anyone has gotten turned on in their major because of an undergraduate research experience, it's due to a fairly close contact probably with a faculty member.

Also, one of the problems with getting authentic research going with an undergraduate is that the faculty members themselves do not and maybe have not had an authentic experience. Their only research may have been in graduate school. It may have been holding on to get this done, because it was part of the degree requirement; if they had had their druthers, they wouldn't have chosen that topic at all.

We should help faculty to know what is or isn't authentic research. Most times people really don't stop to think what goes into research and what would make that experience authentic. I had the advantage of eight years in industry before I started teaching. Research and projects may have been easier for me. But the longer I've been in higher education, the more I realize that there are faculty who never knew what they should have been doing. We have to go back to the first principle of science. We should teach science for wherever we are. In other words, in a rural area we teach it for a rural area. In San Diego, we teach it from the beach. In Maine, we teach it in the snow. We have to have that kind of a perspective. Some higher education faculty aim for something beyond the students. They, the undergraduates particularly, need something beyond them and challenging, but not so far beyond that it turns them off.

As it turns out, the undergraduate experience in research is usually very good. But if the faculty member is not comfortable with this or hasn't the time for it, we should look at the attitude toward research in itself and at what kinds of projects would be appropriate for an undergraduate. If we look at these two questions, we might have an easier time of putting the two together.

BERTRAM: The theologian in me still asks, perhaps over asks, whether some or all of these people in close contact with their professors owe any part of their inclination toward close contact from growing up with a God who is willing to be in close contact with them in Christ. That may be stretching things. Is part of the thrill, the satisfaction of research, the thrill of surprises, imbedded in a God relationship which has taught us to expect the most outrageous surprises? That, too, might be stretching things, but theologians are in the business of stretching things.

FORD (NY): We've been circling around a subject dear to my heart, probably reflecting my Presbyterian/Quaker/Methodist origins and a long string of family members who have engaged in preaching and teaching. When I started out, my goal was to be a teacher. I failed miserably. If I had been successful, I'd be in Cape May, New Jersey watching birds. I landed in teacher education by choice.

In making these remarks I'm influenced by several conversations I've had about the condition of teacher education, Fr. Brungs' concern for the future, and a little anecdote about Msgr. Cassidy, a Dominican, who used to teach at Providence College in the federally funded program focused on young scientists. He taught either Fauci or Gallo -- the one of them who heads the National Cancer Institute. He took great pride in describing that Providence College experience to a group of us at Pope John XXIII Institute in Braintree, with which my college was meeting to discuss a possible alliance. That typifies what a church-related college is and what undergraduate teaching is. As learned and insightful as we may be, it doesn't matter unless we follow Benedict's notion that, if it's important, we'd better bring the young into the picture.

I've been out of direct involvement in teacher education for 20 years. I was a professor of higher education at St. Louis University, and I was reluctantly the director of student teaching. It was a route to becoming a professor of higher education in my first love, the history of American higher education. I'm may be wrong in what I'm going to say. Teacher education has its ups and downs, good times and hard times, for many reasons, part cultural and part the view (and behavior) of departments of education. They have a tendency to alienate in a discipline which is not a discipline.

Being in a medical college and having been raised on a farm, it's easy for me to compare agriculture, medicine, and education and their vaster disciplines. They don't exist in themselves. They are rooted in basic disciplines. The education of the teacher is a function of psychology, philosophy, theosophy, sociology, and from our perspective, theology. That distinguishes us in the church-related college from the non-church-related college.

I'd like to make an important subpoint on that. It may help the church-related question on the board. When I was director of student teaching, I was struck by the difference in placing teachers in Lutheran and Catholic and public and private schools in Missouri and Illinois. I directed a program that grew rapidly and attracted the best students. This was followed up in my experience at Fontbonne College. It was apparent to me, without any solid study of the subject, that the private or the church-related educated teacher had characteristics distinguishing them from those who went to college somewhere in rural Missouri. With all due respect to the state college system, they were old Teachers' Colleges. There were no business schools. There wasn't much science. They were very narrowly conceived then. They're better now. The dedication Sister Joan mentioned, as well as what's required to become a good teacher, made the church-related colleges' teacher a better teacher. Their state in life didn't matter, because they had an infusion of the apostolate of teaching. Somewhere they picked up the Augustinian notion that Christ taught through them, that they were voices of the Spirit.

I live in Bridgeport, Connecticut, and we disarm our students as they enter school. One of the local football coaches was just murdered. The schools are centers for drugs. Teachers and students sell drugs. There's a new superintendent in the city of New York -- I'm very much involved by virtue of our college and the city of New York and its problems -- chosen from Miami Dade in Florida. He's Hispanic; he's a dropout; he understands. We hope it works. He's got a tough assignment. First, he has to disarm the school. Then he has to restore teacher morale. He has to create school boards, and so forth.

It's nice here on the banks of the Mississippi, but let's go back to our campuses and look at our responsibility as deans, physicists, psychologists, theologians, philosophers, and look at our teacher education departments. I'd like you to go home and embrace your teacher education department. If they are pariahs on your faculty, bring them back into the mainstream. If they've been pushed to the physical periphery of your campus, bring them back to the center. Force them, lure them, shake them and cajole them to play their part within the ITEST mainstream that Fr. Brungs and his group represents. Here we're talking only about science. We could say the same thing about international studies. What we don't know about the rest of the world, or about the humanities or about language or about history or about how to read and write a new mathematics and so on!

There seems to be a resurgence of interest in teacher education and new ways to prepare teachers to enter our public and private school classrooms. In Connecticut, for example, one does not need to have a certificate to enter the classroom. There's an alternate route. Of course, the educators and the bureaucracy are fighting it. What else does a Ph.D. in anatomy do but go out and teach anatomy to the rest of our people? So we're all, regardless of the institution, involved in teacher education. I've painted a narrow, uninformed and perhaps too dismal a picture of teacher education. If I've touched a glimmer of truth in any of your campuses, I hope that the point sinks in. Not much will matter unless we serve by going out into our schools.

Fr. Maurice McNamee, now 80, former chairman of English at St. Louis University, called me one day many years ago and said, "Charlie, all of our English majors, who want to be teachers and are very good students, know nothing about teaching English, teaching grammar and about the role of teaching itself." So McNamee, Ford, and others coordinated a course taught by members of the faculty of the English department who gained a pedagogical sense from the pedagogues in the education department. I hope that we produced better English teachers. There was a professor of English who went to a department of education. I hope professors of biology, chemistry, physics, and mathematics draw their educators back into the mainstream of teacher education.

JABLONSKI: One of the things that should characterize our church-related institutions -- and gatherings like this as opposed to our professional scientific meetings -- is our realization that we're led by the God of the covenant who continues to speak to us and to lead us. With that kind of trust, we're doing more than sharing our views. We believe there's something within and beyond us, and therefore, in our institutions as well. When we design a mission statement we state how we're being led within that institution. Perhaps one of the important things for us as scientists is helping to articulate the theology of a science ministry. There's a lot of discussion about the lay ministry and a theology of ministry. What is the theology of a science ministry? We can look at it from a Christological basis in terms of our ministry as complete professionals. That term means some kind of relationship with God, relationship to self and self-knowledge in a holistic way. It includes a service dimension.

It's going to be the Christian laity who will carry out this ministry. We are going to have to enable our lay colleagues with the skills for communicating with theologians in order to have that understanding and to continue it into the future. We don't expect people who haven't had church experience to jump in and start being a member of any of our churches. There are formation programs, such as the rite of Christian initiation for adults. Why not formulate a rite of "science Christian initiation" to help them into an apostolic way of thinking?

Some experiences and frustrations lead people to alienation or misunderstanding. They need help in affirming what they are doing, how they are educating, how they are working in science. This is part of the Christian mission. This is ministry. This is the way we live in the community.

ORNA: I'd like to pick up on what Leanne and Joan were saying. I'm continually struck by the mystery of our profession. Sitting here, I realized that the opposite of love is not hate but fear. What I've heard today of the Galileo debate points to a fearful church reacting to a threat. I heard from many of you that science has nothing to fear from theology and vice versa. That's a great breakthrough in the 20th century and something on which we might base our discussion on and our theme.

We here are obviously all persons dedicated to our profession; we are servants; we view ourselves as serving those to whom we minister. I don't know that my vow of celibacy has anything to do with the time and effort that I put in. I am at times humbled by the tremendous dedication, the time and effort put in by my lay colleagues at the College of New Rochelle. I'm humbled by the effort and time put in by Marie Sherman, who has a family yet spends many hours taking students on field trips and directing research. It points to the mystery of our dedication to our purpose. This is something we are committed to and take the time to do.

SKEHAN: I'll mention what may be unique but certainly is distinctive about the church-related institutions. It follows closely on Leanne's statement. It was brought home to me by a Jew who joined our department of geophysics and geology a few years ago. He has been ecstatic since he came to Boston College. He is a devout Jew, one who likes to talk about the religious matters and other matters of values, including the science. He is able to talk about these things very freely in the present atmosphere. He had been at Columbia University as a full time researcher and did his doctoral studies at the New York State University at Stony Brook. When he came to our campus, he was blessed by surprise because he never expected the freedom to talk about the things that were of greatest value to him. We have a unique resource that many of us take for granted. We don't capitalize on this enough. We are an oasis where we can speak about things that are of greatest value to us. We can speak not only in our field of science but also of our other cherished values, particularly religious values. It's something that we ought not to take for granted.

WHARTON: Two of the groups last night reported on the contribution of church-related schools to science education. Let me go over the similarities of those two reports. One talked about the atmosphere which permeates the church-related institution. The other emphasized the person-centered characteristics of a church-related institution and the greater freedom we have to express our religious views and to integrate our Christian worldview in a holistic way. Those two statements go together. Number one also dealt with issues involving the future of the human race. The third point of the second group emphasized science as a service field with responsible citizenship. Those two ideas go together.

Also, the third point of the first group was the value focus in courses. That ties in with the third point of the second group as a service field and its functional citizenship. But it also ties in with counteracting a negative view of science. Of course, with value focus you can look at either the negative aspects or the positive aspects of science because science has both positive and negative aspects. But with the value focus, I would prefer we concentrate on the positive aspects of science. Question was raised about the uniqueness of church-related schools. One unique thing that ties in with all these is our constituency of students who want to come to church-related schools. If we aren't going to reach out to them, no one else will.

I was talking with Marie Sherman who pointed out that we can't force students to go into science or to become involved, but we can create opportunities to stimulate their interest. We can advertise what can be done in science in the service field -- even if they don't go into science, they need to study science to be responsible citizens -- and present a positive view of science to our constituents.

SMOLARSKI: Many church-related schools have not taken the opportunity to foster interplay between religion, art or humanities section of curricula and the scientific. At Santa Clara there's been a team taught course with a professor in the English department and a professor in the Math department. Students sign up for sections of Calculus I and English I. They must take both. They're both taught by both professors. I don't know how an English prof can teach Calculus I and Calculus II or how a mathematician can explain the literary qualities in English I and II, but they have to do it.

Can we encourage science faculty to get release time to participate in a beginning freshman theology or religious studies course? That might lead to a team taught approach from their perspective as scientists on these questions. If that could be officially concretized in various schools -- at least credit and incentive given to a faculty member to sit in on a course not in their discipline -- it may eventually contribute to the training of theologians in the sciences and scientists in theology.

Earlier, someone mentioned ministering in our schools to the students who have math anxiety or a more generalized scientific anxiety. How do we break down the barrier preventing them from being whole individuals? Students equivalently deny that this area is necessary for their future as human beings and also as believers. We haven't challenged that.

Many church-related schools don't have a strong science department or a strong math curriculum. Yet we state that this is an important aspect of a liberal education. We haven't begun to think about that as a curriculum question or a paradigm question. That needs to be addressed.

COLICELLI: My institution is 90 years old and we've had undergraduate research for just about that whole time. The tradition of Catholic women's colleges (and Catholic colleges in general), filled a need to enable a group of people who were held back. We knew then, and still do, that sometimes women scientists must be better scientists than their male counterparts. We did a lot of extra things but we still needed to do the science. I hope our colleges continue to realize their obligations to enable other under-represented groups in society, especially the Hispanic population. It's tied to our Christian base.

FORD (NY): I address the comment just made about anxiety in mathematics and science. My present provost of the diocesan university dealt with a blue collar student population with a lot of anxieties. Those anxieties are addressed in several strategies. The full answer is a strategy encompassing a core of people willing to leave their departments several hours a week to assist the students who have anxieties in grammar, math and science. The departments can set up introductory courses to address that problem, monitor it and network with other departments so that the student is watched and assisted in a variety of areas. It's a bureaucratic strategy to identify the anxiety and get people willing to work on it. It's an apostolic endeavor to get them over the anxiety and help them move on. I've seen anxious young folks come into our graduate school and leave as super post docs five or six years later because caring people work with them, significantly lessening that anxiety. That is our second line of defense. The first line of defense is in the secondary and elementary schools. We have no choice in that matter. If we don't participate longitudinally in the educational process, we're going to get what we asked for. It will continue.

SHEAHEN: Take the question on the board about the unique contribution of church-related schools. Some of the things I've heard this morning are starting to converge. In Washington, D.C. we joke about the building of the National Academy of Sciences and call it the Science Temple. You go there and you worship. You put out a government report that asks for money. That's the kind of sacrifice that's offered.

The general origin of math and science anxiety is what Elena said a few minutes ago. They fear man, not science. They fear what we've come to know as secular humanism. The perception is that science is the flagship, the wave of the future, of secular humanism. People innately reject that because they innately have a common search for God but they can't get a handle on it. Their flight from secular humanism turns into a flight from science, a math anxiety. As Dennis Smolarski said, we haven't challenged the assumption that science is necessary to overall life.

Jim Skehan's idea that the religious universities are oases in which we are free to pursue our inward feeling for faith represents a unique contribution. Church-related schools are the one place where we can proclaim: "Science is not the flagship of secular humanism. Science is a gift from God. Come into our building and we'll tell you how it all fits together."

BERTRAM: Are you saying that to translate mathematical sciences from "not God" to "gift from God" is not to dethrone them but to promote them?

SHEAHEN: You bet.

FORD (ST. LOUIS): I find Tom's statement intriguing but I'm going to offer a comment on what might be unique about church-related schools that takes a totally different approach. I'm being a little provocative here. When I advise parttime faculty who teach for us in the evening, I point out that teaching is a vocation of justice rather than mercy. We are not merciful in the sense that we do not give grades as gifts. We judge an eye for an eye and a tooth for a tooth. I tell students that we're a church-related institution and that makes it easier to flunk those who get F's. In a secular institution, where science is the be all and the end all, you might succumb to the notion that your worth is determined by the grades you get, by your achievements and such measurements. That may be the way that our society measures worth and value, but not ours. The F I'm giving you has nothing to do with your value as a human being. It has nothing to do with your potential as a human being. It has everything to do with your performance in this class in these few months, and that's it. I'm not saying anything about you, the person. Perhaps you goofed off too much, but you'll be the judge of that. I'm not the Judge. I'm just a judge with a small j. The framework of our university makes that easier for me to do. So church-related institutions can morally flunk anybody.

Let me make an aside here. I don't want to make light of math anxiety. I had math anxiety when I was doing my Ph.D. Can I measure up to that? Is this attainable? Math anxiety is part of the human condition.

CONNELL: I have the same sort of thought. Some students have math and science anxiety. Somewhere along the way, they missed something that they needed, and they truly need help. More of them seem to have grade anxiety -- not just not flunking but getting a B instead of an A. If you've been in a church-related institution, it isn't always possible to say, "But you don't have to get all A's" and have it really penetrate.

EAGAN: I want to pick up on something that Fr. Skehan said, because as a non-Catholic, a non-Christian, a non-Jew, I want to attest to something about freedom in these institutions which we will call church-related. My father was a free thinker, but he insisted that I go to a Jesuit undergraduate college because he felt that genuine intellectual discourse took place in such an institution and that it was free discourse. I have taught and gone to school in every other type of higher education institution in the country. I would underscore that my father was correct. The Jewish colleague of Fr. Skehan's is correct. Free intellectual discourse is much more attainable, much more secure in the church-related schools I know than the many state or secular institutions I'm familiar with.

As I look at what ought to be the unique contribution of church-related schools, I try to understand and explain why I feel that there is more genuine intellectual or scientific discourse in the church-related institutions with which I am familiar. That's why I would insist that the notion of church-related institutions or schools be taken in its broadest terms. Years ago, some wag in my discipline pointed out that it's interesting to look at the history of organizations that are still alive and well in the world since the Protestant Reformation. There are three institutions that are still in existence that were existent when Luther pounded the nails. One is the Roman church, of course, and the Protestant tradition or

Protestant church. The third example is the parliament of the Isle of Man. That parliament is still pretty much the same as it was then. All the rest of the institutions, 58, are universities, most of which, if not all, were religiously founded. Many have long since dropped close familiar religious ties, but Oxford University's colleges still bear the names that attest to their foundation as does Cambridge.

When I try to figure out what protects what I see as my ultimate goal, free intellectual discourse and pursuit of understanding of the universe, I find it in the church-related institutions. I want to take it broadly because that free discourse I'm talking about does occur in places like Harvard and Southern Methodist University. It probably takes place at Southern Cal; it takes place at Northwestern. All of these were founded in the religious tradition. I urge all of you to keep that notion of religious-related schools very broad. I'm familiar only with Jesuit institutions in terms of this orientation. The first words the last president of John Carroll University spoke to our faculty were: "We are first a university, then Catholic, then Jesuit." Some might disagree with that, but that's the tradition I knew at Canisius College a long time ago.

BERTRAM: That brings us to the end of our list. I was almost going to say the end of our rope. We ended with Pat Eagan's returning us to a point on which we began. I remember Dan McLoughlin's provocative remark which was later picked up by his straight man, Charles Ford, asking an apparently embarrassing question. Why is it that church-related colleges don't show up among the top hundred, at least as far as science education goes. I'm provoked to a kind of puckish observation that, at least in North America, the same thing that is said about church-related schools slipping out of the top hundred with respect to science education is true with respect to intercollegiate sports. Yesterday's victory for Notre Dame in a way proves me wrong, but when we look at all the other top hundred teams the church is slipping also in that league. What might seem even more ironic would be for me to say there is a similar phenomenon, not quite as dramatic, with respect to, would you believe it, the profession called theology.

If you ranked theology and its achievements in North America the way in which people might be inclined to rank science education or to rate intercollegiate sports -- in terms of publication, name recognition, how many people are reached by a given theologian -- more and more of those theologians are showing up in non-church-related schools. These schools have more and more provided themselves with faculties of theology or religious studies. That might at least suggest the provocative tentative conclusion that the "church-based" in the so-called First World today is destined to be poor. I don't mean poor in quality, but poor financially. Intercollegiate sports and main line professional publishable theology and the teaching of science and research in science are destined to be expensive. That seems to price the church out of those markets.

The purpose for making a statement like that is largely provocative, but there might be some embarrassing half truth in it. That may bring us back to something that Sr. Rosemary said early in our sessions. This wasn't the way she put it, but it had the effect of picking up on something that Archbishop Camara once said, namely, that the age of miracles is by no means over for Christians. Every Christian is privileged to be able to continue to perform the miracle of making adversity into prosperity. I took you to be saying, Sr. Rosemary, that maybe the very fact that church-related colleges are from one point of view being marginated may only challenge their God given resourcefulness and imaginativeness to make the most of what they seem to have little of. Someone else called that making a sow's ear into a silk purse.

I've been reminded by several things that have just been said in the last hour of a favorite document of mine in the New Testament, the first epistle of Peter. We've talked over and over again about fear. In the first epistle of Peter, the Christians who are under duress for being Christians, some evidently quite explicitly being persecuted for their faith, are told in the Greek timate, often mistranslated in English to "fear" the emperor, to "fear" the king, to "fear" the slave master, and so on. That's a bad translation. A more adequate translation would be "to respect" or even "to revere," perhaps. That is distinguished in the first epistle in Peter from another Greek verb which should be translated "fear" and that's the word phobein, our word phobia.

In that epistle, though the Christians are urged again and again, the Christian wife, for example, who for all we know may even be tyrannized, possibly abused by a pagan husband, is told to respect him. But she is told not to fear him. No one is ever, in the first epistle of Peter, told to fear anybody except theos, God. That is quite remarkable. In that problematic passage where the advice is to the wife, the author says that the very fact that she might respect this disrespectable husband but not be terrorized, never allow herself to be frightened by him -- that very phenomenon might seem so different that he himself will be forced to inquire what makes her that way. More than halfway through the epistle comes a sort of throw away line amid advice to Christian citizens, Christian slaves, Christian wives, Christian husbands. The author says, with respect to the non-Christian environment, the fact that you lose respect for association with those people should not make you fear them. Fearing only God may provoke in them the curiosity to ask a question for which you should all be ready. All of you should be ready to give a reason for the hope that is in you. Very low key evangelization, by the way! Always be ready to give a reason of the hope, in case anyone should ask! The author then adds for good measure, "do that with gentleness and respect."

We've not talked much about evangelization. We have talked about research. We talked about surprise. We talked about curiosity. I suppose listening to people like us talk makes me wonder whether you yourselves don't become objects of curiosity among your colleagues and your students who may at some point, not because your Christianity is that manifest but your goodness is that manifest. Might they be provoked to ask of you the reason of the hope that is in you? I suppose in good theater talk, that may be your one chance for your one good walk-on line. I take Peter to be saying to you, "don't blow it!" In case anyone should ask, be ready to give the reason of the hope that is in you, that you yourself become an object of research. I suppose you can't do that unless you are curious about your colleagues; respectfully you're curious about what makes them tick. You see them as gifts given by a freely giving creator. I can imagine that that would prompt them to ask what makes you care, what makes you keep going, what makes you work long hours in order to keep undergraduate research going.

I wish you every blessing. I've been grateful for your hanging in there, being as participatory and responsible as you've been.

BRUNGS: Bob Bertram has mentioned hope. And I remember, Bob -- I may not have the quotation exact -- that at one of our meetings about 20 years ago, you quoted Horace Bushnell to the effect that power follows the direction of hope. It does not follow money nor fear, but hope. Who should have more hope than we? At our second meeting in March, 1970 we brought together people interested in areas between science and faith. One was Don Shriver, at that time teaching theology at Emory. He had an engineering background. He's presently President of Union Theological Seminary. He said: "You know, I always thought I was out there alone in a foxhole. After this weekend, I find out that there are 35 or 40 other people up here, each in his or her own foxhole. Now that I know I'm not isolated and you know you're not isolated, isn't it time to start digging slit trenches so we can communicate?" One of the basic functions of bringing together 50 people like yourself is the digging of slit trenches. It's been alluded to more than once that the primary effect of such a meeting takes place in the lounge, on the grounds, and in the dining room. The one-tenth that shows up in the Proceedings is the least important one-tenth. The alliances formed, the partnerships and the friendships formed, will lead us on in our hope to serve the Lord through our science, our theology and ourselves.

I want to thank you for coming. I hope that you've all enjoyed yourself. I hope you've been stimulated by each other and by our paper writers. Finally, I wish you Godspeed on your return home.

PARTICIPANTS

Sr. Joan Acker, HM
Borromeo College of Ohio
28700 Euclid Avenue
Wickliffe, OH 44092

Dr. Michael Barnes
Dept. of Religious Studies
Univ. of Dayton -- Zehler Hall
300 College Park
Dayton, OH 45469-0001

Dr. Robert Bertram
Lutheran Sch. of Theology-Chicago
c/o 7039 Westmoreland
St. Louis, Mo. 63103

Brother Lawrence Bradford, OSB
Department of Biology
Benedictine College
Atchison, KS 66002

Terrance G. Brennan
Director of Campus Ministry
Parks College of St. Louis Univ.
Cahokia, IL 62206

Sr. Dorothy Browne, O. P.
8000 S. Linder Ave.
Burbank, IL 60459

Rev. Robert A. Brungs, S. J.
Director: ITEST
221 North Grand Blvd.
St. Louis, Missouri 63103

Dr. James Bundschuh
Dean of Arts and Sciences
Saint Louis University
St. Louis, MO 63103

Rev. Thaddeus Burch, S.J.
Dean of the Graduate School
Marquette University
1404 W. Wisconsin Ave.
Milwaukee, WI 53233

Dr. David Byers
Committee on Science & Human Values NCCB
3211 4th St., N.E.
Washington, D.C. 20017-1194

Dr. Mary Lou Caspers
Department of Chemistry
University of Detroit
4001 W. McNichols
Detroit, MI 48221

Dr. J. Richard Chase
President
Wheaton College
Wheaton, IL 60187

Dr. Elena Colicelli, SC
Department of Chemistry
College of St. Elizabeth
Convent Station, NJ 07961

Sr. Rosemary Connell, csj
6321 Clemens
St. Louis, MO 63105

Dr. John Cross
Department of Psychology
St. Louis University
St. Louis, Mo. 63103

Rev. Charles Currie, S. J.
Bicentennial Office
Georgetown University
37th & O Sts., N. W.
Washington, D. C. 20057

S. Thérèse Dill, SNDdeN
Biology Department
College of Notre Dame of Maryland
4701 North Charles Street
Baltimore, MD 21210

Dr. Patrick L. Eagan
Department of Political Science
John Carroll University
20700 North Park Blvd.
University Hts., OH 44118

Dr. Loretta Findysz
Loyola Academy
1100 N. Laramie Ave.
Wilmette, IL 60091

Dr. Charles E. Ford
Dean of the Graduate School
NY Medical College
Sunshine Cottage-Rm 209
Valhalla, NY 10595

Dr. Charles E. Ford
Department of Mathematics
St. Louis University
St. Louis, Mo. 63103

Dr. Walter W. Fredricks
Department of Biology
Marquette University
Milwaukee, WI 53233

Leanne M. Jablonski, FMI
Department of Biology, S-222
University of Dayton
Dayton, OH 45469-0001

Fr. Donald J. Keefe, SJ
Department of Theology
Marquette University
Milwaukee, WI 53233

Miss Peggy Keilholz
9700 Cisco Dr.
St. Louis, MO 63123

Fr. Gerry Magill
Department of Theology
Saint Louis University
Saint Louis, MO 63103

Dr. Francis J. McGuire
Dean of Enrollment
Loyola College
4501 North Charles Street
Baltimore, MD 21210

Fr. William McInnes, S.J.
Director: ACJU
1726 New Hampshire Ave., N. W.
Washington, D. C. 20009

Fr. Frederick McLeod, S.J.
Department of Theology
St. Louis University
St. Louis, Mo. 63103

Dr. Daniel J. McLoughlin
Dept. of Chemistry, Logan Hall
Xavier University
Cincinnati, OH 45207

Mrs. Bernice Morris
Admin. Asst.: ITEST
221 N. Grand Blvd.
St. Louis, Mo. 63103

Sr. Mary Ellen Murphy, PhD
Dean of the College
St. Joseph's College
Windham, ME 04062

Rev. William H. Nichols, S. J.
Department of Physics
John Carroll University
20700 North Park Blvd.
University Hts., OH 44118

Thad F. Niemira
4924 Sutherland
St. Louis, MO 63109

Sr. Mary Virginia Orna
Professor of Chemistry
College of New Rochelle
New Rochelle, NY 10801

Fr. J. A. Panuska, S. J.
President
University of Scranton
Scranton, PA 18510

Rev. Daniel M. Perrine, S. J.
Department of Chemistry
Loyola College
4501 North Charles Street
Baltimore, MD 21210

S. Marianne Postiglione, RSM
Dir. of Communications: ITEST
221 N. Grand Blvd.
St. Louis, Mo. 63103

Dr. Donald Procaccini
Department of Biology
Emmanuel College
400 The Fenway
Boston, MA 02115

Rev. Donald Reck, S. J.
Campus Minister
Parks College of St. Louis Univ.
Cahokia, IL 62206

Dr. Rustum Roy
Director: STS Program
Penn State U. -- 128 Willard
University Park, Pa. 16802

Dr. M. Angelice Seibert, O.S.U.
Ursuline Sisters of Louisville
3105 Lexington Road
Louisville, KY 40206

Dr. Thomas Sheahen
18708 Woodway Dr.
Derwood, Md. 20855

Mrs. Marie Sherman
7602 Weil
St. Louis, MO 63119

Rev. James W. Skehan, S. J.
Director
Weston Observatory
381 Concord Road
Weston, MA 02193

Rev. Dennis Smolarski, S.J.,
St. Mary's Catholic Church
612 E. Park Ave.
Champaign, IL 61820

Br. Anthony Smulders, CFMM
Assoc. Dean of Sciences
Loyola-Marymount University
7101 West 80th St.
Los Angeles, CA 90045-2699

Fr. John Stack
Department of Religious Studies
St. Joseph College
1678 Asylum Avenue
West Hartford, CT 06117

S. Leona Truchan
Department of Biology
Alverno College
3401 S. 39th Street
Milwaukee, WI 53215

Dr. William Wharton
Prof. of Physics/Geology
Wheaton College
Wheaton, IL 60187-5593

Jeanene Yackey
Chair, Natural Sciences Department
Fontbonne College
2307 S. Lindbergh
St. Louis, MO 63131